THE ROAD TO SERFDOM

The Road to
SERFDOM

F. A. Hayek

Fiftieth Anniversary Edition

WITH A NEW INTRODUCTION BY

Milton Friedman

THE UNIVERSITY OF CHICAGO PRESS

F. A. HAYEK (1899–1992) taught at the
University of London, the University of Chicago,
and the University of Freiburg (Germany). He was awarded
the Nobel Memorial Prize in Economics in 1974
and the Medal of Freedom in 1991.

The University of Chicago Press, Chicago 60637
© 1944 (renewed 1972), 1994 by The University of Chicago
All rights reserved. Published 1994
Printed in the United States of America
03 02 01 00 99 98 97 96 95   3 4 5
ISBN: 0-226-32059-6   (cloth)
0-226-32061-8   (paper)

Library of Congress Cataloging-in-Publication Data

Hayek, Friedrich A. von (Friedrich August), 1899–
    The road to serfdom / Friedrich A. Hayek. — 50th
anniversary ed. / with a new introd. by Milton Friedman.
        p.   cm.
    Originally published: Chicago : University of Chicago Press,
1944.
    Includes bibliographical references and index.
    1. Economic policy.   2. Totalitarianism.   I. Title.
    HD82.H38   1994
    338.9—dc20   94-27675
                                                  CIP

⊚ The paper used in this publication meets the minimum
requirements of the American National Standard for Information
Sciences—Permanence of Paper for Printed Library Materials,
ANSI Z39.48-1984.

To

THE SOCIALISTS OF ALL PARTIES

It is seldom that

liberty of any kind is lost all at once

DAVID HUME

I should have loved freedom,

I believe, at all times, but in the time

in which we live I am ready

to worship it.

A. DE TOCQUEVILLE.

CONTENTS

INTRODUCTION
to the Fiftieth Anniversary Edition by
MILTON FRIEDMAN

THIS book has become a true classic: essential reading for everyone who is seriously interested in politics in the broadest and least partisan sense, a book whose central message is timeless, applicable to a wide variety of concrete situations. In some ways it is even more relevant to the United States today than it was when it created a sensation on its original publication in 1944.

Nearly a quarter of a century ago (1971), I wrote an introduction to a new German edition of *The Road to Serfdom* that illustrates how timeless Hayek's message is. That introduction is equally relevant to this fiftieth anniversary edition of Hayek's classic. Rather than plagiarize myself, I herewith quote it in full before adding a few additional comments.[1]

"Over the years, I have made it a practice to inquire of believers in individualism how they came to depart from the collectivist orthodoxy of our times. For years, the most frequent answer was a reference to the book for which I have the honor of writing this introduction. Professor Hayek's remarkable and vigorous tract was a revelation particularly to the young men and women who had been in the armed forces during the war. Their recent experience had enhanced their appreciation of the value and meaning of individual freedom. In addition, they had observed a collectivist organiza-

---

1. *Der Weg zur Knechtschaft: Den Sozialisten in allen Parteien,* © 1971 (for the new edition) Verlag moderne Industrie AG, 86895 Landsberg am Lech. This was the first edition ever published in Germany, though a German translation of *The Road to Serfdom* was published in Switzerland in 1948.

tion in action. For them, Hayek's predictions about the consequences of collectivism were not simply hypothetical possibilities but visible realities that they had themselves experienced in the military.

"On rereading the book before writing this introduction, I was again impressed with what a magnificent book it is—subtle and closely reasoned yet lucid and clear, philosophical and abstract yet also concrete and realistic, analytical and rational yet animated by high ideals and a vivid sense of mission. Little wonder that it had so great an influence. I was impressed also that its message is no less needed today than it was when it first appeared—on this more later. But its message may not be as immediate or as persuasive to today's youth as to the young men and women who read it when it first appeared. The problems of the war and postwar adjustment that Hayek used to illustrate his timeless central thesis, and the collectivist jargon of the time that he used to document his assertions about the intellectual climate, were familiar to the immediate postwar generation and established an immediate rapport between author and reader. The same collectivist fallacies are abroad and on the rise today, but the immediate issues are different and so is much of the jargon. Today we hear little of 'central planning,' of 'production for use,' of the need for 'conscious direction' of society's resources. Instead the talk is of the urban crisis—solvable it is said only by vastly expanded government programs; of the environmental crisis—produced it is said by rapacious businessmen who must be forced to discharge their social responsibility instead of 'simply' operating their enterprises to make the most profit and requiring also, it is said, vastly expanded government programs; of the consumer crisis—false values stimulated by the selfsame rapacious businessmen seeking profits instead of exercising social responsibility and

INTRODUCTION

of course also requiring expanded government programs to protect the consumer, not least from himself; of the welfare or poverty crisis—here the jargon is still 'poverty in the midst of plenty,' though what is now described as poverty would have been regarded as plenty when that slogan was first widely used.

"Now as then, the promotion of collectivism is combined with the profession of individualist values. Indeed, experience with big government has strengthened this discordant strand. There is wide protest against the 'establishment'; an incredible conformity in the protest against conformity; a widespread demand for freedom to 'do one's own thing,' for individual lifestyles, for participatory democracy. Listening to this strand, one might also believe that the collectivist tide has turned, that individualism is again on the rise. As Hayek so persuasively demonstrates, these values require an individualistic society. They can be achieved only in a liberal order in which government activity is limited primarily to establishing the framework within which individuals are free to pursue their own objectives.[2] The free market is the only mechanism that has ever been discovered for achieving participatory democracy.

"Unfortunately, the relation between the ends and the means remains widely misunderstood. Many of those who profess the most individualistic objectives support collectivist means without recognizing the contradiction. It is tempting to believe that social evils arise from the activities of evil men and that if only good men (like ourselves, naturally) wielded

2. (Added in 1994.) I use the term *liberal*, as Hayek does in the book, and also in his Preface to the 1956 Paperback Edition (p. xxxv below), in the original nineteenth-century sense of limited government and free markets, not in the corrupted sense it has acquired in the United States, in which it means almost the opposite.

power, all would be well. That view requires only emotion and self-praise—easy to come by and satisfying as well. To understand why it is that 'good' men in positions of power will produce evil, while the ordinary man without power but able to engage in voluntary cooperation with his neighbors will produce good, requires analysis and thought, subordinating the emotions to the rational faculty. Surely that is one answer to the perennial mystery of why collectivism, with its demonstrated record of producing tyranny and misery, is so widely regarded as superior to individualism, with its demonstrated record of producing freedom and plenty. The argument for collectivism is simple if false; it is an immediate emotional argument. The argument for individualism is subtle and sophisticated; it is an indirect rational argument. And the emotional faculties are more highly developed in most men than the rational, paradoxically or especially even in those who regard themselves as intellectuals.

"How stands the battle between collectivism and individualism in the West more than a quarter of a century [now half a century] after the publication of Hayek's great tract? The answer is very different in the world of affairs and in the world of ideas.

"In the world of affairs, those of us who were persuaded by Hayek's analysis saw few signs in 1945 of anything but a steady growth of the state at the expense of the individual, a steady replacement of private initiative and planning by state initiative and planning. Yet in practice that movement did not go much farther—not in Britain or in France or in the United States. And in Germany there was a sharp reaction away from the totalitarian controls of the Nazi period and a major move toward a liberal economic policy.

"What produced this unexpected check to collectivism? I believe that two forces were primarily responsible. First, and

INTRODUCTION

this was particularly important in Britain, the conflict between central planning and individual liberty that is Hayek's
theme became patent, particularly when the exigencies of
central planning led to the so-called 'control of engagements' order under which the government had the power to
assign people to occupations. The tradition of liberty, the
liberal values, were still sufficiently strong in Britain so that,
when the conflict occurred, central planning was sacrificed
rather than individual liberty. The second force checking collectivism was simply its inefficiency. Government proved unable to manage enterprises, to organize resources to achieve
stated objectives at reasonable cost. It became mired in bu-
reaucratic confusion and inefficiency. Widespread disillusionment set in about the effectiveness of centralized government in administering programs.

"Unfortunately, the check to collectivism did not check
the growth of government; rather, it diverted its growth to
a different channel. The emphasis shifted from govern-
mentally administered production activities to indirect regulation of supposedly private enterprises and even more to
governmental transfer programs, involving extracting taxes
from some in order to make grants to others—all in the
name of equality and the eradication of poverty but in practice producing an erratic and contradictory mélange of sub-
sidies to special interest groups. As a result, the fraction of
the national income being spent by governments has continued to mount.

"In the world of ideas, the outcome has been even less
satisfactory to a believer in individualism. In one respect,
this is most surprising. Experience in the past quarter century has strongly confirmed the validity of Hayek's central
insight—that coordination of men's activities through central direction and through voluntary cooperation are roads

going in very different directions: the first to serfdom, the second to freedom. That experience has also strongly reinforced a secondary theme—central direction is also a road to poverty for the ordinary man; voluntary cooperation, a road to plenty.

"East and West Germany almost provide a controlled scientific experiment. Here are people of the same blood, the same civilization, the same level of technical skill and knowledge, torn asunder by the accidents of warfare, yet adopting radically different methods of social organization—central direction and the market. The results are crystal clear. East Germany, not West Germany, had to build a wall to keep its citizens from leaving. On its side of the wall, tyranny and misery; on the other side, freedom and affluence.

"In the Middle East, Israel and Egypt offer the same contrast as West and East Germany. In the Far East, Malaya, Singapore, Thailand, Formosa, Hong Kong, and Japan—all relying primarily on free markets—are thriving and their people full of hope; a far call from India, Indonesia, and Communist China—all relying heavily on central planning. Again it is Communist China and not Hong Kong that has to guard its borders against people trying to get out.

"Yet despite this remarkable and dramatic confirmation of Hayek's thesis, the intellectual climate of the West, after a brief interlude in which there were some signs of the resurgence of earlier liberal values, has again started moving in a direction strongly antagonistic to free enterprise, competition, private property and limited government. For a time, Hayek's description of the ruling intellectual attitudes seemed to be growing somewhat obsolete. Today, it rings truer than it did a decade ago. It is hard to know what explains this development. We badly need a new book by Hayek that will give as clear and penetrating an insight into the intellectual developments of the past quarter century as *The Road to Serf-dom* does of earlier developments. Why is it that intellectual classes everywhere almost automatically range themselves on the side of collectivism—even while chanting individualist slogans—and denigrate and revile capitalism? Why is it that the mass media are almost everywhere dominated by this view?

"Whatever the explanation, the fact of growing intellectual support of collectivism—and I believe it is a fact—makes Hayek's book as timely today as it was when it first appeared. Let us hope that a new edition in Germany—which of all countries should be most receptive to its message—will have as much influence as the initial edition had in the United States and the United Kingdom. The battle for freedom must be won over and over again. The socialists in all parties to whom Hayek dedicated his book must once again be persuaded or defeated if they and we are to remain free men."

The penultimate paragraph of my introduction to the German edition is the only one that does not ring fully true today. The fall of the Berlin Wall, the collapse of communism behind the Iron Curtain, and the changing character of China have reduced the defenders of a Marxian-type collectivism to a small, hardy band concentrated in Western universities. Today, there is wide agreement that socialism is a failure, capitalism a success. Yet this apparent conversion of the intellectual community to what might be called a Hayekian view is deceptive. While the talk is about free markets and private property—and it is more respectable than it was a few decades ago to defend near-complete laissez-faire—the bulk of the intellectual community almost automatically favors any expansion of government power so long as it is advertised as a way to protect individuals from big bad corporations, relieve poverty, protect the environment, or promote "equality." The present discussion of a national program of health care provides a striking example. The intellectuals may have learned the words but they do not yet have the tune.

I said at the outset that "in some ways" the message of this book "is even more relevant to the United States today than it was when it created a sensation . . . half a century ago." Intellectual opinion then was far more hostile to its theme than it appears to be now, but practice conformed to it far more than it does today. Government in the post–World War II period was smaller and less intrusive than it is today. Johnson's Great Society programs, including Medicare and Medicaid, and Bush's Clean Air and Americans with Disabilities Acts, were all still ahead, let alone the numerous other extensions of government that Reagan was only able to slow down, not reverse, in his eight years in office. Total government spending—federal state, and local—in the United States has gone from 25 percent of national income in 1950 to nearly 45 percent in 1993.

Much the same has been true in Britain, in one sense more dramatically. The Labour Party, formerly openly socialist, now defends free private markets; and the Conservative Party, once content to administer Labour's socialist policies, has tried to reverse, and to some extent under Margaret Thatcher succeeded in reversing, the extent of government ownership and operation. But Thatcher was unable to call on anything like the reservoir of popular support for liberal values that led to the withdrawal of the "control of engagements" order shortly after World War II. And while there has been a considerable amount of "privatization" there as here, government today spends a larger fraction of the national income and is more intrusive than it was in 1950.

On both sides of the Atlantic, it is only a little overstated to say that we preach individualism and competitive capitalism, and practice socialism.

NOTE ON PUBLISHING HISTORY*

Hayek began working on *The Road to Serfdom* in September 1940, and the book was first published in England on March 10, 1944. Hayek authorized his friend Dr. Fritz Machlup, an Austrian refugee who pursued a distinguished academic career in the United States and was employed, in 1944, at the Office of Alien Property Custodian in Washington, D.C., to sign up the book with an American publisher. Before it was submitted to the University of Chicago Press the book was turned down in the United States by three publishers—whether because they believed it would not sell or, in at least one case, because they considered it "unfit for publication by a reputable house."[3] Undeterred, Machlup showed the page proofs of the British edition to Aaron Director, a former member of the University of Chicago Economics Department who was to return to the university after the war as an economist in the Law School. Subsequently, Frank H. Knight, a distinguished economist at the university, received a set of proofs and presented them to the University of Chicago Press with Director's suggestion that the Press might want to publish the book.

The Press signed a contract with Hayek for American

*Much of this section is based on research carried out by Alex Philipson, promotions manager at the University of Chicago Press.

3. See Hayek's Preface to the 1956 Paperback Edition, n. 2, p. xxxix below.

rights in April 1944, after persuading him to make some changes—"to be specific about the application to the United States . . . instead of slanting the book directly at an audience limited to England," as John Scoon, then editor at the Press, later recalled. "About the time the contract for American rights was signed—the beginning of April—we began to hear about the book in England, which had been published there on March 10. The first printing in England was only 2,000 but it was sold out in about a month. It began to be quoted in Parliament and in newspapers, and a few newspapers over here began mentioning it now and then—but of course we were still uncertain as to how it would appeal to the United States. As a matter of fact, right up until publication date we couldn't get a bookstore even in New York excited about the book."[4]

The Chicago edition was published on September 18, 1944, in a first printing of 2,000 copies, with an introduction by John Chamberlain, then as now a well-known writer and reviewer of books on economic subjects. "The first review that we saw," Scoon went on to say, "was Orville Prescott's in the *New York Times* of September 20, which was neutral and called it 'this sad and angry little book,' but by the time we had seen Henry Hazlitt's front page review in the Sunday *Times Book Review* we had ordered a second printing of 5,000 copies. In a few days we had requests for German, Spanish, Dutch and other translating rights, and on September 27 we ordered a third printing of 5,000 copies, upping it to 10,000 the next day. . . .

"By the first week of October many stores were out of stock and we had a tremendous and intricate job of printing, binding, shipping and allotting to customers in both this

4. Letter to C. Hartley Gratlan, May 2. 1945.

country and Canada. . . . From the start there was great enthusiasm for the book but the sales went by ups and downs. . . .

"Bitterness about the book has increased as time has gone by, rising to new heights as the book has made more of an impression. (People still tend to go off half-cocked about it; why don't they *read* it and find out what Hayek actually says!)" Scoon's comment is still true today.

The *Reader's Digest* published a condensation in April 1945, and more than 600,000 copies of the condensed version were subsequently distributed by the Book of the Month Club. In anticipation of the *Digest's* condensation and also of a lecture tour that Hayek was scheduled to make in the Spring of 1945, the Press tried to arrange for a large seventh printing. However, a paper shortage limited the press run to 10,000 and forced the Press to reduce the size of the book to a pocket-size version. It is a copy from that printing, incidentally, that is in my personal library.

In the fifty years since its publication, the Press has sold over a quarter of a million copies, 81,000 in hardback and 175,000 in paperback. Chicago's first paperback edition was published in 1956. Hayek's son, Lawrence, reports that nearly twenty authorized foreign translations have been published. In addition, underground, unauthorized translations circulated in Russian, Polish, Czech, and possibly other languages, when Eastern Europe was behind the Iron Curtain. There is little doubt that Hayek's writings, and especially this book, were an important intellectual source of the disintegration of faith in communism behind the Iron Curtain, as on our side of it.

Since the fall of the Berlin Wall it has been possible to publish the book openly in the countries and satellites of the former Soviet Union. I know from a variety of sources that there has been an upsurge of interest in Hayek, in general, and *The Road to Serfdom* in particular in those countries.

Since Hayek's death in 1992 there has been increasing recognition of the influence that he exerted in both communist and noncommunist regimes. His publishers can confidently look forward to continuing sales of this remarkable book for as long as freedom of the press prevails—which, despite some erosion since he wrote, is nonetheless more secure than it would otherwise be precisely because of this book.

Stanford, California
April 14, 1994

PREFACE
to the 1976 Reprint Edition

THIS BOOK, written in my spare time from 1940 to 1943, while my mind was still mainly occupied with problems of pure economic theory, has unexpectedly become for me the starting point of more than thirty years' work in a new field. This first attempt in the new direction was caused by my annoyance with the complete misinterpretation in English "progressive" circles of the character of the Nazi movement, an annoyance which led me from a memorandum to the then director of the London School of Economics, Sir William Beveridge, through an article in the *Contemporary Review* for 1938, which at the request of Professor Harry G. Gideonse of the University of Chicago I enlarged for publication in his Public Policy Pamphlets, and which, finally and reluctantly, when I found that all my more competent British colleagues were preoccupied with more urgent problems of the conduct of the war, I expanded into this tract for the times. In spite of the wholly unexpected success of the book—in the case of the initially not-contemplated American edition even greater than in that of the British one—I felt for a long time not altogether happy about it. Though I had frankly declared at the outset of the book that it was a political one, I was made to feel by most of my fellow social scientists that I had used my abilities on the wrong side, and I was myself uncomfortable about the possibility that in going beyond technical economics I might have exceeded my competence. I will not speak here about the fury which the book caused in certain circles, or of the curious difference between its reception in Great Britain and that in the United States—about that I did say something twenty years ago in the Preface to the first American paperback edition. Just to indicate the character of a widespread reaction, I will mention merely that one well-known philosopher, who shall be nameless, wrote to another to reproach him for having lauded this scandalous book, which "of course [he] had not read"!

But though I tried hard to get back to economics proper, I could not free myself of the feeling that the problems on which I had so undesignedly embarked were more challenging and important than those of economic theory, and that much that I had said in my first sketch needed clarification and elaboration. When I wrote the book, I had by no means sufficiently freed myself from all the prejudices and superstitions dominating general opinion, and even less had I learned to avoid all the prevalent confusions of terms and concepts of which I have since become very conscious. And the discussion of the consequences of socialist policies which the book attempts is of course not complete without an adequate account of what an appropriately run market order requires and can achieve. It was to the latter problem that the further work I have since done in the field was mainly devoted. The first result of these efforts of explaining the nature of an order of freedom was a substantial book called *The Constitution of Liberty* (1960) in which I essentially attempted to restate and make more coherent the doctrines of classical nineteenth-century liberalism. The awareness that such a restatement left certain important questions unanswered led me then to a further effort to provide my own answers in a work of three volumes entitled *Law, Legislation, and Liberty*, of which the first volume appeared in 1973.

In the last twenty years, I have, I believe, learned much about the problems discussed in this book, though I don't think I ever reread the book during this time. Having done so now for the purpose of this Preface, I feel no longer apologetic, but for the first time am rather proud of it—and not least of the insight which made me dedicate it 'To the Socialists of All Parties." Indeed, though I have in the interval learned much that I did not know when I wrote it, I was now often surprised by how much I did already see at the beginning of my efforts that later work has confirmed; and though my later efforts will, I hope, be more rewarding to the expert, I am now prepared unhesitatingly to recommend this early book to the general reader who wants a simple and nontechnical introduction to what I believe is still one of the most ominous questions which we have to solve.

The reader will probably ask whether this means that I am still prepared to defend all the main conclusions of this book, and the answer to this is on the whole affirmative. The most important qualification I must add is that during the interval of time terminology has changed and for this reason what I say in the book may be misunderstood. At the time I wrote, socialism meant unambiguously the nationalization of the means of production and the central economic planning which this made possible and necessary. In this sense Sweden, for instance, is today very much less socialistically organized than Great Britain or Austria, though Sweden is commonly regarded as much more socialistic. This is due to the fact that socialism has come to mean chiefly the extensive redistribution of incomes through taxation and the institutions of the welfare state. In the latter kind of socialism the effects I discuss in this book are brought about more slowly, indirectly, and imperfectly. I believe that the ultimate outcome tends to be very much the same, although the process by which it is brought about is not quite the same as that described in this book.

It has frequently been alleged that I have contended that any movement in the direction of socialism is bound to lead to totalitarianism. Even though this danger exists, this is not what the book says. What it contains is a warning that unless we mend the principles of our policy, some very unpleasant consequences will follow which most of those who advocate these policies do not want.

Where I now feel I was wrong in this book is chiefly in that I rather understressed the significance of the experience of communism in Russia—a fault which is perhaps pardonable when it is remembered that when I wrote, Russia was our wartime ally—and that I had not wholly freed myself from all the current interventionist superstitions, and in consequence still made various concessions which I now think unwarranted. And I certainly was not yet fully aware how bad things already were in some respects. I still regarded it, for example, as a rhetorical question when I asked (p. 91), if Hitler had obtained his unlimited powers in a strictly constitutional manner, "who would suggest that the Rule of Law still prevailed in Germany?" only to discover later that professors Hans Kelsen and Harold J. Laski, and probably many other socialist lawyers and political scientists following these influential authors, had maintained precisely this. Quite generally, further study of the contemporary trends of thought and institutions has, if anything, increased my alarm and concern. And both the influence of socialist ideas and the naïve trust in the good intentions of the holders of totalitarian power have markedly increased since I wrote this book.

I have long resented being more widely known by what I

PREFACE 1976

regarded as a pamphlet for the time than by my strictly scientific work. After reexamining what I wrote then in the light of some thirty years' further study of the problems then raised, I no longer do so. Though the book may contain much that I could not, when I wrote it, have convincingly demonstrated, it was a genuine effort to find the truth which I believe has produced insights that will help even those who disagree with me to avoid grave dangers.

F. A. HAYEK

PREFACE
to the 1956 Paperback Edition

ALTHOUGH THIS BOOK might in some respects have been different if I had written it in the first instance with American readers primarily in mind, it has by now made for itself too definite if unexpected a place in this country to make any rewriting advisable. Its republication in a new form, however, more than ten years after its first appearance, is perhaps an appropriate occasion for explaining its original aim and for a few comments on the altogether unforeseen and in many ways curious success it has had in this country.

The book was written in England during the war years and was designed almost exclusively for English readers. Indeed, it was addressed mainly to a very special class of readers in England. It was in no spirit of mockery that I dedicated it "To the Socialists of All Parties." It had its origin in many discussions which, during the preceding ten years, I had with friends and colleagues whose sympathies had been inclined toward the left, and it was in continuation of those arguments that I wrote *The Road to Serfdom*.

When Hitler came into power in Germany, I had already been teaching at the University of London for several years, but I kept in close touch with affairs on the Continent and was able to do so until the outbreak of war. What I had thus seen of the origins and evolution of the various totalitarian movements made me feel that English public opinion, particularly among my friends who held "advanced" views on social matters, completely misconceived the nature of those movements. Even before the war I was led by this to state in a brief essay what became the central argument of this book. But after war broke out I felt that this widespread misunderstanding of the political systems of our enemies, and soon also of our new ally, Russia, constituted a serious danger which had to be met by a more systematic effort. Also, it was already fairly obvious that England herself was likely to experiment after the war with the same kind of policies which I was convinced had contributed so much to destroy liberty elsewhere.

Thus this book gradually took shape as a warning to the socialist intelligentsia of England; with the inevitable delays of wartime production, it finally appeared there early in the spring of 1944. This date will, incidentally, also explain why I felt that in order to get a hearing I had somewhat to restrain myself in my comments on the regime of our wartime ally and to choose my illustrations mainly from developments in Germany.

It seems that the book appeared at a propitious moment, and I can feel only gratification at the success it had in England, which, though very different in kind, was quantitatively no smaller than it was to be in the United States. On the whole, the book was taken in the spirit in which it was written, and its argument was seriously examined by those to whom it was mainly addressed. Excepting only certain of the leading politicians of the Labour party—who, as if to provide an illustration for my remarks on the nationalist tendencies of socialism, attacked the book on the ground that it was written by a foreigner—the thoughtful and receptive manner in which it was generally examined by persons who must have found its conclusions running counter

to their strongest convictions was deeply impressive.[1] The
same applies also to the other European countries where the
book eventually appeared; and its particularly cordial reception by the post-Nazi generation of Germany, when copies
of a translation published in Switzerland at last reached that
country, was one of the unforeseen pleasures I derived from
the publication.

Rather different was the reception the book had in the
United States when it was published here a few months after
its appearance in England. I had given little thought to its
possible appeal to American readers when writing it. It was
then twenty years since I had last been in America as a research student, and during that time I had somewhat lost
touch with the development of American ideas. I could not
be sure how far my argument had direct relevance to the
American scene, and I was not in the least surprised when
the book was in fact rejected by the first three publishing
houses approached.[2] It was certainly most unexpected when,

1. The most representative example of British criticism of the book
from a left-wing point of view is probably Mrs. Barbara Wootton's courte-
ous and frank study, *Freedom under Planning* (London: George Allen & Unwin, 1946). It is often quoted in the United States as an effective refutation
of my argument, though I cannot help feeling that more than one reader
must have gained the impression that, as one American reviewer expressed
it, "it seems substantially to confirm Hayek's thesis" (Chester I. Barnard,
Southern Economic Journal, January, 1946).

2. I did not know then, as has since been admitted by a person advis-
ing one of the firms, that this appears to have been due not to any doubts
of the success of the book but to political prejudice, which went to the extent of representing the book as "unfit for publication by a reputable
house" (see on this the statement by William Miller quoted by W. T.
Couch in "The Sainted Book Burners," *The Freeman*, April, 1955, p. 423,
and also William Miller, *The Book Industry: A Report of the Public Library Inquiry of the Social Science Research Council* [New York: Columbia University
Press, 1949], p. 12).

PREFACE 1956

after the book was brought out by its present publishers, it soon began to sell at a rate almost unprecedented for a book of this kind, not intended for popular consumption.[3] And I was even more surprised by the violence of the reaction from both political wings, by the lavish praise the book received from some quarters no less than by the passionate hatred it appeared to arouse in others.

Contrary to my experience in England, in America the kind of people to whom this book was mainly addressed seem to have rejected it out of hand as a malicious and disingenuous attack on their finest ideals; they appear never to have paused to examine its argument. The language used and the emotion shown in some of the more adverse criticism the book received were indeed rather extraordinary.[4] But scarcely less surprising to me was the enthusiastic welcome accorded to the book by many whom I never expected to read a volume of this type—and from many more of whom I still doubt whether in fact they ever read it. And I must add that occasionally the manner in which it was used vividly brought home to me the truth of Lord Acton's observation that "at all times sincere friends of freedom have been rare, and its triumphs have been due to minorities, that have prevailed by associating themselves with auxiliaries whose objects often differed from their own; and this association,

3. Not a little of this was due to the publication of a condensation of this book in the *Reader's Digest*, and I should like to pay here to the editors of this journal a public testimony to the extremely skillful manner in which this was done without my assistance. It is inevitable that the compression of a complex argument to a fraction of its original length produces some over-simplification, but that it was done without distortion and better than I could have done it myself is a remarkable achievement.

4. To any reader who would like to see a specimen of abuse and invective which is probably unique in contemporary academic discussion I recommend a reading of Professor Herman Finer's *Road to Reaction* (Boston: Little Brown & Co., 1945).

which is always dangerous, has sometimes been disastrous."

It seems hardly likely that this extraordinary difference in the reception of the book on the two sides of the Atlantic is due entirely to a difference in national temperament. I have since become increasingly convinced that the explanation must lie in a difference of intellectual situation at the time when it arrived. In England, and in Europe generally, the problems with which I dealt had long ceased to be abstract questions. The ideals which I examined had long before come down to earth, and even their most enthusiastic adherents had already seen concretely some of the difficulties and unlooked-for results which their application produced. I was thus writing about phenomena of which almost all my European readers had some more or less close experience, and I was merely arguing systematically and consistently what many had already intuitively felt. There was already a disillusionment about these ideals under way, which their critical examination merely made more vocal or explicit.

In the United States, on the other hand, these ideals were still fresh and more virulent. It was only ten or fifteen years earlier—not forty or fifty, as in England—that a large part of the intelligentsia had caught the infection. And, in spite of the experimentation of the New Deal, their enthusiasm for the new kind of rationally constructed society was still largely unsoiled by practical experience. What to most Europeans had in some measure become *vieux jeux* was to the American radicals still the glittering hope of a better world which they had embraced and nourished during the recent years of the Great Depression.

Opinion moves fast in the United States, and even now it is difficult to remember how comparatively short a time it was before *The Road to Serfdom* appeared that the most extreme kind of economic planning had been seriously advocated and the model of Russia held up for imitation by men who were soon to play an important role in public affairs. It would be easy enough to give chapter and verse for this, but it would be invidious now to single out individuals. Be it enough to mention that in 1934 the newly established National Planning Board devoted a good deal of attention to the example of planning provided by these four countries: Germany, Italy, Russia, and Japan. Ten years later we had of course learned to refer to these same countries as "totalitarian," had fought a long war with three of them, and were soon to start a "cold war" with the fourth. Yet the contention of this book that the political development in those countries had something to do with their economic policies was then still indignantly rejected by the advocates of planning in this country. It suddenly became the fashion to deny that the inspiration of planning had come from Russia and to contend, as one of my eminent critics put it, that it was "a plain fact that Italy, Russia, Japan, and Germany all reached totalitarianism by very different roads."

The whole intellectual climate in the United States at the time *The Road to Serfdom* appeared was thus one in which it was bound either profoundly to shock or greatly to delight the members of sharply divided groups. In consequence, in spite of its apparent success, the book has not had here the kind of effect I should have wished or which it has had elsewhere. It is true that its main conclusions are today widely accepted. If twelve years ago it seemed to many almost sacrilege to suggest that fascism and communism are merely variants of the same totalitarianism which central control of all economic activity tends to produce, this has become almost a commonplace. It is now even widely recognized that democratic socialism is a very precarious and unstable affair,

ridden with internal contradictions and everywhere producing results most distasteful to many of its advocates.

For this sobered mood the lessons of events and more
popular discussions of the problem[5] are certainly more responsible than this book. Nor was my general thesis as such
original when it was published. Although similar but earlier
warnings may have been largely forgotten, the dangers inherent in the policies which I criticized had been pointed out
again and again. Whatever merits this book possesses consist
not in the reiteration of this thesis but in the patient and
detailed examination of the reasons why economics planning will produce such unlooked-for results and of the process by which they come about.

It is for this reason that I rather hope that the time may
now be more favorable in America for a serious consideration of the true argument of the book than it was when it
first appeared. I believe that what is important in it still has
to render its service, although I recognize that the hot socialism against which it was mainly directed—that organized
movement toward a deliberate organization of economic life
by the state as the chief owner of the means of production—is nearly dead in the Western world. The century of
socialism in this sense probably came to an end around 1948.
Many of its illusions have been discarded even by its leaders,
and elsewhere as well as in the United States the very name
has lost much of its attraction. Attempts will no doubt be
made to rescue the name for movements which are less dogmatic, less doctrinaire, and less systematic. But an argument
applicable solely against those clear-cut conceptions of social
reform which characterized the socialist movements of the
past might today well appear as tilting against windmills.

5. The most effective of these was undoubtedly George Orwell's *1984*.
The author had earlier kindly reviewed this book.

Yet though hot socialism is probably a thing of the past, some of its conceptions have penetrated far too deeply into the whole structure of current thought to justify complacency. If few people in the Western world now want to remake society from the bottom according to some ideal blueprint, a great many still believe in measures which, though not designed completely to remodel the economy, in their aggregate effect may well unintentionally produce this result. And, even more than at the time when I wrote this book, the advocacy of policies which in the long run cannot be reconciled with the preservation of a free society is no longer a party matter. That hodgepodge of ill-assembled and often inconsistent ideals which under the name of the Welfare State has largely replaced socialism as the goal of the reformers needs very careful sorting-out if its results are not to be very similar to those of full-fledged socialism. This is not to say that some of its aims are not both practicable and laudable. But there are many ways in which we can work toward the same goal, and in the present state of opinion there is some danger that our impatience for quick results may lead us to choose instruments which, though perhaps more efficient for achieving the particular ends, are not compatible with the preservation of a free society. The increasing tendency to rely on administrative coercion and discrimination where a modification of the general rules of law might, perhaps more slowly, achieve the same object, and to resort to direct state controls or to the creation of monopolistic institutions where judicious use of financial inducements might evoke spontaneous efforts is still a powerful legacy of the socialist period which is likely to influence policy for a long time to come.

Just because in the years ahead of us political ideology is not likely to aim at a clearly defined goal but toward piecemeal change, a full understanding of the process through which certain kinds of measures can destroy the bases of an economy based on the market and gradually smother the creative powers of a free civilization seems now of the greatest importance. Only if we understand why and how certain kinds of economic controls tend to paralyze the driving forces of a free society, and which kinds of measures are particularly dangerous in this respect, can we hope that social experimentation will not lead us into situations none of us want.

It is as a contribution to this task that this book is intended. I hope that at least in the quieter atmosphere of the present it will be received as what it was meant to be, not as an exhortation to resistance against any improvement or experimentation, but as a warning that we should insist that any modification in our arrangements should pass certain tests (described in the central chapter on the Rule of Law) before we commit ourselves to courses from which withdrawal may be difficult.

The fact that this book was originally written with only the British public in mind does not appear to have seriously affected its intelligibility for the American reader. But there is one point of phraseology which I ought to explain here to forestall any misunderstanding. I use throughout the term "liberal" in the original, nineteenth-century sense in which it is still current in Britain. In current American usage it often means very nearly the opposite of this. It has been part of the camouflage of leftish movements in this country, helped by the muddleheadedness of many who really believe in liberty, that "liberal" has come to mean the advocacy of almost every kind of government control. I am still puzzled why those in the United States who truly believe in liberty should not only have allowed the left to appropriate this almost indispensable term but should even have assisted by beginning to use it themselves as a term of opprobrium. This seems to be particularly regrettable because of the consequent tendency of many true liberals to describe themselves as conservatives.

It is true, of course, that in the struggle against the believers in the all-powerful state the true liberal must sometimes make common cause with the conservative, and in some circumstances, as in contemporary Britain, he has hardly any other way of actively working for his ideals. But true liberalism is still distinct from conservatism, and there is danger in the two being confused. Conservatism, though a necessary element in any stable society, is not a social program; in its paternalistic, nationalistic, and power-adoring tendencies it is often closer to socialism than true liberalism; and with its traditionalistic, anti-intellectual, and often mystical propensities it will never, except in short periods of disillusionment, appeal to the young and all those others who believe that some changes are desirable if this world is to become a better place. A conservative movement, by its very nature, is bound to be a defender of established privilege and to lean on the power of government for the protection of privilege. The essence of the liberal position, however, is the denial of all privilege, if privilege is understood in its proper and original meaning of the state granting and protecting rights to some which are not available on equal terms to others.

Perhaps a further word of apology is required for my allowing this book to reappear in entirely unchanged form after the lapse of almost twelve years. I have many times tried to revise it, and there are numerous points I should like to explain at greater length or to state more cautiously or to fortify by more illustration and proof. But all attempts at rewriting only proved that I could never again produce as short a book covering as much of the field; and it seems to me that, whatever other merits it may have, its relative brevity is its greatest. I have thus been forced to the conclusion that whatever I want to add to the argument I must attempt in separate studies. I have begun to do so in various essays, some of which provide a more searching discussion of certain philosophical and economic issues on which the present book only touches.[6] On the special question of the roots of the ideas here criticized and of their connection with some of the most powerful and impressive intellectual movements of this age, I have commented in another volume.[7] And before long I hope to supplement the all-too-brief central chapter of this book by a more extensive treatment of the relation between equality and justice.[8]

There is one particular topic, however, on which the reader will with justice expect me to comment on this occasion, yet which I could even less treat adequately without writing a new book. Little more than a year after *The Road to Serfdom* first appeared, Great Britain had a socialist government which remained in power for six years. And the question of how far this experience has confirmed or refuted my apprehensions is one which I must try to answer at least briefly. If anything, this experience has strengthened my concern and, I believe I may add, has taught the reality of the difficulties I pointed out to many for whom an abstract argument would never have carried conviction. Indeed, it was not long after the Labour government came into

6. *Individualism and Economic Order* (Chicago, 1948).

7. *The Counter Revolution of Science* (Glencoe, Ill., 1952).

8. An advance sketch of my treatment of this subject has been published by the National Bank of Egypt in the form of four lectures on *The Political Ideal of the Rule of Law* (Cairo, 1955).

power that some of the issues which my critics in America dismissed as bogeys became in Great Britain main topics of political discussion. Soon even official documents were gravely discussing the danger of totalitarianism raised by the policy of economic planning. There is no better illustration of the manner in which the inherent logic of their policies drove an unwilling socialist government into the kind of coercion it disliked than the following passage in the *Economic Survey for 1947* (which the Prime Minister presented to Parliament in February of that year) and its sequel:

> There is an essential difference between totalitarian and democratic planning. The former subordinates all individual desires and preferences to the demand of the State. For this purpose, it uses various methods of compulsion upon the individual which deprive him of his freedom of choice. Such methods may be necessary even in a democratic country during the extreme emergency of a great war. Thus the British people gave their war time Government the power to direct labour. But in normal times the people of a democratic country will not give up their freedom of choice to their Government. A democratic Government must therefore conduct its economic planning in a manner which preserves the maximum possible freedom of choice to the individual citizen.

The interesting point about this profession of laudable intentions is that six months later the same government found itself in peacetime forced to put the conscription of labor back on the statute book. It hardly diminishes the significance of this when it is pointed out that the power was in fact never used because, if it is known that the authorities have power to coerce, few will wait for actual coercion. But it is rather difficult to see how the government could have persisted in its illusions when in the same document it claims that it was now for "the Government to say what is the best use for the resources in the national interest" and to "lay

PREFACE 1956

down the economic task for the nation: it must say which things are the most important and what the objectives of policy ought to be."

Of course, six years of socialist government in England have not produced anything resembling a totalitarian state. But those who argue that this has disproved the thesis of *The Road to Serfdom* have really missed one of its main points: that the most important change which extensive government control produces is a psychological change, an alteration in the character of the people. This is necessarily a slow affair, a process which extends not over a few years but perhaps over one or two generations. The important point is that the political ideals of a people and its attitude toward authority are as much the effect as the cause of the political institutions under which it lives. This means, among other things, that even a strong tradition of political liberty is no safeguard if the danger is precisely that new institutions and policies will gradually undermine and destroy that spirit. The consequences can of course be averted if that spirit reasserts itself in time and the people not only throw out the party which has been leading them further and further in the dangerous direction but also recognize the nature of the danger and resolutely change their course. There is not yet much ground to believe that the latter has happened in England.

Yet the change undergone by the character of the British people, not merely under its Labour government but in the course of the much longer period during which it has been enjoying the blessings of a paternalistic welfare state, can hardly be mistaken. These changes are not easily demonstrated but are clearly felt if one lives in the country. In illustration, I will cite a few significant passages from a sociological survey dealing with the impact of the surfeit of regulation on the mental attitudes of the young. It is concerned with the situation before the Labour government came into power, in fact, about the time this book was first published, and deals mainly with the effects of those wartime regulations which the Labour government made permanent:

> It is above all in the city that the province of the optional is felt as dwindling away to nothing. At school, in the place of work, on the journey to and fro, even in the very equipment and provisioning of the home, many of the activities normally possible to human beings are either forbidden or enjoined. Special agencies, called Citizen's Advice Bureaus, are set up to steer the bewildered through the forest of rules, and to indicate to the persistent the rare clearings where a private person may still make a choice. . . . [The town lad] is conditioned not to lift a finger without refering mentally to the book of words first. A time-budget of an ordinary city youth for an ordinary working day would show the he spends great stretches of his waking hour going through motions that have been predetermined for him by directives in whose framing he has had no part, whose precise intention he seldom understands, and of whose appropriateness he cannot judge. . . . The inference that what the city lad needs is more discipline and tighter control is too hasty. It would be nearer the mark to say that he is suffering from an overdose of control already. . . . Surveying his parents and his older brothers or sisters he finds them as regulation-bound as himself. He sees them so acclimatised to that state that they seldom plan and carry out under their own steam any new social excursion or enterprise. He thus looks forward to no future period at which a sinewy faculty of responsibility is likely to be of service to himself or others. . . . [The young people] are obliged to stomach so much external and, as it seems to them meaningless control that they seek escape and recuperation in an absence of discipline as complete as they can make it.[9]

9. L. J. Barnes, *Youth Service in an English County: A Report Prepared for King George's Jubilee Trust* (London, 1945).

Is it too pessimistic to fear that a generation grown up under these conditions is unlikely to throw off the fetters to which it has grown used? Or does this description not rather fully bear out De Tocqueville's prediction of the "new kind of servitude" when

> after having thus successively taken each member of the community in its powerful grasp, and fashioned him at will, the supreme power then extends its arm over the whole community. It covers the surface of society with a network of small complicated rules, minute and uniform, through which the most original minds and the most energetic characters cannot penetrate to rise above the crowd. The will of man is not shattered but softened, bent and guided; men are seldom forced by it to act, but they are constantly restrained from acting. Such a power does not destroy, but it prevents existence; it does not tyrannize, but it compresses, enervates, extinguishes, and stupefies a people, till each nation is reduced to be nothing better than a flock of timid and industrial animals, of which government is the shepherd.—I have always thought that servitude of the regular, quiet, and gentle kind which I have just described might be combined more easily than is commonly believed with some of the outward forms of freedom and that it might even establish itself under the wing of the sovereignty of the people.[10]

What De Tocqueville did not consider was how long such a government would remain in the hands of benevolent despots when it would be so much more easy for any group of ruffians to keep itself indefinitely in power by disregarding all the traditional decencies of political life.

10. A. de Tocqueville, *Democracy in America*, Part II, Book IV, chap. vi. The whole chapter should be read in order to realize with what acute insight De Tocqueville was able to foresee the psychological effects of the modern welfare state. It was, incidentally, De Tocqueville's frequent reference to the "new servitude" which suggested the title of the present book.

Perhaps I should also remind the reader that I have never accused the socialist parties of deliberately aiming at a totalitarian regime or even suspected that the leaders of the old socialist movements might ever show such inclinations. What I have argued in this book, and what the British experience convinces me even more to be true, is that the unforeseen but inevitable consequences of socialist planning create a state of affairs in which, if the policy is to be pursued, totalitarian forces will get the upper hand. I explicitly stress that "socialism can be put into practice only by methods of which most socialists disapprove" and even add that in this "the old socialist parties were inhibited by their democratic ideals" and that "they did not possess the ruthlessness required for the performance of their chosen task." I am afraid the impression one gained under the Labour government was that these inhibitions were if anything weaker among the British socialists than they had been among their German fellow-socialists twenty-five years earlier. Certainly the German Social Democrats, in the comparable period of the 1920's, under equally or more difficult economic conditions. never approached as closely to totalitarian planning as the British Labour government has done.

Since I cannot here examine the effect of these policies in detail, I will rather quote the summary judgments of other observers who may be less suspect of preconceived opinions. Some of the most damning, in fact, come from men who not long before had themselves been members of the Labour party. Thus Mr. Ivor Thomas, in a book apparently intended to explain why he left that party, comes to the conclusion that "from the point of view of fundamental human liberties there is little to choose between communism, socialism, and national socialism. They all are examples of the collectivist or totalitarian state . . . in its essentials not only is completed socialism the same as communism but it hardly differs from fascism."[11]

The most serious development is the growth of a measure of arbitrary administrative coercion and the progressive destruction of the cherished foundation of British liberty, the Rule of Law, for exactly the reasons here discussed in chapter 6. This process had of course started long before the last Labour government came into power and had been accentuated by the war. But the attempts at economic planning under the Labour government carried it to a point which makes it doubtful whether it can be said that the Rule of Law still prevails in Britain. The "New Despotism" of which a Lord Chief Justice had warned Britain as long as twenty-five years ago is, as *The Economist* recently observed, no longer a mere danger but an established fact.[12] It is a despotism exercised by a thoroughly conscientious and honest bureaucracy for what they sincerely believe is the good of the country. But it is nevertheless an arbitrary government, in practice free from effective parliamentary control; and its machinery would be as effective for any other than the beneficent purposes for which it is now used. I doubt whether it was much exaggerated when recently an eminent British jurist, in a careful analysis of these trends, came to the conclusions that "in Britain to-day, we live on the edge of dictatorship. Transition would be easy, swift, and it could be accomplished with complete legality. Already so many steps have been taken in this direction, due to the complete-

11. *The Socialist Tragedy* (London: Latimer House Ltd., 1949), pp. 241 and 242.

12. In an article in the issue of June 19, 1954, discussing the *Report on the Public Inquiry Ordered by the Minister of Agriculture into the Disposal of Land at Crichel Down* (Cmd. 9176; London: H.M. Stationery Office, 1954), a document deserving the most careful study by all those interested in the psychology of a planning bureaucracy.

ness of power possessed by the Government of the day, and the absence of any real check such as the terms of a written constitution or the existence of an effective second chamber, that those still to be taken are small in comparison."[13]

For a more detailed analysis of the economic policies of the British Labour government and its consequences I cannot do better than refer the reader to Professor John Jewkes's *Ordeal by Planning* (London: Macmillan & Co., 1948). It is the best discussion known to me of a concrete instance of the phenomena discussed in general terms in this book. It supplements it better than anything I could add here and spells out a lesson which is of significance far beyond Great Britain.

It seems now unlikely that, even when another Labour government should come into power in Great Britain, it would resume the experiments in large-scale nationalization and planning. But in Britain, as elsewhere in the world, the defeat of the onslaught of systematic socialism has merely given those who are anxious to preserve freedom a breathing space in which to re-examine our ambitions and to discard all those parts of the socialist inheritance which are a danger to a free society. Without such a revised conception of our social aims, we are likely to continue to drift in the same direction in which outright socialism would merely have carried us a little faster.

F. A. HAYEK

13. G. W. Keeton, *The Passing of Parliament* (London, 1952).

PREFACE
to the 1944 Edition

WHEN A PROFESSIONAL student of social affairs writes a political book, his first duty is plainly to say so. This is a political book. I do not wish to disguise this by describing it, as I might perhaps have done, by the more elegant and ambitious name of an essay in social philosophy. But, whatever the name, the essential point remains that all I shall have to say is derived from certain ultimate values. I hope I have adequately discharged in the book itself a second and no less important duty: to make it clear beyond doubt what these ultimate values are on which the whole argument depends.

There is, however, one thing I want to add to this. Though this is a political book, I am as certain as anyone can be that the beliefs set out in it are not determined by my personal interests. I can discover no reason why the kind of society which seems to me desirable should offer greater advantages to me than to the great majority of the people of my country. In fact, I am always told by my socialist colleagues that as an economist I should occupy a much more important position in the kind of society to which I am opposed—provided, of course, that I could bring myself to accept their views. I feel equally certain that my opposition to these views is not due to their being different from those with which I have grown up, since they are the very views which I held as a young man and which have led me to make the study of economics my profession. For those who, in the current fashion, seek interested motives in every profession of a political opinion, I may, perhaps, be allowed to add that

PREFACE 1944

I have every possible reason for *not* writing or publishing this book. It is certain to offend many people with whom I wish to live on friendly terms; it has forced me to put aside work for which I feel better qualified and to which I attach greater importance in the long run; and, above all, it is certain to prejudice the reception of the results of the more strictly academic work to which all my inclinations lead me.

If in spite of this I have come to regard the writing of this book as a duty which I must not evade, this was mainly due to a peculiar and serious feature of the discussions of problems of future economic policy at the present time, of which the public is scarcely sufficiently aware. This is the fact that the majority of economists have now for some years been absorbed by the war machine, and silenced by their official positions, and that in consequence public opinion on these problems is to an alarming extent guided by amateurs and cranks, by people who have an ax to grind or a pet panacea to sell. In these circumstances one who still has the leisure for literary work is hardly entitled to keep to himself apprehensions which current tendencies must create in the minds of many who cannot publicly express them—though in different circumstances I should have gladly left the discussion of questions of national policy to those who are both better authorized and better qualified for the task.

The central argument of this book was first sketched in an article entitled "Freedom and the Economic System," which appeared in the *Contemporary Review* for April, 1938, and was later reprinted in an enlarged form as one of the "Public Policy Pamphlets" edited by Professor H. D. Gideonse for the University of Chicago Press (1939). I have to thank the editors and publishers of both these publications for permission to reproduce certain passages from them.

F. A. HAYEK

The Road to Serfdom

Introduction

*Few discoveries are more irritating than
those which expose the pedigree of ideas.*
—LORD ACTON

CONTEMPORARY events differ from history in that we
do not know the results they will produce. Looking
back, we can assess the significance of past occurrences and trace the consequences they have brought in
their train. But while history runs its course, it is not history
to us. It leads us into an unknown land, and but rarely can
we get a glimpse of what lies ahead. It would be different if
it were given to us to live a second time through the same
events with all the knowledge of what we have seen before. How different would things appear to us; how important and often alarming would changes seem that we now
scarcely notice! It is probably fortunate that man can never
have this experience and knows of no laws which history
must obey.

Yet, although history never quite repeats itself, and just
because no development is inevitable, we can in a measure
learn from the past to avoid a repetition of the same process.
One need not be a prophet to be aware of impending dangers. An accidental combination of experience and interest
will often reveal events to one man under aspects which few
yet see.

The following pages are the product of an experience as
near as possible to twice living through the same period—
or at least twice watching a very similar evolution of ideas.
While this is an experience one is not likely to gain in one
country, it may in certain circumstances be acquired by living

in turn for long periods in different countries. Though the influences to which the trend of thought is subject in most civilized nations are to a large extent similar, they do not necessarily operate at the same time or at the same speed. Thus, by moving from one country to another, one may sometimes twice watch similar phases of intellectual development. The senses have then become peculiarly acute. When one hears for a second time opinions expressed or measures advocated which one has first met twenty or twenty-five years ago, they assume a new meaning as symptoms of a definite trend. They suggest, if not the necessity, at least the probability, that developments will take a similar course.

It is necessary now to state the unpalatable truth that it is Germany whose fate we are in some danger of repeating. The danger is not immediate, it is true, and conditions in England and the United States are still so remote from those witnessed in recent years in Germany as to make it difficult to believe that we are moving in the same direction. Yet, though the road be long, it is one on which it becomes more difficult to turn back as one advances. If in the long run we are the makers of our own fate, in the short run we are the captives of the ideas we have created. Only if we recognize the danger in time can we hope to avert it.

It is not to the Germany of Hitler, the Germany of the present war, that England and the United States bear yet any resemblance. But students of the currents of ideas can hardly fail to see that there is more than a superficial similarity between the trend of thought in Germany during and after the last war and the present current of ideas in the democracies. There exists now in these countries certainly the same determination that the organization of the nation which has been achieved for purposes of defense shall be retained for the purposes of creation. There is the same contempt for nineteenth-century liberalism, the same spurious "realism" and even cynicism, the same fatalistic acceptance of "inevitable trends." And at least nine out of every ten of the lessons which our most vociferous reformers are so anxious we should learn from this war are precisely the lessons which the Germans did learn from the last war and which have done much to produce the Nazi system. We shall have opportunity in the course of this book to show that there are a large number of other points where at an interval of fifteen to twenty-five years we seem to follow the example of Germany. Although one does not like to be reminded, it is not so many years since the socialist policy of that country was generally held up by progressives as an example to be imitated, just as in more recent years Sweden has been the model country to which progressive eyes were directed. All those whose memory goes further back know how deeply for at least a generation before the last war German thought and German practice influenced ideals and policy in England and, to some extent, in the United States.

The author has spent about half of his adult life in his native Austria, in close touch with German intellectual life, and the other half in the United States and England. In the latter period he has become increasingly convinced that at least some of the forces which have destroyed freedom in Germany are also at work here and that the character and the source of this danger are, if possible, even less understood than they were in Germany. The supreme tragedy is still not seen that in Germany it was largely people of good will, men who were admired and held up as models in the democratic countries, who prepared the way for, if they did not actually create, the forces which now stand for everything they detest. Yet our chance of averting a similar fate depends on our facing the danger and on our being prepared to revise even our most cherished hopes and ambitions if they should prove to be the source of the danger. There are few signs yet that we have the intellectual courage to admit to ourselves that we may have been wrong. Few are ready to recognize that the rise of fascism and naziism was not a reaction against the socialist trends of the preceding period but a necessary outcome of those tendencies. This is a truth which most people were unwilling to see even when the similarities of many of the repellent features of the internal regimes in communist Russia and National Socialist Germany were widely recognized. As a result, many who think themselves infinitely superior to the aberrations of naziism, and sincerely hate all its manifestations, work at the same time for ideals whose realization would lead straight to the abhorred tyranny.

All parallels between developments in different countries are, of course, deceptive; but I am not basing my argument mainly on such parallels. Nor am I arguing that these developments are inevitable. If they were, there would be no point in writing this. They can be prevented if people realize in time where their efforts may lead. But until recently there was little hope that any attempt to make them see the danger would be successful. It seems, however, as if the time were now ripe for a fuller discussion of the whole issue. Not only is the problem now more widely recognized; there are also special reasons which at this juncture make it imperative that we should face the issues squarely.

It will, perhaps, be said that this is not the time to raise an issue on which opinions clash sharply. But the socialism of which we speak is not a party matter, and the questions which we are discussing have little to do with the questions at dispute between political parties. It does not affect our problem that some groups may want less socialism than others; that some want socialism mainly in the interest of one group and others in that of another. The important point is that, if we take the people whose views influence developments, they are now in the democracies in some measure all socialists. If it is no longer fashionable to emphasize that "we are all socialists now," this is so merely because the fact is too obvious. Scarcely anybody doubts that we must continue to move toward socialism, and most people are merely trying to deflect this movement in the interest of a particular class or group.

It is because nearly everybody wants it that we are moving in this direction. There are no objective facts which make it inevitable. We shall have to say something about the alleged inevitability of "planning" later. The main question is where this movement will lead us. Is it not possible that if the people whose convictions now give it an irresistible momentum began to see what only a few yet apprehend, they would recoil in horror and abandon the quest which for half a century has engaged so many people of good will? Where these common beliefs of our generation will lead us is a problem not for one party but for every one of us—a problem of the most momentous significance. Is there a greater tragedy imaginable than that, in our endeavor consciously to shape our future in accordance with high ideals, we should in fact unwittingly produce the very opposite of what we have been striving for?

There is an even more pressing reason why at this time we should seriously endeavor to understand the forces which have created National Socialism: that this will enable us to understand our enemy and the issue at stake between us. It cannot be denied that there is yet little recognition of the positive ideals for which we are fighting. We know that we are fighting for freedom to shape our life according to our own ideas. That is a great deal, but not enough. It is not enough to give us the firm beliefs which we need to resist an enemy who uses propaganda as one of his main weapons not only in the most blatant but also in the most subtle forms. It is still more insufficient when we have to counter this propaganda among the people in the countries under his control and elsewhere, where the effect of this propaganda will not disappear with the defeat of the Axis powers. It is not enough if we are to show to others that what we are fighting for is worth their support, and it is not enough to guide us in the building of a new world safe against the dangers to which the old one has succumbed.

It is a lamentable fact that the democracies in their dealings with the dictators before the war, not less than in their attempts at propaganda and in the discussion of their war aims, have shown an inner insecurity and uncertainty of aim which can be explained only by confusion about their own ideals and the nature of the differences which separated them from the enemy. We have been misled as much because we have refused to believe that the enemy was sincere in the profession of some beliefs which we shared as because we believed in the sincerity of some of his other claims. Have not the parties of the Left as well as those of the Right been deceived by believing that the National Socialist party was in the service of the capitalists and opposed to all forms of socialism? How many features of Hitler's system have not been recommended to us for imitation from the most unexpected quarters, unaware that they are an integral part of that system and incompatible with the free society we hope to preserve? The number of dangerous mistakes we have made before and since the outbreak of war because we do not understand the opponent with whom we are faced is appalling. It seems almost as if we did not want to understand the development which has produced totalitarianism because such an understanding might destroy some of the dearest illusions to which we are determined to cling.

We shall never be successful in our dealings with the Germans until we understand the character and the growth of the ideas which now govern them. The theory which is once again put forth, that the Germans as such are inherently vicious, is hardly tenable and not very creditable to those who hold it. It dishonors the long series of Anglo-Saxon thinkers who during the last hundred years have gladly taken over what was best, and not only what was best, in German thought. It overlooks the fact that, when eighty years ago John Stuart Mill was writing his great essay *On Liberty*, he drew his inspiration, more than from any other men, from two Germans—Goethe and Wilhelm von Humboldt[1]—and forgets the fact that two of the most influential intellectual forebears of National Socialism—Thomas Carlyle and Houston Stewart Chamberlain—were a Scot and an Englishman. In its cruder forms this view is a disgrace to those who by maintaining it adopt the worst features of German racial theories.

The problem is not why the Germans as such are vicious, which congenitally they are probably no more than other peoples, but to determine the circumstances which during the last seventy years have made possible the progressive growth and the ultimate victory of a particular set of ideas,

1. As some people may think this statement exaggerated, the testimony of Lord Morley may be worth quoting, who in his *Recollections* speaks of the "acknowledged point" that the main argument of the essay *On Liberty* "was not original but came from Germany."

and why in the end this victory has brought the most vicious elements among them to the top. Mere hatred of everything German instead of the particular ideas which now dominate the Germans is, moreover, very dangerous, because it blinds those who indulge in it against a real threat. It is to be feared that this attitude is frequently merely a kind of escapism, caused by an unwillingness to recognize tendencies which are not confined to Germany and by a reluctance to re-examine, and if necessary to discard, beliefs which we have taken over from the Germans and by which we are still as much deluded as the Germans were. It is doubly dangerous because the contention that only the peculiar wickedness of the Germans has produced the Nazi system is likely to become the excuse for forcing on us the very institutions which have produced that wickedness.

The interpretation of the developments in Germany and Italy about to be proffered in this book is very different from that given by most foreign observers and by the majority of exiles from those countries. But if this interpretation is correct, it will also explain why it is almost impossible for a person who, like most of the exiles and the foreign correspondents of English and American newspapers, holds the now prevalent socialist views to see those events in the proper perspective. The superficial and misleading view which sees in National Socialism merely a reaction fomented by those whose privileges or interests were threatened by the advance of socialism was naturally supported by all those who, although they were at one time active in the movement of ideas that has led to National Socialism, have stopped at some point of that development and, by the conflict into which this brought them with the Nazis, were forced to leave their country. But the fact that they were numerically the only significant opposition to the Nazis means no more than that in the wider sense practically all Germans had become socialists and that liberalism in the old sense had been driven out by socialism. As we hope to show, the conflict in existence between the National Socialist "Right" and the "Left" in Germany is the kind of conflict that will always arise between rival socialist factions. If this interpretation is correct, it means, however, that many of those socialist refugees, in clinging to their beliefs, are now, though with the best will in the world, helping to lead their adopted country the way which Germany has gone.

I know that many of my Anglo-Saxon friends have sometimes been shocked by the semi-Fascist views they would occasionally hear expressed by German refugees, whose genuinely socialist convictions could not be doubted. But while these observers put this down to the others' being Germans, the true explanation is that they were socialists whose experience had carried them several stages beyond that yet reached by socialists in England and America. It is true, of course, that German socialists have found much support in their country from certain features of the Prussian tradition; and this kinship between Prussianism and socialism, in which in Germany both sides gloried, gives additional support to our main contention.[2] But it would be a mistake to believe that the specific German rather than the socialist element produced totalitarianism. It was the prevalence of so-

2. That there did exist a certain kinship between socialism and the organization of the Prussian state, consciously organized from the top as in no other country, is undeniable and was freely recognized already by the early French socialists. Long before the ideal of running the whole state on the same principles as a single factory was to inspire nineteenth-century socialism, the Prussian poet Novalis had already deplored that "no other state has ever been administered so much like a factory as Prussia since the death of Frederick William" (cf. Novalis [Friedrich von Hardenberg], *Glauben und Liebe, oder der König und die Königin* [1798]).

cialist views and not Prussianism that Germany had in common with Italy and Russia—and it was from the masses and not from the classes steeped in the Prussian tradition, and favored by it, that National Socialism arose.

1

The Abandoned Road

*A program whose basic thesis is, not that the system
of free enterprise for profit has failed in this generation, but
that it has not yet been tried.*
—F. D. ROOSEVELT

WHEN the course of civilization takes an unexpected turn—when, instead of the continuous progress which we have come to expect, we find ourselves threatened by evils associated by us with past ages of barbarism—we naturally blame anything but ourselves. Have we not all striven according to our best lights, and have not many of our finest minds incessantly worked to make this a better world? Have not all our efforts and hopes been directed toward greater freedom, justice, and prosperity? If the outcome is so different from our aims—if, instead of freedom and prosperity, bondage and misery stare us in the face—is it not clear that sinister forces must have foiled our intentions, that we are the victims of some evil power which must be conquered before we can resume the road to better things? However much we may differ when we name the culprit—whether it is the wicked capitalist or the vicious spirit of a particular nation, the stupidity of our elders, or a social system not yet, although we have struggled against it for a half a century, fully overthrown—we all are, or at least were until recently, certain of one thing: that the leading ideas which during the last generation have become common to most people of good will and have determined the major changes in our social life cannot have been wrong. We are ready to accept almost any explanation of the present

13

crisis of our civilization except one: that the present state of the world may be the result of genuine error on our own part and that the pursuit of some of our most cherished ideals has apparently produced results utterly different from those which we expected.

While all our energies are directed to bring this war to a victorious conclusion, it is sometimes difficult to remember that even before the war the values for which we are now fighting were threatened here and destroyed elsewhere. Though for the time being the different ideals are represented by hostile nations fighting for their existence, we must not forget that this conflict has grown out of a struggle of ideas within what, not so long ago, was a common European civilization and that the tendencies which have culminated in the creation of the totalitarian systems were not confined to the countries which have succumbed to them. Though the first task must now be to win the war, to win it will only gain us another opportunity to face the basic problems and to find a way of averting the fate which has overtaken kindred civilizations.

Now, it is somewhat difficult to think of Germany and Italy, or of Russia, not as different worlds but as products of a development of thought in which we have shared; it is, at least so far as our enemies are concerned, easier and more comforting to think that they are entirely different from us and that what happened there cannot happen here. Yet the history of these countries in the years before the rise of the totalitarian system showed few features with which we are not familiar. The external conflict is a result of a transformation of European thought in which others have moved so much faster as to bring them into irreconcilable conflict with our ideals, but which has not left us unaffected.

15

THE ABANDONED ROAD

That a change of ideas and the force of human will have made the world what it is now, though men did not foresee the results, and that no spontaneous change in the facts obliged us thus to adapt our thought is perhaps particularly difficult for the Anglo-Saxon nations to see, just because in this development they have, fortunately for them, lagged behind most of the European peoples. We still think of the ideals which guide us, and have guided us for the past generation, as ideals only to be realized in the future and are not aware how far in the last twenty-five years they have already transformed not only the world but also our own countries. We still believe that until quite recently we were governed by what are vaguely called nineteenth-century ideas or the principle of laissez faire. Compared with some other countries, and from the point of view of those impatient to speed up the change, there may be some justification for such belief. But although until 1931 England and America had followed only slowly on the path on which others had led, even by then they had moved so far that only those whose memory goes back to the years before the last war know what a liberal world has been like.[1]

The crucial point of which our people are still so little aware is, however, not merely the magnitude of the changes

1. Even in that year the Macmillan Report could already speak of "the change of outlook of the government of this country in recent times, its growing preoccupation, irrespective of party, with the management of the like of the people" and add that "Parliament finds itself increasingly engaged in legislation which has for its conscious aim the regulation of the day-to-day affairs of the community and now intervenes in matters formerly thought to be entirely outside its scope." This could be said before, later in the same year, England finally took the headlong plunge and, in the short space of the inglorious years 1931–39, transformed its economic system beyond recognition.

which have taken place during the last generation but the fact that they mean a complete change in the direction of the evolution of our ideas and social order. For at least twenty-five years before the specter of totalitarianism became a real threat, we had progressively been moving away from the basic ideas on which Western civilization has been built. That this movement on which we have entered with such high hopes and ambitions should have brought us face to face with the totalitarian horror has come as a profound shock to this generation, which still refuses to connect the two facts. Yet this development merely confirms the warnings of the fathers of the liberal philosophy which we still profess. We have progressively abandoned that freedom in economic affairs without which personal and political freedom has never existed in the past. Although we had been warned by some of the greatest political thinkers of the nineteenth century, by De Tocqueville and Lord Acton, that socialism means slavery, we have steadily moved in the direction of socialism. And now that we have seen a new form of slavery arise before our eyes, we have so completely forgotten the warning that it scarcely occurs to us that the two things may be connected.[2]

How sharp a break not only with the recent past but with the whole evolution of Western civilization the modern trend toward socialism means becomes clear if we consider it not merely against the background of the nineteenth cen-

2. Even much more recent warnings which have proved dreadfully true have been almost entirely forgotten. It is not yet thirty years since Hilaire Belloc, in a book which explains more of what has happened since in Germany than most works written after the event, explained that "the effect of Socialist doctrine on Capitalist society is to produce a third thing different from either of its two begetters—to wit, the Servile State" (*The Servile State* [1913; 3d ed., 1927], p. xiv).

tury but in a longer historical perspective. We are rapidly abandoning not the views merely of Cobden and Bright, of Adam Smith and Hume, or even of Locke and Milton, but one of the salient characteristics of Western civilization as it has grown from the foundations laid by Christianity and the Greeks and Romans. Not merely nineteenth- and eighteenth-century liberalism, but the basic individualism inherited by us from Erasmus and Montaigne, from Cicero and Tacitus, Pericles and Thucydides, is progressively relinquished.

The Nazi leader who described the National Socialist revolution as a counter-Renaissance spoke more truly than he probably knew. It was the decisive step in the destruction of that civilization which modern man had built up from the age of the Renaissance and which was, above all, an individualist civilization. Individualism has a bad name today, and the term has come to be connected with egotism and selfishness. But the individualism of which we speak in contrast to socialism and all other forms of collectivism has no necessary connection with these. Only gradually in the course of this book shall we be able to make clear the contrast between the two opposing principles. But the essential features of that individualism which, from elements provided by Christianity and the philosophy of classical antiquity, was first fully developed during the Renaissance and has since grown and spread into what we know as Western civilization—are the respect for the individual man *qua* man, that is, the recognition of his own views and tastes as supreme in his own sphere, however narrowly that may be circumscribed, and the belief that it is desirable that men should develop their own individual gifts and bents. "Freedom" and "liberty" are now words so worn with use and abuse that one must hesitate to employ them to express the ideals for which they stood during that period. "Tolerance" is, perhaps, the only word which still preserves the full meaning of the principle which during the whole of this period was in the ascendant and which only in recent times has again been in decline, to disappear completely with the rise of the totalitarian state.

The gradual transformation of a rigidly organized hierarchic system into one where men could at least attempt to shape their own life, where man gained the opportunity of knowing and choosing between different forms of life, is closely associated with the growth of commerce. From the commercial cities of northern Italy the new view of life spread with commerce to the west and north, through France and the southwest of Germany to the Low Countries and the British Isles, taking firm root wherever there was no despotic political power to stifle it. In the Low Countries and Britain it for a long time enjoyed its fullest development and for the first time had an opportunity to grow freely and to become the foundation of the social and political life of these countries. And it was from there that in the late seventeenth and eighteenth centuries it again began to spread in a more fully developed form to the West and East, to the New World and to the center of the European continent, where devastating wars and political oppression had largely submerged the earlier beginnings of a similar growth.[3]

During the whole of this modern period of European history the general direction of social development was one of freeing the individual from the ties which had bound him to the customary or prescribed ways in the pursuit of his ordi-

---

3. The most fateful of these developments, pregnant with consequences not yet extinct, was the subjection and partial destruction of the German bourgeoisie by the territorial princes in the fifteenth and sixteenth centuries.

nary activities. The conscious realization that the spontaneous and uncontrolled efforts of individuals were capable of producing a complex order of economic activities could come only after this development had made some progress. The subsequent elaboration of a consistent argument in favor of economic freedom was the outcome of a free growth of economic activity which had been the undesigned and unforeseen by-product of political freedom.

Perhaps the greatest result of the unchaining of individual energies was the marvelous growth of science which followed the march of individual liberty from Italy to England and beyond. That the inventive faculty of man had been no less in earlier periods is shown by the many highly ingenious automatic toys and other mechanical contrivances constructed while industrial technique still remained stationary and by the development in some industries which, like mining or watch-making, were not subject to restrictive controls. But the few attempts toward a more extended industrial use of mechanical inventions, some extraordinarily advanced, were promptly suppressed, and the desire for knowledge was stifled, so long as the dominant views were held to be binding for all: the beliefs of the great majority on what was right and proper were allowed to bar the way of the individual innovator. Only since industrial freedom opened the path to the free use of new knowledge, only since everything could be tried—if somebody could be found to back it at his own risk—and, it should be added, as often as not from outside the authorities officially intrusted with the cultivation of learning, has science made the great strides which in the last hundred and fifty years have changed the face of the world.

As is so often true, the nature of our civilization has been seen more clearly by its enemies than by most of its friends:

"the perennial Western malady, the revolt of the individual against the species," as that nineteenth-century totalitarian, Auguste Comte, has described it, was indeed the force which built our civilization. What the nineteenth century added to the individualism of the preceding period was merely to make all classes conscious of freedom, to develop systematically and continuously what had grown in a haphazard and patchy manner, and to spread it from England and Holland over most of the European continent.

The result of this growth surpassed all expectations. Wherever the barriers to the free exercise of human ingenuity were removed, man became rapidly able to satisfy ever widening ranges of desire. And while the rising standard soon led to the discovery of very dark spots in society, spots which men were no longer willing to tolerate, there was probably no class that did not substantially benefit from the general advance. We cannot do justice to this astonishing growth if we measure it by our present standards, which themselves result from this growth and now make many defects obvious. To appreciate what it meant to those who took part in it, we must measure it by the hopes and wishes men held when it began: and there can be no doubt that its success surpassed man's wildest dreams, that by the beginning of the twentieth century the workingman in the Western world had reached a degree of material comfort, security, and personal independence which a hundred years before had seemed scarcely possible.

What in the future will probably appear the most significant and far-reaching effect of this success is the new sense of power over their own fate, the belief in the unbounded possibilities of improving their own lot, which the success already achieved created among men. With the success grew ambition—and man had every right to be ambitious. What had been an inspiring promise seemed no longer enough, the rate of progress far too slow; and the principles which had made this progress possible in the past came to be regarded more as obstacles to speedier progress, impatiently to be brushed away, than as the conditions for the preservation and development of what had already been achieved.

There is nothing in the basic principles of liberalism to make it a stationary creed; there are no hard-and-fast rules fixed once and for all. The fundamental principle that in the ordering of our affairs we should make as much use as possible of the spontaneous forces of society, and resort as little as possible to coercion, is capable of an infinite variety of applications. There is, in particular, all the difference between deliberately creating a system within which competition will work as beneficially as possible and passively accepting institutions as they are. Probably nothing has done so much harm to the liberal cause as the wooden insistence of some liberals on certain rough rules of thumb, above all the principle of laissez faire. Yet, in a sense, this was necessary and unavoidable. Against the innumerable interests which could show that particular measures would confer immediate and obvious benefits on some, while the harm they caused was much more indirect and difficult to see, nothing short of some hard-and-fast rule would have been effective. And since a strong presumption in favor of industrial liberty had undoubtedly been established, the temptation to present it as a rule which knew no exceptions was too strong always to be resisted.

But, with this attitude taken by many popularizers of the liberal doctrine, it was almost inevitable that, once their position was penetrated at some points, it should soon collapse as a whole. The position was further weakened by the inevitably slow progress of a policy which aimed at a gradual improvement of the institutional framework of a free society. This progress depended on the growth of our understanding of the social forces and the conditions most favorable to their working in a desirable manner. Since the task was to assist, and where necessary to supplement, their operation, the first requisite was to understand them. The attitude of the liberal toward society is like that of the gardener who tends a plant and, in order to create the conditions most favorable to its growth, must know as much as possible about its structure and the way it functions.

No sensible person should have doubted that the crude rules in which the principles of economic policy of the nineteenth century were expressed were only a beginning—that we had yet much to learn and that there were still immense possibilities of advancement on the lines on which we had moved. But this advance could come only as we gained increasing intellectual mastery of the forces of which we had to make use. There were many obvious tasks, such as our handling of the monetary system and the prevention or control of monopoly, and an even greater number of less obvious but hardly less important tasks to be undertaken in other fields, where there could be no doubt that the governments possessed enormous powers for good and evil; and there was every reason to expect that, with a better understanding of the problems, we should some day be able to use these powers successfully.

But while the progress toward what is commonly called "positive" action was necessarily slow, and while for the immediate improvement liberalism had to rely largely on the gradual increase of wealth which freedom brought about, it had constantly to fight proposals which threatened this progress. It came to be regarded as a "negative" creed because it could offer to particular individuals little more than a share in the common progress—a progress which came to be taken more and more for granted and was no longer recognized as the result of the policy of freedom. It might even be said that the very success of liberalism became the cause of its decline. Because of the success already achieved, man became increasingly unwilling to tolerate the evils still with him which now appeared both unbearable and unnecessary.

Because of the growing impatience with the slow advance of liberal policy, the just irritation with those who used liberal phraseology in defense of antisocial privileges, and the boundless ambition seemingly justified by the material improvements already achieved, it came to pass that toward the turn of the century the belief in the basic tenets of liberalism was more and more relinquished. What had been achieved came to be regarded as a secure and imperishable possession, acquired once and for all. The eyes of the people became fixed on the new demands, the rapid satisfaction of which seemed to be barred by the adherence to the old principles. It became more and more widely accepted that further advance could be expected not along the old lines within the general framework which had made past progress possible but only by a complete remodeling of society. It was no longer a question of adding to or improving the existing machinery but of completely scrapping and replacing it. And, as the hope of the new generation came to be centered on something completely new, interest in and understanding of the functioning of the existing society rapidly declined; and, with the decline of the understanding of the way in which the free system worked, our awareness of what depended on its existence also decreased.

This is not the place to discuss how this change in outlook was fostered by the uncritical transfer to the problems of society of habits of thought engendered by the preoccupation with technological problems, the habits of thought of the natural scientist and the engineer, and how these at the same time tended to discredit the results of the past study of society which did not conform to their prejudices and to impose ideals of organization on a sphere to which they are not appropriate.[4] All we are here concerned to show is how completely, though gradually and by almost imperceptible steps, our attitude toward society has changed. What at every stage of this process of change had appeared a difference of degree only has in its cumulative effect already brought about a fundamental difference between the older liberal attitude toward society and the present approach to social problems. The change amounts to a complete reversal of the trend we have sketched, an entire abandonment of the individualist tradition which has created Western civilization.

According to the views now dominant, the question is no longer how we can make the best use of the spontaneous forces found in a free society. We have in effect undertaken to dispense with the forces which produced unforeseen results and to replace the impersonal and anonymous mechanism of the market by collective and "conscious" direction of all social forces to deliberately chosen goals. The difference cannot be better illustrated than by the extreme position

4. The author has made an attempt to trace the beginning of this development in two series of articles on "Scientism and the Study of Society" and "The Counter-Revolution of Science" which appeared in *Economica*, 1941–44.

THE ABANDONED ROAD

taken in a widely acclaimed book on whose program of so-called "planning for freedom" we shall have to comment yet more than once. "We have never had to set up and direct," writes Dr. Karl Mannheim, "the entire system of nature as we are forced to do today with society. . . . Mankind is tending more and more to regulate the whole of its social life, although it has never attempted to create a second nature."[5]

It is significant that this change in the trend of ideas has coincided with a reversal of the direction in which ideas have traveled in space. For over two hundred years English ideas had been spreading eastward. The rule of freedom which had been achieved in England seemed destined to spread throughout the world. By about 1870 the reign of these ideas had probably reached its easternmost expansion. From then onward it began to retreat, and a different set of ideas, not really new but very old, began to advance from the East. England lost her intellectual leadership in the political and social sphere and became an importer of ideas. For the next sixty years Germany became the center from which the ideas destined to govern the world in the twentieth century spread east and west. Whether it was Hegel or Marx, List or Schmoller, Sombart or Mannheim, whether it was socialism in its more radical form or merely "organization" or "planning" of a less radical kind, German ideas were everywhere readily imported and German institutions imitated.

Although most of the new ideas, and particularly socialism, did not originate in Germany, it was in Germany that they were perfected and during the last quarter of the nineteenth and the first quarter of the twentieth century that they reached their fullest development. It is now often for-

5. *Man and Society in an Age of Reconstruction* (1940), p. 175.

gotten how very considerable was the lead which Germany had during this period in the development of the theory and practice of socialism; that a generation before socialism became a serious issue in this country, Germany had a large socialist party in her parliament and that until not very long ago the doctrinal development of socialism was almost entirely carried on in Germany and Austria, so that even today Russian discussion largely carries on where the Germans left off. Most English and American socialists are still unaware that the majority of the problems they begin to discover were thoroughly discussed by German socialists long ago.

The intellectual influence which German thinkers were able to exercise during this period on the whole world was supported not merely by the great material progress of Germany but even more by the extraordinary reputation which German thinkers and scientists had earned during the preceding hundred years when Germany had once more become an integral and even leading member of the common European civilization. But it soon served to assist the spreading from Germany of ideas directed against the foundations of that civilization. The Germans themselves—or at least those among them who spread these ideas—were fully aware of the conflict: what had been the common heritage of European civilization became to them, long before the Nazis, "Western" civilization—where "Western" was no longer used in the old sense of Occident but had come to mean west of the Rhine. "Western" in this sense was liberalism and democracy, capitalism and individualism, free trade and any form of internationalism or love of peace.

But in spite of the ill-concealed contempt of an ever increasing number of Germans for those "shallow" Western ideals, or perhaps because of it, the people of the West continued to import German ideas and were even induced to

THE ABANDONED ROAD

believe that their own former convictions had merely been rationalizations of selfish interests, that free trade was a doctrine invented to further British interests, and that the political ideals of England and America were hopelessly outmoded and a thing to be ashamed of.

2
The Great Utopia

*What has always made the state a hell on earth has
been precisely that man has tried to make it his heaven.*
—F. HÖLDERLIN

THAT socialism has displaced liberalism as the doctrine held by the great majority of progressives does not simply mean that people had forgotten the warnings of the great liberal thinkers of the past about the consequences of collectivism. It has happened because they were persuaded of the very opposite of what these men had predicted. The extraordinary thing is that the same socialism that was not only early recognized as the gravest threat to freedom, but quite openly began as a reaction against the liberalism of the French Revolution, gained general acceptance under the flag of liberty. It is rarely remembered now that socialism in its beginnings was frankly authoritarian. The French writers who laid the foundations of modern socialism had no doubt that their ideas could be put into practice only by strong dictatorial government. To them socialism meant an attempt to "terminate the revolution" by a deliberate reorganization of society on hierarchical lines and by the imposition of a coercive "spiritual power." Where freedom was concerned, the founders of socialism made no bones about their intentions. Freedom of thought they regarded as the root-evil of nineteenth-century society, and the first of modern planners, Saint-Simon, even predicted that those who did not obey his proposed planning boards would be "treated as cattle."

Only under the influence of the strong democratic currents preceding the revolution of 1848 did socialism begin to ally itself with the forces of freedom. But it took the new "democratic socialism" a long time to live down the suspicions aroused by its antecedents. Nobody saw more clearly than De Tocqueville that democracy as an essentially individualist institution stood in an irreconcilable conflict with socialism:

"Democracy extends the sphere of individual freedom," he said in 1848; "socialism restricts it. Democracy attaches all possible value to each man; socialism makes each man a mere agent, a mere number. Democracy and socialism have nothing in common but one word: equality. But notice the difference: while democracy seeks equality in liberty, socialism seeks equality in restraint and servitude."[1]

To allay these suspicions and to harness to its cart the strongest of all political motives—the craving for freedom—socialism began increasingly to make use of the promise of a "new freedom." The coming of socialism was to be the leap from the realm of necessity to the realm of freedom. It was to bring "economic freedom," without which the political freedom already gained was "not worth having." Only socialism was capable of effecting the consummation of the age-long struggle for freedom, in which the attainment of political freedom was but a first step.

The subtle change in meaning to which the word "freedom" was subjected in order that this argument should sound plausible is important. To the great apostles of political freedom the word had meant freedom from coercion, freedom from the arbitrary power of other men, release from the ties which left the individual no choice but obedi-

1. "Discours prononcé à l'assemblée constituante le 12 septembre 1848 sur la question du droit au travail," *Œuvres complètes d'Alexis de Tocqueville* (1866), IX, 546.

ence to the orders of a superior to whom he was attached. The new freedom promised, however, was to be freedom from necessity, release from the compulsion of the circumstances which inevitably limit the range of choice of all of us, although for some very much more than for others. Before man could be truly free, the "despotism of physical want" had to be broken, the "restraints of the economic system" relaxed.

Freedom in this sense is, of course, merely another name for power[2] or wealth. Yet, although the promises of this new freedom were often coupled with irresponsible promises of a great increase in material wealth in a socialist society, it was not from such an absolute conquest of the niggardliness of nature that economic freedom was expected. What the promise really amounted to was that the great existing disparities in the range of choice of different people were to disappear. The demand for the new freedom was thus only another name for the old demand for an equal distribution of wealth. But the new name gave the socialists another word in common with the liberals, and they exploited it to the full. And, although the word was used in a different sense by the two groups, few people noticed this and still fewer asked themselves whether the two kinds of freedom promised could really be combined.

2. The characteristic confusion of freedom with power, which we shall meet again and again throughout this discussion, is too big a subject to be thoroughly examined here. As old as socialism itself, it is so closely allied with it that almost seventy years ago a French scholar, discussing its Saint-Simonian origins, was led to say that this theory of liberty "est à elle seule tout le socialisme" (Paul Janet, *Saint-Simon et le Saint-Simonisme* [1878], p. 26 n.). The most explicit defender of this confusion is, significantly, the leading philosopher of American left-wingism, John Dewey, according to whom "liberty is the effective power to do specific things" so that "the demand for liberty is demand for power" ("Liberty and Social Control," *Social Frontier,* November, 1935, p. 41).

There can be no doubt that the promise of greater freedom has become one of the most effective weapons of socialist propaganda and that the belief that socialism would bring freedom is genuine and sincere. But this would only heighten the tragedy if it should prove that what was promised to us as the Road to Freedom was in fact the High Road to Servitude. Unquestionably, the promise of more freedom was responsible for luring more and more liberals along the socialist road, for blinding them to the conflict which exists between the basic principles of socialism and liberalism, and for often enabling socialists to usurp the very name of the old party of freedom. Socialism was embraced by the greater part of the intelligentsia as the apparent heir of the liberal tradition: therefore it is not surprising that to them the idea of socialism's leading to the opposite of liberty should appear inconceivable.

In recent years, however, the old apprehensions of the unforeseen consequences of socialism have once more been strongly voiced from the most unexpected quarters. Observer after observer, in spite of the contrary expectation with which he approached his subject, has been impressed with the extraordinary similarity in many respects of the conditions under "fascism" and "communism." While "progressives" in England and elsewhere were still deluding themselves that communism and fascism represented opposite poles, more and more people began to ask themselves whether these new tyrannies were not the outcome of the same tendencies. Even communists must have been somewhat shaken by such testimonies as that of Max Eastman, Lenin's old friend, who found himself compelled to admit that "instead of being better, Stalinism is worse than fascism, more ruthless, barbarous, unjust, immoral, anti-democratic, unredeemed by any hope or scruple," and that it is "better described as superfascist"; and when we find the same author recognizing that Stalinism *is* socialism, in the sense of being an inevitable although unforeseen political accompaniment of nationalization and collectivization which he had relied upon as part of his plan for erecting a classless society,"[3] his conclusion clearly achieves wider significance.

Mr. Eastman's case is perhaps the most remarkable, yet he is by no means the first or the only sympathetic observer of the Russian experiment to form similar conclusions. Several years earlier W. H. Chamberlin, who in twelve years in Russia as an American correspondent had seen all his ideals shattered, summed up the conclusions of his studies there and in Germany and Italy in the statement that "socialism is certain to prove, in the beginning at least, the road NOT to freedom, but to dictatorship and counter-dictatorships, to civil war of the fiercest kind. Socialism achieved and maintained by democratic means seems definitely to belong to the world of utopias."[4] Similarly a British writer, F. A. Voigt, after many years of close observation of developments in Europe as a foreign correspondent, concludes that "Marxism has led to Fascism and National Socialism, because, in all essentials, it is Fascism and National Socialism."[5] And Walter Lippmann has arrived at the conviction that "the generation to which we belong is now learning from experience what happens when men retreat from freedom to a coercive organization of their affairs. Though they promise themselves a more abundant life, they must in practice renounce it; as the organized direction increases, the variety of ends must

3. *Stalin's Russia and the Crisis of Socialism* (1940), p. 82.
4. *A False Utopia* (1937), pp. 202–3.
5. *Unto Caesar* (1939), p. 95.

THE GREAT UTOPIA

give way to uniformity. That is the nemesis of the planned society and the authoritarian principle in human affairs."[6]

Many more similar statements from people in a position to judge might be selected from publications of recent years, particularly from those by men who as citizens of the now totalitarian countries have lived through the transformation and have been forced by their experience to revise many cherished beliefs. We shall quote as one more example a German writer who expresses the same conclusion perhaps more justly than those already quoted.

"The complete collapse of the belief in the attainability of freedom and equality through Marxism," writes Peter Drucker, "has forced Russia to travel the same road toward a totalitarian, purely negative, non-economic society of unfreedom and inequality which Germany has been following. Not that communism and fascism are essentially the same. Fascism is the stage reached after communism has proved an illusion, and it has proved as much an illusion in Stalinist Russia as in pre-Hitler Germany."[7]

No less significant is the intellectual history of many of the Nazi and Fascist leaders. Everyone who has watched the growth of these movements in Italy[8] or in Germany has been struck by the number of leading men, from Mussolini downward (and not excluding Laval and Quisling), who began as socialists and ended as Fascists or Nazis. And what is true of the leaders is even more true of the rank and file of the movement. The relative ease with which a young

6. *Atlantic Monthly*, November, 1936, p. 552.
7. *The End of Economic Man* (1939), p. 230.
8. An illuminating account of the intellectual history of many of the Fascist leaders will be found in Robert Michels (himself a former Marxist Fascist), *Sozialismus und Faszismus* (Munich, 1925), II, 264–66, 311–12.

communist could be converted into a Nazi or vice versa was generally known in Germany, best of all to the propagandists of the two parties. Many a university teacher during the 1930's has seen English and American students return from the Continent uncertain whether they were communists or Nazis and certain only that they hated Western liberal civilization.

It is true, of course, that in Germany before 1933, and in Italy before 1922, communists and Nazis or Fascists clashed more frequently with each other than with other parties. They competed for the support of the same type of mind and reserved for each other the hatred of the heretic. But their practice showed how closely they are related. To both, the real enemy, the man with whom they had nothing in common and whom they could not hope to convince, is the liberal of the old type. While to the Nazi the communist, and to the communist the Nazi, and to both the socialist, are potential recruits who are made of the right timber, although they have listened to false prophets, they both know that there can be no compromise between them and those who really believe in individual freedom.

Lest this be doubted by people misled by official propaganda from either side, let me quote one more statement from an authority that ought not to be suspect. In an article under the significant title of "The Rediscovery of Liberalism," Professor Eduard Heimann, one of the leaders of German religious socialism, writes: "Hitlerism proclaims itself as both true democracy and true socialism, and the terrible truth is that there is a grain of truth for such claims—an infinitesimal grain, to be sure, but at any rate enough to serve as a basis for such fantastic distortions. Hitlerism even goes so far as to claim the role of protector of Christianity, and the terrible truth is that even this gross misinterpretation is able to make some impression. But one fact stands out with perfect clarity in all the fog: Hitler has never claimed to represent true liberalism. Liberalism then has the distinction of being the doctrine most hated by Hitler."[9] It should be added that this hatred had little occasion to show itself in practice merely because, by the time Hitler came to power, liberalism was to all intents and purposes dead in Germany. And it was socialism that had killed it.

While to many who have watched the transition from socialism to fascism at close quarters the connection between the two systems has become increasingly obvious, in the democracies the majority of people still believe that socialism and freedom can be combined. There can be no doubt that most socialists here still believe profoundly in the liberal ideal of freedom and that they would recoil if they became convinced that the realization of their program would mean the destruction of freedom. So little is the problem yet seen, so easily do the most irreconcilable ideals still live together, that we can still hear such contradictions in terms as "individualist socialism" seriously discussed. If this is the state of mind which makes us drift into a new world, nothing can be more urgent than that we should seriously examine the real significance of the evolution that has taken place elsewhere. Although our conclusions will only confirm the apprehensions which others have already expressed, the reasons why this development cannot be regarded as accidental will not appear without a rather full examination of the main aspects

9. *Social Research*, Vol. VIII, No. 4 (November, 1941). It deserves to be recalled in this connection that, whatever may have been his reasons, Hitler thought it expedient to declare in one of his public speeches as late as February, 1941, that "basically National Socialism and Marxism are the same" (cf. the *Bulletin of International News* [published by the Royal Institute of International Affairs], XVIII, No. 5, 269).

of this transformation of social life. That democratic socialism, the great utopia of the last few generations, is not only
unachievable, but that to strive for it produces something so
utterly different that few of those who now wish it would be
prepared to accept the consequences, many will not believe
until the connection has been laid bare in all its aspects.

3
Individualism and Collectivism

The socialists believe in two things which are
absolutely different and perhaps even contradictory:
freedom and organization.
—ÉLIE HALÉVY

BEFORE we can progress with our main problem, an obstacle has yet to be surmounted. A confusion largely responsible for the way in which we are drifting into things which nobody wants must be cleared up. This confusion concerns nothing less than the concept of socialism itself. It may mean, and is often used to describe, merely the ideals of social justice, greater equality, and security, which are the ultimate aims of socialism. But it means also the particular method by which most socialists hope to attain these ends and which many competent people regard as the only methods by which they can be fully and quickly attained. In this sense socialism means the abolition of private enterprise, of private ownership of the means of production, and the creation of a system of "planned economy" in which the entrepreneur working for profit is replaced by a central planning body.

There are many people who call themselves socialists, although they care only about the first, who fervently believe in those ultimate aims of socialism but neither care nor understand how they can be achieved, and who are merely certain that they must be achieved, whatever the cost. But to nearly all those to whom socialism is not merely a hope but an object of practical politics, the characteristic methods of modern socialism are as essential as the ends themselves.

37

Many people, on the other hand, who value the ultimate
ends of socialism no less than the socialists refuse to support
socialism because of the dangers to other values they see in
the methods proposed by the socialists. The dispute about
socialism has thus become largely a dispute about means and
not about ends—although the question whether the different ends of socialism can be simultaneously achieved is also
involved.

This would be enough to create confusion. And the confusion has been further increased by the common practice
of denying that those who repudiate the means value the
ends. But this is not all. The situation is still more complicated by the fact that the same means, the "economic planning" which is the prime instrument of socialist reform, can
be used for many other purposes. We must centrally direct
economic activity if we want to make the distribution of income conform to current ideas of social justice. "Planning,"
therefore, is wanted by all those who demand that "production for use" be substituted for production for profit. But
such planning is no less indispensable if the distribution of
incomes is to be regulated in a way which to us appears to be
the opposite of just. Whether we should wish that more of
the good things of this world should go to some racial élite,
the Nordic men, or the members of a party or an aristocracy,
the methods which we shall have to employ are the same as
those which could insure an equalitarian distribution.

It may, perhaps, seem unfair to use the term "socialism"
to describe its methods rather than its aims, to use for a
particular method a term which for many people stands for
an ultimate ideal. It is probably preferable to describe the
methods which can be used for a great variety of ends as
collectivism and to regard socialism as a species of that ge-
nus. Yet, although to most socialists only one species of col-

lectivism will represent true socialism, it must always be remembered that socialism is a species of collectivism and that
therefore everything which is true of collectivism as such
must apply also to socialism. Nearly all the points which are
disputed between socialists and liberals concern the methods
common to all forms of collectivism and not the particular
ends for which socialists want to use them; and all the consequences with which we shall be concerned in this book follow from the methods of collectivism irrespective of the ends
for which they are used. It must also not be forgotten that
socialism is not only by far the most important species of
collectivism or "planning" but that it is socialism which has
persuaded liberal-minded people to submit once more to
that regimentation of economic life which they had overthrown because, in the words of Adam Smith, it puts governments in a position where "to support themselves they
are obliged to be oppressive and tyrannical."[1]

The difficulties caused by the ambiguities of the common
political terms are not yet over if we agree to use the term
"collectivism" so as to include all types of "planned economy," whatever the end of planning. The meaning of this
term becomes somewhat more definite if we make it clear
that we mean that sort of planning which is necessary to realize any given distributive ideals. But, as the idea of central economic planning owes its appeal largely to this very
vagueness of its meaning, it is essential that we should agree
on its precise sense before we discuss its consequences.

"Planning" owes its popularity largely to the fact that everybody desires, of course, that we should handle our common problems as rationally as possible and that, in so doing,

1. Quoted in Dugald Stewart's *Memoir of Adam Smith* from a memorandum written by Smith in 1755.

we should use as much foresight as we can command. In this sense everybody who is not a complete fatalist is a planner, every political act is (or ought to be) an act of planning, and there can be differences only between good and bad, between wise and foresighted and foolish and shortsighted planning. An economist, whose whole task is the study of how men actually do and how they might plan their affairs, is the last person who could object to planning in this general sense. But it is not in this sense that our enthusiasts for a planned society now employ this term, nor merely in this sense that we must plan if we want the distribution of income or wealth to conform to some particular standard. According to the modern planners, and for their purposes, it is not sufficient to design the most rational permanent framework within which the various activities would be conducted by different persons according to their individual plans. This liberal plan, according to them, is no plan—and it is, indeed, not a plan designed to satisfy particular views about who should have what. What our planners demand is a central direction of all economic activity according to a single plan, laying down how the resources of society should be "consciously directed" to serve particular ends in a definite way.

The dispute between the modern planners and their opponents is, therefore, *not* a dispute on whether we ought to choose intelligently between the various possible organizations of society; it is not a dispute on whether we ought to employ foresight and systematic thinking in planning our common affairs. It is a dispute about what is the best way of so doing. The question is whether for this purpose it is better that the holder of coercive power should confine himself in general to creating conditions under which the knowledge and initiative of individuals are given the best scope so that *they* can plan most successfully; or whether a rational utilization of our resources requires *central* direction and organization of all our activities according to some consciously constructed "blueprint." The socialists of all parties have appropriated the term "planning" for planning of the latter type, and it is now generally accepted in this sense. But though this is meant to suggest that this is the only rational way of handling our affairs, it does not, of course, prove this. It remains the point on which the planners and the liberals disagree.

It is important not to confuse opposition against this kind of planning with a dogmatic laissez faire attitude. The liberal argument is in favor of making the best possible use of the forces of competition as a means of co-ordinating human efforts, not an argument for leaving things just as they are. It is based on the conviction that, where effective competition can be created, it is a better way of guiding individual efforts than any other. It does not deny, but even emphasizes, that, in order that competition should work beneficially, a carefully thought-out legal framework is required and that neither the existing nor the past legal rules are free from grave defects. Nor does it deny that, where it is impossible to create the conditions necessary to make competition effective, we must resort to other methods of guiding economic activity. Economic liberalism is opposed, however, to competition's being supplanted by inferior methods of co-ordinating individual efforts. And it regards competition as superior not only because it is in most circumstances the most efficient method known but even more because it is the only method by which our activities can be adjusted to each other without coercive or arbitrary intervention of authority. Indeed, one of the main arguments in favor of competition is that it dispenses with the need for "conscious social control" and that it gives the individuals a chance to decide whether the prospects of a particular occupation are sufficient to compensate for the disadvantages and risks connected with it.

The successful use of competition as the principle of social organization precludes certain types of coercive interference with economic life, but it admits of others which sometimes may very considerably assist its work and even requires certain kinds of government action. But there is good reason why the negative requirements, the points where coercion must not be used, have been particularly stressed. It is necessary in the first instance that the parties in the market should be free to sell and buy at any price at which they can find a partner to the transaction and that anybody should be free to produce, sell, and buy anything that may be produced or sold at all. And it is essential that the entry into the different trades should be open to all on equal terms and that the law should not tolerate any attempts by individuals or groups to restrict this entry by open or concealed force. Any attempt to control prices or quantities of particular commodities deprives competition of its power of bringing about an effective co-ordination of individual efforts, because price changes then cease to register all the relevant changes in circumstances and no longer provide a reliable guide for the individual's actions.

This is not necessarily true, however, of measures merely restricting the allowed methods of production, so long as these restrictions affect all potential producers equally and are not used as an indirect way of controlling prices and quantities. Though all such controls of the methods of production impose extra costs (i.e., make it necessary to use more resources to produce a given output), they may be well

worth while. To prohibit the use of certain poisonous sub-
stances or to require special precautions in their use, to limit
working hours or to require certain sanitary arrangements,
is fully compatible with the preservation of competition. The
only question here is whether in the particular instance the
advantages gained are greater than the social costs which
they impose. Nor is the preservation of competition incompatible with an extensive system of social services—so long
as the organization of these services is not designed in such
a way as to make competition ineffective over wide fields.

It is regrettable, though not difficult to explain, that in
the past much less attention has been given to the positive
requirements of a successful working of the competitive system than to these negative points. The functioning of a competition not only requires adequate organization of certain
institutions like money, markets, and channels of information—some of which can never be adequately provided by
private enterprise—but it depends, above all, on the existence of an appropriate legal system, a legal system designed
both to preserve competition and to make it operate as beneficially as possible. It is by no means sufficient that the law
should recognize the principle of private property and freedom of contract; much depends on the precise definition of
the right of property as applied to different things. The systematic study of the forms of legal institutions which will
make the competitive system work efficiently has been sadly
neglected; and strong arguments can be advanced that serious shortcomings here, particularly with regard to the law
of corporations and of patents, not only have made competition work much less effectively than it might have done but
have even led to the destruction of competition in many
spheres.

There are, finally, undoubted fields where no legal arrangements can create the main condition on which the usefulness of the system of competition and private property depends: namely, that the owner benefits from all the useful services rendered by his property and suffers for all the damages caused to others by its use. Where, for example, it is impracticable to make the enjoyment of certain services dependent on the payment of a price, competition will not produce the services; and the price system becomes similarly ineffective when the damage caused to others by certain uses of property cannot be effectively charged to the owner of that property. In all these instances there is a divergence between the items which enter into private calculation and those which affect social welfare; and, whenever this divergence becomes important, some method other than competition may have to be found to supply the services in question. Thus neither the provision of signposts on the roads nor, in most circumstances, that of the roads themselves can be paid for by every individual user. Nor can certain harmful effects of deforestation, of some methods of farming, or of the smoke and noise of factories be confined to the owner of the property in question or to those who are willing to submit to the damage for an agreed compensation. In such instances we must find some substitute for the regulation by the price mechanism. But the fact that we have to resort to the substitution of direct regulation by authority where the conditions for the proper working of competition cannot be created does not prove that we should suppress competition where it can be made to function.

To create conditions in which competition will be as effective as possible, to supplement it where it cannot be made effective, to provide the services which, in the words of Adam Smith, "though they may be in the highest degree advantageous to a great society, are, however, of such a nature, that the profit could never repay the expense to any individual or small number of individuals"—these tasks provide, indeed, a wide and unquestioned field for state activity. In no system that could be rationally defended would the state just do nothing. An effective competitive system needs an intelligently designed and continuously adjusted legal framework as much as any other. Even the most essential prerequisite of its proper functioning, the prevention of fraud and deception (including exploitation of ignorance), provides a great and by no means yet fully accomplished object of legislative activity.

The task of creating a suitable framework for the beneficial working of competition had, however, not yet been carried very far when states everywhere turned from it to that of supplanting competition by a different and irreconcilable principle. The question was no longer one of making competition work and of supplementing it but of displacing it altogether. It is important to be quite clear about this: the modern movement for planning is a movement against competition as such, a new flag under which all the old enemies of competition have rallied. And although all sorts of interests are now trying to reestablish under this flag privileges which the liberal era swept away, it is socialist propaganda for planning which has restored to respectability among liberal-minded people opposition to competition and which has effectively lulled the healthy suspicion which any attempt to smother competition used to arouse.[2] What in

2. Of late, it is true, some academic socialists, under the spur of criticism and animated by the same fear of the extinction of freedom in a centrally planned society, have devised a new kind of "competitive socialism" which they hope will avoid the difficulties and dangers of central planning

effect unites the socialists of the Left and the Right is this common hostility to competition and their common desire to replace it by a directed economy. Though the terms "capitalism" and "socialism" are still generally used to describe the past and the future forms of society, they conceal rather than elucidate the nature of the transition through which we are passing.

Yet, though all the changes we are observing tend in the direction of a comprehensive central direction of economic activity, the universal struggle against competition promises to produce in the first instance something in many respects even worse, a state of affairs which can satisfy neither planners nor liberals: a sort of syndicalist or "corporative" organization of industry, in which competition is more or less suppressed but planning is left in the hands of the independent monopolies of the separate industries. This is the inevitable first result of a situation in which the people are united in their hostility to competition but agree on little else. By destroying competition in industry after industry, this policy puts the consumer at the mercy of the joint monopolist action of capitalists and workers in the best organized industries. Yet, although this is a state of affairs which in wide fields has already existed for some time, and al-

---

and combine the abolition of private property with the full retention of individual freedom. Although some discussion of this new kind of socialism has taken place in learned journals, it is hardly likely to recommend itself to practical politicians. If it ever did, it would not be difficult to show (as the author has attempted elsewhere—see *Economica*, 1940) that these plans rest on a delusion and suffer from an inherent contradiction. It is impossible to assume control over all the productive resources without also deciding for whom and by whom they are to be used. Although under this so-called "competitive socialism" the planning by the central authority would take somewhat more roundabout forms, its effects would not be fundamentally different, and the element of competition would be little more than a sham.

though much of the muddled (and most of the interested)
agitation for planning aims at it, it is not a state which is
likely to persist or can be rationally justified. Such independent planning by industrial monopolies would, in fact, produce effects opposite to those at which the argument for
planning aims. Once this stage is reached, the only alternative to a return to competition is the control of the monopolies by the state—a control which, if it is to be made effective,
must become progressively more complete and more detailed. It is this stage we are rapidly approaching. When,
shortly before the war, a weekly magazine pointed out that
there were many signs that British leaders, at least, were
growing accustomed to thinking in terms of national development by controlled monopolies, this was probably a true
estimate of the position as it then existed. Since then this
process has been greatly accelerated by the war, and its
grave defects and dangers will become increasingly obvious
as time goes on.

The idea of complete centralization of the direction of
economic activity still appalls most people, not only because
of the stupendous difficulty of the task, but even more because of the horror inspired by the idea of everything being
directed from a single center. If we are, nevertheless, rapidly moving toward such a state, this is largely because most
people still believe that it is must be possible to find some
middle way between "atomistic" competition and central direction. Nothing, indeed, seems at first more plausible, or is
more likely to appeal to reasonable people, than the idea
that our goal must be neither the extreme decentralization
of free competition nor the complete centralization of a
single plan but some judicious mixture of the two methods.
Yet mere common sense proves a treacherous guide in the
field. Although competition can bear some admixture of

regulation, it cannot be combined with planning to any extent we like without ceasing to operate as an effective guide to production. Nor is "planning" a medicine which, taken in small doses, can produce the effects for which one might hope from its thoroughgoing application. Both competition and central direction become poor and inefficient tools if they are incomplete; they are alternative principles used to solve the same problem, and a mixture of the two means that neither will really work and that the result will be worse than if either system had been consistently relied upon. Or, to express it differently, planning and competition can be combined only by planning for competition but not by planning against competition.

It is of the utmost importance to the argument of this book for the reader to keep in mind that the planning against which all our criticism is directed is solely the planning against competition—the planning which is to be substituted for competition. This is the more important, as we cannot, within the scope of this book, enter into a discussion of the very necessary planning which is required to make competition as effective and beneficial as possible. But as in current usage "planning" has become almost synonymous with the former kind of planning, it will sometimes be inevitable for the sake of brevity to refer to it simply as planning, even though this means leaving to our opponents a very good word meriting a better fate.

4

The "Inevitability" of Planning

We were the first to assert that the more complicated the forms assumed by civilization, the more restricted the freedom of the individual must become.
—BENITO MUSSOLINI

I T IS a revealing fact that few planners are content to say that central planning is desirable. Most of them affirm that we can no longer choose but are compelled by circumstances beyond our control to substitute planning for competition. The myth is deliberately cultivated that we are embarking on the new course not out of free will but because competition is spontaneously eliminated by technological changes which we neither can reverse nor should wish to prevent. This argument is rarely developed at any length—it is one of the assertions taken over by one writer from another until, by mere iteration, it has come to be accepted as an established fact. It is, nevertheless, devoid of foundation. The tendency toward monopoly and planning is not the result of any "objective facts" beyond our control but the product of opinions fostered and propagated for half a century until they have come to dominate all our policy.

Of the various arguments employed to demonstrate the inevitability of planning, the one most frequently heard is that technological changes have made competition impossible in a constantly increasing number of fields and that the only choice left to us is between control of production by private monopolies and direction by the government. This belief derives mainly from the Marxist doctrine of the "concentration of industry," although, like so many Marxist ideas, it is now found in many circles which have received it at third or fourth hand and do not know whence it derives.

The historical fact of the progressive growth of monopoly during the last fifty years and the increasing restriction of the field in which competition rules is, of course, not disputed—although the extent of the phenomenon is often greatly exaggerated.[1] The important question is whether this development is a necessary consequence of the advance of technology or whether it is simply the result of the policies pursued in most countries. We shall presently see that the actual history of this development strongly suggests the latter. But we must first consider in how far modern technological developments are of such a kind as to make the growth of monopolies in wide fields inevitable.

The alleged technological cause of the growth of monopoly is the superiority of the large firm over the small, owing to the greater efficiency of modern methods of mass production. Modern methods, it is asserted, have created conditions in the majority of industries where the production of the large firm can be increased at decreasing costs per unit, with the result that the large firms are everywhere underbidding and driving out the small ones; this process must go on until in each industry only one or at most a few giant firms are left. This argument singles out one effect sometimes accompanying technological progress; it disregards others which work in the opposite direction; and it receives little support from a serious study of the facts. We cannot here investigate this question in detail and must be content to accept the best evidence available. The most com-

1. For a fuller discussion of these problems see Professor Lionel Robbins' essay, "The Inevitability of Monopoly," *The Economic Basis of Class Conflict* (1939), pp. 45–80.

prehensive study of the facts undertaken in recent times is that by the Temporary National Economic Committee on the *Concentration of Economic Power*. The final report of this committee (which certainly cannot be accused of an undue liberal bias) arrives at the conclusion that the view according to which the greater efficiency of large-scale production is the cause of the disappearance of competition "finds scant support in any evidence that is now at hand."[2] And the detailed monograph on the question which was prepared for the committee sums up the answer in this statement:

"The superior efficiency of large establishments has not been demonstrated; the advantages that are supposed to destroy competition have failed to manifest themselves in many fields. Nor do the economies of size, where they exist, invariably necessitate monopoly. . . . The size or the sizes of the optimum efficiency may be reached long before the major part of a supply is subjected to such control. The conclusions that the advantage of large-scale production must lead inevitably to the abolition of competition cannot be accepted. It should be noted, moreover, that monopoly is frequently the product of factors other than the lower costs of greater size. It is attained through collusive agreement and promoted by public policies. When these agreements are invalidated and when these policies are reversed, competitive conditions can be restored."[3]

An investigation of conditions in England would lead to very similar results. Anyone who has observed how aspiring monopolists regularly seek and frequently obtain the assistance of the power of the state to make their control effective

2. *Final Report and Recommendations of the Temporary National Economic Committee* (77th Cong., 1st sess.; Senate Document No. 35 [1941]), p. 89.

3. C. Wilcox, *Competition and Monopoly in American Industry* (Temporary National Economic Committee Monograph, No. 21 [1940]), p. 314.

can have little doubt that there is nothing inevitable about this development.

This conclusion is strongly supported by the historical order in which the decline of competition and the growth of monopoly manifested themselves in different countries. If they were the result of technological developments or a necessary product of the evolution of "capitalism," we should expect them to appear first in the countries with the most advanced economic system. In fact, they appeared first during the last third of the nineteenth century in what were then comparatively young industrial countries, the United States and Germany. In the latter country especially, which came to be regarded as the model country typifying the necessary evolution of capitalism, the growth of cartels and syndicates has since 1878 been systematically fostered by deliberate policy. Not only the instrument of protection but direct inducements and ultimately compulsion were used by the governments to further the creation of monopolies for the regulation of prices and sales. It was here that, with the help of the state, the first great experiment in "scientific planning" and "conscious organization of industry" led to the creation of giant monopolies, which were represented as inevitable growths fifty years before the same was done in Great Britain. It is largely due to the influence of German socialist theoreticians, particularly Sombart, generalizing from the experience of their country, that the inevitable development of the competitive system into "monopoly capitalism" became widely accepted. That in the United States a highly protectionist policy made a somewhat similar development possible seemed to confirm this generalization. The development of Germany, however, more than that of the United States, came to be regarded as representative of a universal tendency; and it became a commonplace to speak—to quote a widely read political essay of recent date—of "Germany where all the social and political forces of modern civilization have reached their most advanced form."[4]

How little there was of inevitability in all this, and how much is the result of deliberate policy, becomes clear when we consider the position in England until 1931 and the development since that year in which Great Britain also embarked upon a policy of general protection. It is only a dozen years since, except for a few industries which had obtained protection earlier, British industry was on the whole as competitive as, perhaps, at any time in its history. And, although during the 1920's it suffered severely from incompatible policies followed with regard to wages and to money, at least the years up to 1929 compare with regard to employment and general activity not unfavorably with the 1930's. It is only since the transition to protection and the general change in British economic policy accompanying it that the growth of monopolies has proceeded at an amazing rate and has transformed British industry to an extent the public has scarcely yet realized. To argue that this development has anything to do with the technological progress during this period, that technological necessities which in Germany operated in the 1880's and 1890's made themselves felt here in the 1930's, is not much less absurd than the claim, implied in a statement of Mussolini, that Italy had to abolish individual freedom before other European people because its civilization had marched so far in advance of the rest!

In so far as England is concerned, the thesis that the change in opinion and policy merely follows an inexorable change in the facts can be given a certain appearance of

4. Reinhold Niebuhr, *Moral Man and Immoral Society* (1932).

truth, just because the nation has followed at a distance the intellectual developments elsewhere. It could thus be argued that monopolistic organization of industry grew up in spite of the fact that public opinion still favored competition but that outside events frustrated their wishes. The true relation between theory and practice becomes, however, clear as soon as we look to the prototype of this development—Germany. That *there* the suppression of competition was a matter of deliberate policy, that it was undertaken in the service of the ideal which we now call planning, there can be no doubt. In the progressive advance toward a completely planned society the Germans, and all the people who are imitating their example, are merely following the course which nineteenth-century thinkers, particularly Germans, have mapped out for them. The intellectual history of the last sixty or eighty years is indeed a perfect illustration of the truth that in social evolution nothing is inevitable but thinking makes it so.

The assertion that modern technological progress makes planning inevitable can also be interpreted in a different manner. It may mean that the complexity of our modern industrial civilization creates new problems with which we cannot hope to deal effectively except by central planning. In a sense this is true—yet not in the wide sense in which it is claimed. It is, for example, a commonplace that many of the problems created by a modern town, like many other problems caused by close contiguity in space, are not adequately solved by competition. But it is not these problems, like those of the "public utilities," etc., that are uppermost in the minds of those who invoke the complexity of modern civilization as an argument for central planning. What they generally suggest is that the increasing difficulty of obtaining a coherent picture of the complete economic process makes it indispensable that things should be co-ordinated by some central agency if social life is not to dissolve in chaos.

This argument is based on a complete misapprehension of the working of competition. Far from being appropriate only to comparatively simple conditions, it is the very complexity of the division of labor under modern conditions which makes competition the only method by which such co-ordination can be adequately brought about. There would be no difficulty about efficient control or planning were conditions so simple that a single person or board could effectively survey all the relevant facts. It is only as the factors which have to be taken into account become so numerous that it is impossible to gain a synoptic view of them that decentralization becomes imperative. But, once decentralization is necessary, the problem of co-ordination arises—a co-ordination which leaves the separate agencies free to adjust their activities to the facts which only they can know and yet brings about a mutual adjustment of their respective plans. As decentralization has become necessary because nobody can consciously balance all the considerations bearing on the decisions of so many individuals, the co-ordination can clearly be effected not by "conscious control" but only by arrangements which convey to each agent the information he must possess in order effectively to adjust his decisions to those of others. And because all the details of the changes constantly affecting the conditions of demand and supply of the different commodities can never be fully known, or quickly enough be collected and disseminated, by any one center, what is required is some apparatus of registration which automatically records all the relevant effects of individual actions and whose indications are at the same time the resultant of, and the guide for, all the individual decisions.

This is precisely what the price system does under competition, and what no other system even promises to accomplish. It enables entrepreneurs, by watching the movement of comparatively few prices, as an engineer watches the hands of a few dials, to adjust their activities to those of their fellows. The important point here is that the price system will fulfil this function only if competition prevails, that is, if the individual producer has to adapt himself to price changes and cannot control them. The more complicated the whole, the more dependent we become on that division of knowledge between individuals whose separate efforts are co-ordinated by the impersonal mechanism for transmitting the relevant information known by us as the price system.

It is no exaggeration to say that if we had had to rely on conscious central planning for the growth of our industrial system, it would never have reached the degree of differentiation, complexity, and flexibility it has attained. Compared with this method of solving the economic problem by means of decentralization plus automatic co-ordination, the more obvious method of central direction is incredibly clumsy, primitive, and limited in scope. That the division of labor has reached the extent which makes modern civilization possible we owe to the fact that it did not have to be consciously created but that man tumbled on a method by which the division of labor could be extended far beyond the limits within which it could have been planned. Any further growth of its complexity, therefore, far from making central direction more necessary, makes it more important than ever that we should use a technique which does not depend on conscious control.

There is yet another theory which connects the growth of monopolies with technological progress, and which uses arguments almost opposite to those we have just considered; though not often clearly stated, it has also exercised considerable influence. It contends not that modern technique destroys competition but that, on the contrary, it will be impossible to make use of many of the new technological possibilities unless protection against competition is granted, i.e., a monopoly is conferred. This type of argument is not necessarily fraudulent, as the critical reader will perhaps suspect: the obvious answer—that if a new technique for satisfying our wants is really better, it ought to be able to stand up against all competition—does not dispose of all instances to which this argument refers. No doubt in many cases it is used merely as a form of special pleading by interested parties. Even more often it is probably based on a confusion between technical excellence from a narrow engineering point of view and desirability from the point of view of society as a whole.

There remains, however, a group of instances where the argument has some force. It is, for example, at least conceivable that the British automobile industry might be able to supply a car cheaper and better than cars used to be in the United States if everyone in England were made to use the same kind of car or that the use of electricity for all purposes could be made cheaper than coal or gas if everybody could be made to use only electricity. In instances like these it is at least possible that we might all be better off and should prefer the new situation if we had the choice—but that no individual ever gets the choice, because the alternative is either that we should all use the same cheap car (or all should use only electricity) or that we should have the choice between these things with each of them at a much higher price. I do not know whether this is true in either of the instances given. But it must be admitted that it is possible that, by compulsory standardization or the prohibition of variety beyond a certain degree, abundance might be increased in some fields more than sufficiently to compensate for the restriction of the choice of the consumer. It is even conceivable that a new invention may be made some day whose adoption would seem unquestionably beneficial but which could be used only if many or all people were made to avail themselves of it at the same time.

Whether such instances are of any great or lasting importance, they are certainly not instances where it could be legitimately claimed that technical progress makes central direction inevitable. They would merely make it necessary to choose between gaining a particular advantage by compulsion and not obtaining it—or, in most instances, obtaining it a little later, when further technical advance has overcome the particular difficulties. It is true that in such situations we may have to sacrifice a possible immediate gain as the price of our freedom—but we avoid, on the other hand, the necessity of making future developments dependent upon the knowledge which particular people now possess. By sacrificing such possible present advantages, we preserve an important stimulus to further progress. Though in the short run the price we have to pay for variety and freedom of choice may sometimes be high, in the long run even material progress will depend on this very variety, because we can never predict from which of the many forms in which a good or service can be provided something better may develop. It cannot, of course, be asserted that the preservation of freedom at the expense of some addition to our present material comfort will be thus rewarded in all instances. But the argument for freedom is precisely that we ought to leave room for the unforeseeable free growth. It applies, therefore, no less when, on the basis of our present knowledge, compulsion would seem to bring only advantages, and although in a particular instance it may actually do no harm.

In much of the current discussion on the effects of technological progress this progress is presented to us as if it were something outside us which could compel us to use the new knowledge in a particular way. While it is true, of course, that inventions have given us tremendous power, it is absurd to suggest that we must use this power to destroy our most precious inheritance: liberty. It does mean, however, that if we want to preserve it, we must guard it more jealously than ever and that we must be prepared to make sacrifices for it. While there is nothing in modern technological developments which forces us toward comprehensive economic planning, there is a great deal in them which makes infinitely more dangerous the power a planning authority would possess.

While there can thus be little doubt that the movement toward planning is the result of deliberate action and that there are no external necessities which force us to it, it is worth inquiring why so large a proportion of the technical experts should be found in the front rank of the planners. The explanation of this phenomenon is closely connected with an important fact which the critics of the planners should always keep in mind: that there is little question that almost every one of the technical ideals of our experts could be realized within a comparatively short time if to achieve them were made the sole aim of humanity. There is an infinite number of good things, which we all agree are highly desirable as well as possible, but of which we cannot hope to achieve more than a few within our lifetime, or which we can hope to achieve only very imperfectly. It is the frustration of his ambitions in his own field which makes the

specialist revolt against the existing order. We all find it difficult to bear to see things left undone which everybody must
admit are both desirable and possible. That these things cannot all be done at the same time, that any one of them can
be achieved only at the sacrifice of others, can be seen only
by taking into account factors which fall outside any specialism, which can be appreciated only by a painful intellectual
effort—the more painful as it forces us to see against a wider
background the objects to which most of our labors are directed and to balance them against others which lie outside
our immediate interest and for which, for that reason, we
care less.

Every one of the many things which, considered in isola-
tion, it would be possible to achieve in a planned society creates enthusiasts for planning who feel confident that they
will be able to instil into the directors of such a society their
sense of the value of the particular objective; and the hopes
of some of them would undoubtedly be fulfilled, since a
planned society would certainly further some objectives
more than is the case at present. It would be foolish to deny
that the instances of planned or semiplanned societies which
we know do furnish illustrations in point, good things which
the people of these countries owe entirely to planning. The
magnificent motor roads in Germany and Italy are an instance often quoted—even though they do not represent a
kind of planning not equally possible in a liberal society. But
it is equally foolish to quote such instances of technical excellence in particular fields as evidence of the general superiority of planning. It would be more correct to say that such
extreme technical excellence out of line with general conditions is evidence of a misdirection of resources. Anyone
who has driven along the famous German motor roads and
found the amount of traffic on them less than on many a

secondary road in England can have little doubt that, so far as peace purposes are concerned, there was little justification for them. Whether it was not a case where the planners decided in favor of "guns" instead of "butter" is another matter.[5] But by our standards there is little ground for enthusiasm.

The illusion of the specialist that in a planned society he would secure more attention to the objectives for which he cares most is a more general phenomenon than the term "specialist" at first suggests. In our predilections and interests we are all in some measure specialists. And we all think that our personal order of values is not merely personal but that in a free discussion among rational people we would convince the others that ours is the right one. The lover of the countryside who wants above all that its traditional appearance should be preserved and that the blots already made by industry on its fair face should be removed, no less than the health enthusiast who wants all the picturesque but insanitary old cottages cleared away, or the motorist who wishes the country cut up by big motor roads, the efficiency fanatic who desires the maximum of specialization and mechanization no less than the idealist who for the development of personality wants to preserve as many independent craftsmen as possible, all know that their aim can be fully achieved only by planning—and they all want planning for that reason. But, of course, the adoption of the social planning for which they clamor can only bring out the concealed conflict between their aims.

The movement for planning owes its present strength largely to the fact that, while planning is in the main still an ambition, it unites almost all the single-minded idealists, all

5. But as I am correcting this the news comes that maintenance work on the German motor roads has been suspended!

the men and women who have devoted their lives to a single task. The hopes they place in planning, however, are the result not of a comprehensive view of society but rather of a very limited view and often the result of a great exaggeration of the importance of the ends they place foremost. This is not to underrate the great pragmatic value of this type of men in a free society like ours, which makes them the subject of just admiration. But it would make the very men who are most anxious to plan society the most dangerous if they were allowed to do so—and the most intolerant of the planning of others. From the saintly and single-minded idealist to the fanatic is often but a step. Though it is the resentment of the frustrated specialist which gives the demand for planning its strongest impetus, there could hardly be a more unbearable—and more irrational—world than one in which the most eminent specialists in each field were allowed to proceed unchecked with the realization of their ideals. Nor can "co-ordination," as some planners seem to imagine, become a new specialism. The economist is the last to claim that he has the knowledge which the co-ordinator would need. His plea is for a method which effects such co-ordination without the need for an omniscient dictator. But that means precisely the retention of some such impersonal, and often unintelligible, checks on individual efforts as those against which all specialists chafe.

5
Planning and Democracy

The statesman who should attempt to direct private people in what manner they ought to employ their capitals, would not only load himself with a most unnecessary attention, but assume an authority which could safely be trusted to no council and senate whatever, and which would nowhere be so dangerous as in the hands of a man who had folly and presumption enough to fancy himself fit to exercise it.

—ADAM SMITH

THE common features of all collectivist systems may be described, in a phrase ever dear to socialists of all schools, as the deliberate organization of the labors of society for a definite social goal. That our present society lacks such "conscious" direction toward a single aim, that its activities are guided by the whims and fancies of irresponsible individuals, has always been one of the main complaints of its socialist critics.

In many ways this puts the basic issue very clearly. And it directs us at once to the point where the conflict arises between individual freedom and collectivism. The various kinds of collectivism, communism, fascism, etc., differ among themselves in the nature of the goal toward which they want to direct the efforts of society. But they all differ from liberalism and individualism in wanting to organize the whole of society and all its resources for this unitary end and in refusing to recognize autonomous spheres in which the ends of the individuals are supreme. In short, they are totalitarian in the true sense of this new word which we have adopted to describe the unexpected but nevertheless inseparable manifestations of what in theory we call collectivism.

The "social goal," or "common purpose," for which society is to be organized is usually vaguely described as the "common good," the "general welfare," or the "general interest." It does not need much reflection to see that these terms have no sufficiently definite meaning to determine a particular course of action. The welfare and the happiness of millions cannot be measured on a single scale of less and more. The welfare of a people, like the happiness of a man, depends on a great many things that can be provided in an infinite variety of combinations. It cannot be adequately expressed as a single end, but only as a hierarchy of ends, a comprehensive scale of values in which every need of every person is given its place. To direct all our activities according to a single plan presupposes that every one of our needs is given its rank in an order of values which must be complete enough to make it possible to decide among all the different courses which the planner has to choose. It presupposes, in short, the existence of a complete ethical code in which all the different human values are allotted their due place.

The conception of a complete ethical code is unfamiliar, and it requires some effort of imagination to see what it involves. We are not in the habit of thinking of moral codes as more or less complete. The fact that we are constantly choosing between different values without a social code prescribing how we ought to choose does not surprise us and does not suggest to us that our moral code is incomplete. In our society there is neither occasion nor reason why people should develop common views about what should be done in such situations. But where all the means to be used are the property of society and are to be used in the name of society according to a unitary plan, a "social" view about what ought to be done must guide all decisions. In such a world we should soon find that our moral code is full of gaps.

We are not concerned here with the question whether it would be desirable to have such a complete ethical code. It may merely be pointed out that up to the present the growth of civilization has been accompanied by a steady diminution of the sphere in which individual actions are bound by fixed rules. The rules of which our common moral code consists have progressively become fewer and more general in character. From the primitive man, who was bound by an elaborate ritual in almost every one of his daily activities, who was limited by innumerable taboos, and who could scarcely conceive of doing things in a way different from his fellows, morals have more and more tended to become merely limits circumscribing the sphere within which the individual could behave as he liked. The adoption of a common ethical code comprehensive enough to determine a unitary economic plan would mean a complete reversal of this tendency.

The essential point for us is that no such complete ethical code exists. The attempt to direct all economic activity according to a single plan would raise innumerable questions to which the answer could be provided only by a moral rule, but to which existing morals have no answer and where there exists no agreed view on what ought to be done. People will have either no definite views or conflicting views on such questions, because in the free society in which we have lived there has been no occasion to think about them and still less to form common opinions about them.

Not only do we not possess such an all-inclusive scale of values: it would be impossible for any mind to comprehend the infinite variety of different needs of different people which compete for the available resources and to attach a definite weight to each. For our problem it is of minor importance whether the ends for which any person cares comprehend only his own individual needs, or whether they include the needs of his closer or even those of his more distant fellows—that is, whether he is egoistic or altruistic in the ordinary senses of these words. The point which is so important is the basic fact that it is impossible for any man to survey more than a limited field, to be aware of the urgency of more than a limited number of needs. Whether his interests center round his own physical needs, or whether he takes a warm interest in the welfare of every human being he knows, the ends about which he can be concerned will always be only an infinitesimal fraction of the needs of all men.

This is the fundamental fact on which the whole philosophy of individualism is based. It does not assume, as is often asserted, that man is egoistic or selfish or ought to be. It merely starts from the indisputable fact that the limits of our powers of imagination make it impossible to include in our scale of values more than a sector of the needs of the whole society, and that, since, strictly speaking, scales of value can exist only in individual minds, nothing but partial scales of values exist—scales which are inevitably different and often inconsistent with each other. From this the individualist concludes that the individuals should be allowed, within defined limits, to follow their own values and preferences rather than somebody else's; that within these spheres the individual's system of ends should be supreme and not subject to any dictation by others. It is this recognition of the individual as the ultimate judge of his ends, the belief that as far as possible his own views ought to govern his actions, that forms the essence of the individualist position.

PLANNING AND DEMOCRACY

This view does not, of course, exclude the recognition of social ends, or rather of a coincidence of individual ends which makes it advisable for men to combine for their pursuit. But it limits such common action to the instances where individual views coincide; what are called "social ends" are for it merely identical ends of many individuals—or ends to the achievement of which individuals are willing to contribute in return for the assistance they receive in the satisfaction of their own desires. Common action is thus limited to the fields where people agree on common ends. Very frequently these common ends will not be ultimate ends to the individuals but means which different persons can use for different purposes. In fact, people are most likely to agree on common action where the common end is not an ultimate end to them but a means capable of serving a great variety of purposes.

When individuals combine in a joint effort to realize ends they have in common, the organizations, like the state, that they form for this purpose are given their own system of ends and their own means. But any organization thus formed remains one "person" among others, in the case of the state much more powerful than any of the others, it is true, yet still with its separate and limited sphere in which alone its ends are supreme. The limits of this sphere are determined by the extent to which the individuals agree on particular ends; and the probability that they will agree on a particular course of action necessarily decreases as the scope of such action extends. There are certain functions of the state on the exercise of which there will be practical unanimity among its citizens; there will be others on which there will be agreement of a substantial majority; and so on, until we come to fields where, although each individual might wish the state to act in some way, there will be almost as many views about what the government should do as there are different people.

We can rely on voluntary agreement to guide the action of the state only so long as it is confined to spheres where agreement exists. But not only when the state undertakes direct control in fields where there is no such agreement is it bound to suppress individual freedom. We can unfortunately not indefinitely extend the sphere of common action and still leave the individual free in his own sphere. Once the communal sector, in which the state controls all the means, exceeds a certain proportion of the whole, the effects of its actions dominate the whole system. Although the state controls directly the use of only a large part of the available resources, the effects of its decisions on the remaining part of the economic system become so great that indirectly it controls almost everything. Where, as was, for example, true in Germany as early as 1928, the central and local authorities directly control the use of more than half the national income (according to an official German estimate then, 53 per cent), they control indirectly almost the whole economic life of the nation. There is, then, scarcely an individual end which is not dependent for its achievement on the action of the state, and the "social scale of values" which guides the state's action must embrace practically all individual ends.

It is not difficult to see what must be the consequences when democracy embarks upon a course of planning which in its execution requires more agreement than in fact exists. The people may have agreed on adopting a system of directed economy because they have been convinced that it will produce great prosperity. In the discussions leading to the decision, the goal of planning will have been described by some such term as "common welfare," which only conceals the absence of real agreement on the ends of planning. Agreement will in fact exist only on the mechanism to be used. But it is a mechanism which can be used only for a common end; and the question of the precise goal toward which all activity is to be directed will arise as soon as the executive power has to translate the demand for a single plan into a particular plan. Then it will appear that the agreement on the desirability of planning is not supported by agreement on the ends the plan is to serve. The effect of the people's agreeing that there must be central planning, without agreeing on the ends, will be rather as if a group of people were to commit themselves to take a journey together without agreeing where they want to go: with the result that they may all have to make a journey which most of them do not want at all. That planning creates a situation in which it is necessary for us to agree on a much larger number of topics than we have been used to, and that in a planned system we cannot confine collective action to the tasks on which we can agree but are forced to produce agreement on everything in order that any action can be taken at all, is one of the features which contributes more than most to determining the character of a planned system.

It may be the unanimously expressed will of the people that its parliament should prepare a comprehensive economic plan, yet neither the people nor its representatives need therefore be able to agree on any particular plan. The inability of democratic assemblies to carry out what seems to be a clear mandate of the people will inevitably cause dissatisfaction with democratic institutions. Parliaments come to be regarded as ineffective "talking shops," unable or incompetent to carry out the tasks for which they have been chosen. The conviction grows that if efficient planning is to be done, the direction must be "taken out of politics" and placed in the hands of experts—permanent officials or in-dependent autonomous bodies.

The difficulty is well known to socialists. It will soon be half a century since the Webbs began to complain of "the increased incapacity of the House of Commons to cope with its work."[1] More recently, Professor Laski has elaborated the argument:

"It is common ground that the present parliamentary machine is quite unsuited to pass rapidly a great body of complicated legislation. The National Government, indeed, has in substance admitted this by implementing its economy and tariff measures not by detailed debate in the House of Commons but by a wholesale system of delegated legislation. A Labour Government would, I presume, build upon the amplitude of this precedent. It would confine the House of Commons to the two functions it can properly perform: the ventilation of grievances and the discussion of general principles of its measures. Its Bills would take the form of general formulae conferring wide powers on the appropriate government departments; and those powers would be exercised by Order in Council which could, if desired, be attacked in the House by means of a vote of no confidence. The necessity and value of delegated legislation has recently been strongly reaffirmed by the Donoughmore Committee; and its extension is inevitable if the process of socialisation is not to be wrecked by the normal methods of obstruction which existing parliamentary procedure sanctions."

And to make it quite clear that a socialist government must not allow itself to be too much fettered by democratic procedure, Professor Laski at the end of the same article raised the question "whether in a period of transition to So-

1. Sidney and Beatrice Webb, *Industrial Democracy* (1897), p. 800 n.

PLANNING AND DEMOCRACY

cialism, a Labour Government can risk the overthrow of its measures as a result of the next general election"—and left it significantly unanswered.[2]

It is important clearly to see the causes of this admitted ineffectiveness of parliaments when it comes to a detailed administration of the economic affairs of a nation. The fault is neither with the individual representatives nor with parliamentary institutions as such but with the contradictions inherent in the task with which they are charged. They are not asked to act where they can agree, but to produce agreement on everything—the whole direction of the resources of the nation. For such a task the system of majority decision is, however, not suited. Majorities will be found where it is a choice between limited alternatives; but it is a superstition to believe that there must be a majority view on everything. There is no reason why there should be a majority in favor of any one of the different possible courses of positive action if their number is legion. Every member of the legislative assembly might prefer some particular plan for the direction of economic activity to no plan, yet no one plan may appear preferable to a majority to no plan at all.

2. H. J. Laski, "Labour and the Constitution," *New Statesman and Nation*, No. 81 (new ser.), September 10, 1932, p. 277. In a book (*Democracy in Crisis* [1933], particularly p. 87) in which Professor Laski later elaborated these ideas, his determination that parliamentary democracy must not be allowed to form an obstacle to the realization of socialism is even more plainly expressed: not only would a socialist government "take vast powers and legislate under them by ordinance and decree" and "suspend the classic formulae of normal opposition" but the "continuance of parliamentary government would depend on its [i.e., the Labour government's] possession of guarantees from the Conservative Party that its work of transformation would not be disrupted by repeal in the event of its defeat at the polls"!

As Professor Laski invokes the authority of the Donoughmore Committee, it may be worth recalling that Professor Laski was a member of that committee and presumably one of the authors of its report.

Nor can a coherent plan be achieved by breaking it up into parts and voting on particular issues. A democratic assembly voting and amending a comprehensive economic plan clause by clause, as it deliberates on an ordinary bill, makes nonsense. An economic plan, to deserve the name, must have a unitary conception. Even if a parliament could, proceeding step by step, agree on some scheme, it would certainly in the end satisfy nobody. A complex whole in which all the parts must be most carefully adjusted to each other cannot be achieved through a compromise between conflicting views. To draw up an economic plan in this fashion is even less possible than, for example, successfully to plan a military campaign by democratic procedure. As in strategy it would become inevitable to delegate the task to the experts.

Yet the difference is that, while the general who is put in charge of a campaign is given a single end to which, for the duration of the campaign, all the means under his control have to be exclusively devoted, there can be no such single goal given to the economic planner, and no similar limitation of the means imposed upon him. The general has not got to balance different independent aims against each other; there is for him only one supreme goal. But the ends of an economic plan, or of any part of it, cannot be defined apart from the particular plan. It is the essence of the economic problem that the making of an economic plan involves the choice between conflicting or competing ends— different needs of different people. But which ends do so conflict, which will have to be sacrificed if we want to achieve certain others, in short, which are the alternatives between which we must choose, can only be known to those who know all the facts; and only they, the experts, are in a position to decide which of the different ends are to be given preference. It is inevitable that they should impose their scale of preferences on the community for which they plan.

This is not always clearly recognized, and delegation is usually justified by the technical character of the task. But this does not mean that only the technical detail is delegated, or even that the inability of parliaments to understand the technical detail is the root of the difficulty.[3] Alterations in the structure of civil law are no less technical and no more difficult to appreciate in all their implications; yet nobody has yet seriously suggested that legislation there should be delegated to a body of experts. The fact is that in these fields legislation does not go beyond general rules on which true

---

3. It is instructive in this connection briefly to refer to the government document in which in recent years these problems have been discussed. As long as thirteen years ago, that is before England finally abandoned economic liberalism, the process of delegating legislative powers had already been carried to a point where it was felt necessary to appoint a committee to investigate "what safeguards are desirable or necessary to secure the sovereignty of Law." In its report the Donoughmore Committee (*Report of the [Lord Chancellor's] Committee in Ministers' Powers*, Cmd. 4060 [1932]) showed that even at that date Parliament had resorted "to the practice of wholesale and indiscriminate delegation" but regarded this (it was before we had really glanced into the totalitarian abyss!) as an inevitable and relatively innocuous development. And it is probably true that delegation as such need not be a danger to freedom. The interesting point is why delegation had become necessary on such a scale. First place among the causes enumerated in the report is given to the fact that "Parliament nowadays passes so many laws every year" and that "much of the detail is so technical as to be unsuitable for Parliamentary discussion." But if this were all there would be no reason why the detail should not be worked out *before* rather than after Parliament passes a law. What is probably in many cases a much more important reason why, "if Parliament were not willing to delegate law-making power, Parliament would be unable to pass the kind and quantity of legislation which public opinion requires" is innocently revealed in the little sentence that "many of the laws affect people's lives so closely that elasticity is essential"! What does this mean if not conferment of arbitrary power— power limited by no fixed principles and which in the opinion of Parliament cannot be limited by definite and unambiguous rules?

majority agreement can be achieved, while in the direction of economic activity the interests to be reconciled are so divergent that no true agreement is likely to be reached in a democratic assembly.

It should be recognized, however, that it is not the delegation of law-making power as such which is so objectionable. To oppose delegation as such is to oppose a symptom instead of the cause and, as it may be a necessary result of other causes, to weaken the case. So long as the power that is delegated is merely the power to make general rules, there may be very good reasons why such rules should be laid down by local rather than by the central authority. The objectionable feature is that delegation is so often resorted to because the matter in hand cannot be regulated by general rules but only by the exercise of discretion in the decision of particular cases. In these instances delegation means that some authority is given power to make with the force of law what to all intents and purposes are arbitrary decisions (usually described as "judging the case on its merits").

The delegation of particular technical tasks to separate bodies, while a regular feature, is yet only the first step in the process whereby a democracy which embarks on planning progressively relinquishes its powers. The expedient of delegation cannot really remove the causes which make all the advocates of comprehensive planning so impatient with the impotence of democracy. The delegation of particular powers to separate agencies creates a new obstacle to the achievement of a single co-ordinated plan. Even if, by this expedient, a democracy should succeed in planning every sector of economic activity, it would still have to face the problem of integrating these separate plans into a unitary whole. Many separate plans do not make a planned whole—in fact, as the planners ought to be the first to admit, they may be worse than no plan. But the democratic legislature will long hesitate to relinquish the decisions on really vital issues, and so long as it does so it makes it impossible for anyone else to provide the comprehensive plan. Yet agreement that planning is necessary, together with the inability of democratic assemblies to produce a plan, will evoke stronger and stronger demands that the government or some single individual should be given powers to act on their own responsibility. The belief is becoming more and more widespread that, if things are to get done, the responsible authorities must be freed from the fetters of democratic procedure.

The cry for an economic dictator is a characteristic stage in the movement toward planning. It is now several years since one of the most acute of foreign students of England, the late Élie Halévy, suggested that, "if you take a composite photograph of Lord Eustace Percy, Sir Oswald Mosley, and Sir Stafford Cripps, I think you would find this common feature—you would find them all agreeing to say: 'We are living in economic chaos and we cannot get out of it except under some kind of dictatorial leadership.'"[4] The number of influential public men whose inclusion would not materially alter the features of the "composite photograph" has since grown considerably.

In Germany, even before Hitler came into power, the movement had already progressed much further. It is important to remember that, for some time before 1933, Germany had reached a stage in which it had, in effect, had to be governed dictatorially. Nobody could then doubt that for the time being democracy had broken down and that sincere democrats like Brüning were no more able to govern demo-

4. "Socialism and the Problems of Democratic Parliamentarism," *International Affairs*, XIII, 501.

cratically than Schleicher or von Papen. Hitler did not have to destroy democracy; he merely took advantage of the decay of democracy and at the critical moment obtained the support of many to whom, though they detested Hitler, he yet seemed the only man strong enough to get things done.

The argument by which the planners usually try to reconcile us with this development is that, so long as democracy retains ultimate control, the essentials of democracy are not affected. Thus Karl Mannheim writes:

"The only [*sic*] way in which a planned society differs from that of the nineteenth century is that more and more spheres of social life, and ultimately each and all of them, are subjected to state control. But if a few controls can be held in check by parliamentary sovereignty, so can many. . . . In a democratic state sovereignty can be boundlessly strengthened by plenary powers without renouncing democratic control."[5]

This belief overlooks a vital distinction. Parliament can, of course, control the execution of tasks where it can give definite directions, where it has first agreed on the aim and merely delegates the working-out of the detail. The situation is entirely different when the reason for the delegation is that there is no real agreement on the ends, when the body charged with the planning has to choose between ends of whose conflict parliament is not even aware, and when the most that can be done is to present to it a plan which has to be accepted or rejected as a whole. There may and probably will be criticism; but as no majority can agree on an alternative plan, and the parts objected to can almost always be rep-

5. *Man and Society in an Age of Reconstruction* (1940), p. 340.

resented as essential parts of the whole, it will remain quite ineffective. Parliamentary discussion may be retained as a useful safety valve and even more as a convenient medium through which the official answers to complaints are disseminated. It may even prevent some flagrant abuses and successfully insist on particular shortcomings being remedied. But it cannot direct. It will at best be reduced to choosing the persons who are to have practically absolute power. The whole system will tend toward that plebiscitarian dictatorship in which the head of the government is from time to time confirmed in his position by popular vote, but where he has all the powers at his command to make certain that the vote will go in the direction he desires.

It is the price of democracy that the possibilities of conscious control are restricted to the fields where true agreement exists and that in some fields things must be left to chance. But in a society which for its functioning depends on central planning this control cannot be made dependent on a majority's being able to agree; it will often be necessary that the will of a small minority be imposed upon the people, because this minority will be the largest group able to agree among themselves on the question at issue. Democratic government has worked successfully where, and so long as, the functions of government were, by a widely accepted creed, restricted to fields where agreement among a majority could be achieved by free discussion; and it is the great merit of the liberal creed that it reduced the range of subjects on which agreement was necessary to one on which it was likely to exist in a society of free men. It is now often said that democracy will not tolerate "capitalism." If "capitalism" means here a competitive system based on free disposal over private property, it is far more important to realize that only

within this system is democracy possible. When it becomes
dominated by a collectivist creed, democracy will inevitably
destroy itself.

We have no intention, however, of making a fetish of democracy. It may well be true that our generation talks and
thinks too much of democracy and too little of the values
which it serves. It cannot be said of democracy, as Lord Acton truly said of liberty, that it "is not a means to a higher
political end. It is itself the highest political end. It is not for
the sake of a good public administration that it is required,
but for the security in the pursuit of the highest objects of
civil society, and of private life." Democracy is essentially a
means, a utilitarian device for safeguarding internal peace
and individual freedom. As such it is by no means infallible
or certain. Nor must we forget that there has often been
much more cultural and spiritual freedom under an autocratic rule than under some democracies—and it is at least
conceivable that under the government of a very homogeneous and doctrinaire majority democratic government
might be as oppressive as the worst dictatorship. Our point,
however, is not that dictatorship must inevitably extirpate
freedom but rather that planning leads to dictatorship because dictatorship is the most effective instrument of coercion and the enforcement of ideals and, as such, essential if
central planning on a large scale is to be possible. The clash
between planning and democracy arises simply from the fact
that the latter is an obstacle to the suppression of freedom
which the direction of economic activity requires. But in so
far as democracy ceases to be a guaranty of individual freedom, it may well persist in some form under a totalitarian
regime. A true "dictatorship of the proletariat," even if democratic in form, if it undertook centrally to direct the eco-

PLANNING AND DEMOCRACY

nomic system, would probably destroy personal freedom as completely as any autocracy has ever done.

The fashionable concentration on democracy as the main value threatened is not without danger. It is largely responsible for the misleading and unfounded belief that, so long as the ultimate source of power is the will of the majority, the power cannot be arbitrary. The false assurance which many people derive from this belief is an important cause of the general unawareness of the dangers which we face. There is no justification for the belief that, so long as power is conferred by democratic procedure, it cannot be arbitrary; the contrast suggested by this statement is altogether false: it is not the source but the limitation of power which prevents it from being arbitrary. Democratic control *may* prevent power from becoming arbitrary, but it does not do so by its mere existence. If democracy resolves on a task which necessarily involves the use of power which cannot be guided by fixed rules, it must become arbitrary power.

6
Planning and the Rule of Law

*Recent studies in the sociology of law once more confirm
that the fundamental principle of formal law by which every case
must be judged according to general rational precepts, which
have as few exceptions as possible and are based on logical
subsumptions, obtains only for the liberal
competitive phase of capitalism.*
—KARL MANNHEIM

NOTHING distinguishes more clearly conditions in a free country from those in a country under arbitrary government than the observance in the former of the great principles known as the Rule of Law. Stripped of all technicalities, this means that government in all its actions is bound by rules fixed and announced beforehand—rules which make it possible to foresee with fair certainty how the authority will use its coercive powers in given circumstances and to plan one's individual affairs on the basis of this knowledge.[1] Though this ideal can never be perfectly achieved, since legislators as well as those to whom the administration of the law is intrusted are fallible men, the

1. According to the classical exposition by A. V. Dicey in *The Law of the Constitution* (8th ed.), p. 198, the Rule of Law "means, in the first place, the absolute supremacy or predominance of regular law as opposed to the influence of arbitrary power, and excludes the existence of arbitrariness, of prerogative, or even of wide discretionary authority on the part of government." Largely as a result of Dicey's work the term has, however, in England acquired a narrower technical meaning which does not concern us here. The wider and older meaning of the concept of the rule or reign of law, which in England had become an established tradition which was more taken for granted than discussed, has been most fully elaborated, just because it raised what were new problems there, in the early nineteenth-century discussion in Germany about the nature of the *Rechtsstaat*.

essential point, that the discretion left to the executive organs wielding coercive power should be reduced as much as possible, is clear enough. While every law restricts individual freedom to some extent by altering the means which people may use in the pursuit of their aims, under the Rule of Law the government is prevented from stultifying individual efforts by *ad hoc* action. Within the known rules of the game the individual is free to pursue his personal ends and desires, certain that the powers of government will not be used deliberately to frustrate his efforts.

The distinction we have drawn before between the creation of a permanent framework of laws within which the productive activity is guided by individual decisions and the direction of economic activity by a central authority is thus really a particular case of the more general distinction between the Rule of Law and arbitrary government. Under the first the government confines itself to fixing rules determining the conditions under which the available resources may be used, leaving to the individuals the decision for what ends they are to be used. Under the second the government directs the use of the means of production to particular ends. The first type of rules can be made in advance, in the shape of *formal rules* which do not aim at the wants and needs of particular people. They are intended to be merely instrumental in the pursuit of people's various individual ends. And they are, or ought to be, intended for such long periods that it is impossible to know whether they will assist particular people more than others. They could almost be described as a kind of instrument of production, helping people to predict the behavior of those with whom they must collaborate, rather than as efforts toward the satisfaction of particular needs.

Economic planning of the collectivist kind necessarily

involves the very opposite of this. The planning authority cannot confine itself to providing opportunities for unknown people to make whatever use of them they like. It cannot tie itself down in advance to general and formal rules which prevent arbitrariness. It must provide for the actual needs of people as they arise and then choose deliberately between them. It must constantly decide questions which cannot be answered by formal principles only, and, in making these decisions, it must set up distinctions of merit between the needs of different people. When the government has to decide how many pigs are to be raised or how many busses are to be run, which coal mines are to operate, or at what prices shoes are to be sold, these decisions cannot be deduced from formal principles or settled for long periods in advance. They depend inevitably on the circumstances of the moment, and, in making such decisions, it will always be necessary to balance one against the other the interests of various persons and groups. In the end somebody's views will have to decide whose interests are more important; and these views must become part of the law of the land, a new distinction of rank which the coercive apparatus of government imposes upon the people.

The distinction we have just used between formal law or justice and substantive rules is very important and at the same time most difficult to draw precisely in practice. Yet the general principle involved is simple enough. The difference between the two kinds of rules is the same as that between laying down a Rule of the Road, as in the Highway Code, and ordering people where to go; or, better still, between providing signposts and commanding people which road to take. The formal rules tell people in advance what action the state will take in certain types of situation, defined in general

83

terms, without reference to time and place or particular people. They refer to typical situations into which anyone may get and in which the existence of such rules will be useful for a great variety of individual purposes. The knowledge that in such situations the state will act in a definite way, or require people to behave in a certain manner, is provided as a means for people to use in making their own plans. Formal rules are thus merely instrumental in the sense that they are expected to be useful to yet unknown people, for purposes for which these people will decide to use them, and in circumstances which cannot be foreseen in detail. In fact, that we do *not* know their concrete effect, that we do *not* know what particular ends these rules will further, or which particular people they will assist, that they are merely given the form most likely on the whole to benefit all the people affected by them, is the most important criterion of formal rules in the sense in which we here use this term. They do not involve a choice between particular ends or particular people, because we just cannot know beforehand by whom and in what way they will be used.

In our age, with its passion for conscious control of everything, it may appear paradoxical to claim as a virtue that under one system we shall know less about the particular effect of the measures the state takes than would be true under most other systems and that a method of social control should be deemed superior because of our ignorance of its precise results. Yet this consideration is in fact the rationale of the great liberal principle of the Rule of Law. And the apparent paradox dissolves rapidly when we follow the argument a little further.

This argument is twofold; the first is economic and can here only briefly be stated. The state should confine itself to establishing rules applying to general types of situations and should allow the individuals freedom in everything which depends on the circumstances of time and place, because only the individuals concerned in each instance can fully known these circumstances and adapt their actions to them. If the individuals are to be able to use their knowledge effectively in making plans, they must be able to predict actions of the state which may affect these plans. But if the actions of the state are to be predictable, they must be determined by rules fixed independently of the concrete circumstances which can be neither foreseen nor taken into account beforehand: and the particular effects of such actions will be unpredictable. If, on the other hand, the state were to direct the individual's actions so as to achieve particular ends, its action would have to be decided on the basis of the full circumstances of the moment and would therefore be unpredictable. Hence the familiar fact that the more the state "plans," the more difficult planning becomes for the individual.

The second, moral or political, argument is even more directly relevant to the point under discussion. If the state is precisely to foresee the incidence of its actions, it means that it can leave those affected no choice. Wherever the state can exactly foresee the effects on particular people of alternative courses of action, it is also the state which chooses between the different ends. It we want to create new opportunities open to all, to offer chances of which people can make what use they like, the precise results cannot be foreseen. General rules, genuine laws as distinguished from specific orders, must therefore be intended to operate in circumstances which cannot be foreseen in detail, and, therefore, their effect on particular ends or particular people cannot be known beforehand. It is in this sense alone that it is at all possible for the legislator to be impartial. To be impartial means to have no answer to certain questions—to the kind of questions which, if we have to decide them, we decide by tossing a coin. In a world where everything was precisely foreseen, the state could hardly do anything and remain impartial.

Where the precise effects of government policy on particular people are known, where the government aims directly at such particular effects, it cannot help knowing these effects, and therefore it cannot be impartial. It must, of necessity, take sides, impose its valuations upon people and, instead of assisting them in the advancement of their own ends, choose the ends for them. As soon as the particular effects are foreseen at the time a law is made, it ceases to be a mere instrument to be used by the people and becomes instead an instrument used by the lawgiver upon the people and for his ends. The state ceases to be a piece of utilitarian machinery intended to help individuals in the fullest development of their individual personality and becomes a "moral" institution—where "moral" is not used in contrast to immoral but describes an institution which imposes on its members its views on all moral questions, whether these views be moral or highly immoral. In this sense the Nazi or any other collectivist state is "moral," while the liberal state is not.

Perhaps it will be said that all this raises no serious problem because in the kind of questions which the economic planner would have to decide he need not and should not be guided by his individual prejudices but could rely on the general conviction of what is fair and reasonable. This contention usually receives support from those who have experience of planning in a particular industry and who find that there is no insuperable difficulty about arriving at a decision which all those immediately interested will accept as fair. The reason why this experience proves nothing is, of course, the selection of the "interests" concerned when planning is confined to a particular industry. Those most immediately interested in a particular issue are not necessarily the best judges of the interests of society as a whole. To take only the most characteristic case: when capital and labor in an industry agree on some policy of restriction and thus exploit the consumers, there is usually no difficulty about the division of the spoils in proportion to former earnings or on some similar principle. The loss which is divided between thousands or millions is usually either simply disregarded or quite inadequately considered. If we want to test the usefulness of the principle of "fairness" in deciding the kind of issues which arise in economic planning, we must apply it to some question where the gains and the losses are seen equally clearly. In such instances it is readily recognized that no general principle such as fairness can provide an answer. When we have to choose between higher wages for nurses or doctors and more extensive services for the sick, more milk for children and better wages for agricultural workers, or between employment for the unemployed or better wages for those already employed, nothing short of a complete system of values in which every want of every person or group has a definite place is necessary to provide an answer.

In fact, as planning becomes more and more extensive, it becomes regularly necessary to qualify legal provisions increasingly by reference to what is "fair" or "reasonable"; this means that it becomes necessary to leave the decision of the concrete case more and more to the discretion of the judge or authority in question. One could write a history of the decline of the Rule of Law, the disappearance of the *Rechts-staat*, in terms of the progressive introduction of these vague formulas into legislation and jurisdiction, and of the increasing arbitrariness and uncertainty of, and the consequent disrespect for, the law and the judicature, which in these circumstances could not but become an instrument of policy. It is important to point out once more in this connection that this process of the decline of the Rule of Law had been going on steadily in Germany for some time before Hitler came into power and that a policy well advanced toward totalitarian planning had already done a great deal of the work which Hitler completed.

There can be no doubt that planning necessarily involves deliberate discrimination between particular needs of different people, and allowing one man to do what another must be prevented from doing. It must lay down by a legal rule how well off particular people shall be and what different people are to be allowed to have and do. It means in effect a return to the rule of status, a reversal of the "movement of progressive societies" which, in the famous phrase of Sir Henry Maine, "has hitherto been a movement from status to contract." Indeed, the Rule of Law, more than the rule of contract, should probably be regarded as the true opposite of the rule of status. It is the rule of Law, in the sense of the rule of formal law, the absence of legal privileges of particular people designated by authority, which safeguards that equality before the law which is the opposite of arbitrary government.

A necessary, and only apparently paradoxical, result of this is that formal equality before the law is in conflict, and in fact incompatible, with any activity of the government deliberately aiming at material or substantive equality of different people, and that any policy aiming directly at a substantive ideal of distributive justice must lead to the destruction of the Rule of Law. To produce the same result for different people, it is necessary to treat them differently. To give different people the same objective opportunities is not to give them the same subjective chance. It cannot be denied that the Rule of Law produces economic inequality—all that can be claimed for it is that this inequality is not designed to affect particular people in a particular way. It is very significant and characteristic that socialists (and Nazis) have always protested against "merely" formal justice, that they have always objected to a law which had no views on how well off particular people ought to be,[2] and that they have always demanded a "socialization of the law," attacked the independence of judges, and at the same time given their support to all such movements as the *Freirechtsschule* which undermined the Rule of Law.

It may even be said that for the Rule of Law to be effective it is more important that there should be a rule applied always without exceptions than what this rule is. Often the content of the rule is indeed of minor importance, provided the same rule is universally enforced. To revert to a former example: it does not matter whether we all drive on the left- or on the right-hand side of the road so long as we all do the same. The important thing is that the rule enables us to predict other people's behavior correctly, and this requires that it should apply to all cases—even if in a particular instance we feel it to be unjust.

The conflict between formal justice and formal equality

2. It is therefore not altogether false when the legal theorist of National Socialism, Carl Schmitt, opposes to the liberal *Rechtstaat* (i.e., the Rule of Law) the National Socialist ideal of the *gerechte Staat* ("the just state")—only that the sort of justice which is opposed to formal justice necessarily implies discrimination between persons.

before the law, on the one hand, and the attempts to realize various ideals of substantive justice and equality, on the other, also accounts for the widespread confusion about the concept of "privilege" and its consequent abuse. To mention only the most important instance of this abuse—the application of the term "privilege" to property as such. It would indeed be privilege if, for example, as has sometimes been the case in the past, landed property were reserved to members of the nobility. And it is privilege if, as is true in our time, the right to produce or sell particular things is reserved to particular people designated by authority. But to call private property as such, which all can acquire under the same rules, a privilege, because only some succeed in acquiring it, is depriving the word "privilege" of its meaning.

The unpredictability of the particular effects, which is the distinguishing characteristic of the formal laws of a liberal system, is also important because it helps us to clear up another confusion about the nature of this system: the belief that its characteristic attitude is inaction of the state. The question whether the state should or should not "act" or "interfere" poses an altogether false alternative, and the term "laissez faire" is a highly ambiguous and misleading description of the principles on which a liberal policy is based. Of course, every state must act and every action of the state interferes with something or other. But that is not the point. The important question is whether the individual can foresee the action of the state and make use of this knowledge as a datum in forming his own plans, with the result that the state cannot control the use made of its machinery and that the individual knows precisely how far he will be protected against interference from others, or whether the state is in a position to frustrate individual efforts. The state controlling weights and measures (or preventing fraud and deception in any other way) is certainly acting, while the state permitting the use of violence, for example, by strike pickets, is inactive. Yet it is in the first case that the state observes liberal principles and in the second that it does not. Similarly with respect to most of the general and permanent rules which the state may establish with regard to production, such as building regulations or factory laws: these may be wise or unwise in the particular instance, but they do not conflict with liberal principles so long as they are intended to be permanent and are not used to favor or harm particular people. It is true that in these instances there will, apart from the long-run effects which cannot be predicted, also be short-run effects on particular people which may be clearly known. But with this kind of laws the short-run effects are in general not (or at least ought not to be) the guiding consideration. As these immediate and predictable effects become more important compared with the long-run effects, we approach the border line where the distinction, however clear in principle, becomes blurred in practice.

The Rule of Law was consciously evolved only during the liberal age and is one of its greatest achievements, not only as a safeguard but as the legal embodiment of freedom. As Immanuel Kant put it (and Voltaire expressed it before him in very much the same terms), "Man is free if he needs to obey no person but solely the laws." As a vague ideal it has, however, existed at least since Roman times, and during the last few centuries it has never been so seriously threatened as it is today. The idea that there is no limit to the powers of the legislator is in part a result of popular sovereignty and democratic government. It has been strengthened by the be-

PLANNING AND THE RULE OF LAW

lief that, so long as all actions of the state are duly authorized by legislation, the Rule of Law will be preserved. But this is completely to misconceive the meaning of the Rule of Law. This rule has little to do with the question whether all actions of government are legal in the juridical sense. They may well be and yet not conform to the Rule of Law. The fact that someone has full legal authority to act in the way he does gives no answer to the question whether the law gives him power to act arbitrarily or whether the law prescribes un-equivocally how he has to act. It may well be that Hitler has obtained his unlimited powers in a strictly constitutional manner and that whatever he does is therefore legal in the juridical sense. But who would suggest for that reason that the Rule of Law still prevails in Germany?

To say that in a planned society the Rule of Law cannot hold is, therefore, not to say that the actions of the govern-ment will not be legal or that such a society will necessarily be lawless. It means only that the use of the government's coercive powers will no longer be limited and determined by pre-established rules. The law can, and to make a central direction of economic activity possible must, legalize what to all intents and purposes remains arbitrary action. If the law says that such a board or authority may do what it pleases, anything that board or authority does is legal—but its ac-tions are certainly not subject to the Rule of Law. By giving the government unlimited powers, the most arbitrary rule can be made legal; and in this way a democracy may set up the most complete despotism imaginable.[3]

3. The conflict is thus *not*, as it has often been misconceived in nine-teenth-century discussions, one between liberty and law. As John Locke had already made clear, there can be no liberty without law. The conflict is be-tween different kinds of law—law so different that it should hardly be

If, however, the law is to enable authorities to direct economic life, it must give them powers to make and enforce decisions in circumstances which cannot be foreseen and on principles which cannot be stated in generic form. The consequence is that, as planning extends, the delegation of legislative powers to divers boards and authorities becomes increasingly common. When before the last war, in a case to which the late Lord Hewart has recently drawn attention, Mr. Justice Darling said that "Parliament had enacted only last year that the Board of Agriculture in acting as they did should be no more impeachable than Parliament itself," this was still a rare thing. It has since become an almost daily occurrence. Constantly the broadest powers are conferred on new authorities which, without being bound by fixed rules, have almost unlimited discretion in regulating this or that activity of the people.

The Rule of Law thus implies limits to the scope of legislation: it restricts it to the kind of general rules known as formal law and excludes legislation either directly aimed at particular people or at enabling anybody to use the coercive power of the state for the purpose of such discrimination. It means, not that everything is regulated by law, but, on the contrary, that the coercive power of the state can be used only in cases defined in advance by the law and in such a way that it can be foreseen how it will be used. A particular en-

---

called by the same name: one is the law of the Rule of Law, general principles laid down beforehand, the "rules of the game" which enable individuals to foresee how the coercive apparatus of the state will be used, or what he and his fellow-citizens will be allowed to do, or made to do, in stated circumstances. The other kind of law gives in effect the authority power to do what it thinks fit to do. Thus the Rule of Law could clearly not be preserved in a democracy that undertook to decide every conflict of interests not according to rules previously laid down but "on its merits."

actment can thus infringe the Rule of Law. Anyone ready to deny this would have to contend that whether the Rule of Law prevails today in Germany, Italy, or Russia depends on whether the dictators have obtained their absolute power by constitutional means.[4]

Whether, as in some countries, the main applications of the Rule of Law are laid down in a bill of rights or in a constitutional code, or whether the principle is merely a firmly established tradition, matters comparatively little. But it will readily be seen that, whatever form it takes, any such recognized limitations of the powers of legislation imply the recognition of the inalienable right of the individual, inviolable rights of man.

It is pathetic but characteristic of the muddle into which many of our intellectuals have been led by the conflicting

4. Another illustration of an infringement of the Rule of Law by legislation is the case of the bill of attainder, familiar in the history of England. The form which the Rule of Law takes in criminal law is usually expressed by the Latin tag *nulla poena sine lege*—no punishment without a law expressly prescribing it. The essence of this rule is that the law must have existed as a general rule before the individual case arose to which it is to be applied. Nobody would argue that, when in a famous case in Henry VIII's reign Parliament resolved with respect to the Bishop of Rochester's cook that "the said Richard Rose shall be boiled to death without having the advantage of his clergy," this act was performed under the Rule of Law. But while the Rule of Law had become an essential part of criminal procedure in all liberal countries, it cannot be preserved in totalitarian regimes. There, as E. B. Ashton has well expressed it, the liberal maxim is replaced by the principles *nullum crimen sine poena*—no "crime" must remain without punishment, whether the law explicitly provides for it or not. "The rights of the state do not end with punishing law breakers. The community is entitled to whatever may seem necessary to the protection of its interests—of which observance of the law, as it stands, is only one of the more elementary requirements" (E. B. Ashton, *The Fascist, His State and Mind* [1937], p. 119). What is an infringement of "the interests of the community" is, of course, decided by the authorities.

ideals in which they believe that a leading advocate of the most comprehensive central planning like H. G. Wells should at the same time write an ardent defense of the rights of man. The individual rights which Mr. Wells hopes to preserve would inevitably obstruct the planning which he desires. To some extent he seems to realize the dilemma, and we find therefore the provisions of his proposed "Declaration of the Rights of Man" so hedged about with qualifications that they lose all significance. While, for instance, his declaration proclaims that every man "shall have the right to buy and sell without any discriminatory restrictions anything which may be lawfully bought and sold," which is admirable, he immediately proceeds to make the whole provision nugatory by adding that it applies only to buying and selling "in such quantities and with such reservations as are compatible with the common welfare." But since, of course, all restrictions ever imposed upon buying or selling anything are supposed to be necessary in the interest of the "common welfare," there is really no restriction which this clause effectively prevents and no right of the individual that is safeguarded by it.

Or, to take another basic clause, the declaration states that every man "may engage in any lawful occupation" and that "he is entitled to paid employment and to a free choice whenever there is any variety of employment open to him." It is not stated, however, who is to decide whether a particular employment is "open" to a particular person, and the added provision that "he may suggest employment for himself and have his claim publicly considered, accepted or dismissed," shows that Mr. Wells is thinking in terms of an authority which decides whether a man is "entitled" to a particular position—which certainly means the opposite of free choice of occupation. And how in a planned world "freedom of travel and migration" is to be secured when not only the means of communication and currencies are controlled but also the location of industries planned, or how the freedom of the press is to be safeguarded when the supply of paper and all the channels of distribution are controlled by the planning authority, are questions to which Mr. Wells provides as little answer as any other planner.

In this respect much more consistency is shown by the more numerous reformers who, ever since the beginning of the socialist movement, have attached the "metaphysical" idea of individual rights and insisted that in a rationally ordered world there will be no individual rights but only individual duties. This, indeed, has become the much more common attitude of our so-called "progressives," and few things are more certain to expose one to the reproach of being a reactionary than if one protests against a measure on the grounds that it is a violation of the rights of the individual. Even a liberal paper like the *Economist* was a few years ago holding up to us the example of the French, of all people, who had learned the lesson that "democratic government no less than dictatorship must always [*sic*] have plenary powers *in posse*, without sacrificing their democratic and representative character. There is no restrictive penumbra of individual rights that can never be touched by government in administrative matters whatever the circumstances. There is no limit to the power of ruling which can and should be taken by a government freely chosen by the people and can be fully and openly criticised by an opposition."

This may be inevitable in wartime, when, of course, even free and open criticism is necessarily restricted. But the "always" in the statement quoted does not suggest that the *Economist* regards it as a regrettable wartime necessity. Yet as a permanent institution this view is certainly incompatible with the preservation of the Rule of Law, and it leads straight to the totalitarian state. It is, however, the view which all those who want the government to direct economic life must hold.

How even a formal recognition of individual rights, or of the equal rights of minorities, loses all significance in a state which embarks on a complete control of economic life, has been amply demonstrated by the experience of the various Central European countries. It has been shown there that it is possible to pursue a policy of ruthless discrimination against national minorities by the use of recognized instruments of economic policy without ever infringing the letter of the statutory protection of minority rights. This oppression by means of economic policy was greatly facilitated by the fact that particular industries or activities were largely in the hands of a national minority, so that many a measure aimed ostensibly against an industry or class was in fact aimed at a national minority. But the almost boundless possibilities for a policy of discrimination and oppression provided by such apparently innocuous principles as "government control of the development of industries" have been amply demonstrated to all those desirous of seeing how the political consequences of planning appear in practice.

7

Economic Control and Totalitarianism

The control of the production of wealth is the
control of human life itself.
—HILAIRE BELLOC

MOST planners who have seriously considered the practical aspects of their task have little doubt that a directed economy must be run on more or less dictatorial lines. That the complex system of interrelated activities, if it is to be consciously directed at all, must be directed by a single staff of experts, and that ultimate responsibility and power must rest in the hands of a commander-in-chief whose actions must not be fettered by democratic procedure, is too obvious a consequence of underlying ideas of central planning not to command fairly general assent. The consolation our planners offer us is that this authoritarian direction will apply "only" to economic matters. One of the most prominent economic planners, Stuart Chase, assures us, for instance, that in a planned society "political democracy can remain if it confines itself to all but economic matter." Such assurances are usually accompanied by the suggestion that, by giving up freedom in what are, or ought to be, the less important aspects of our lives, we shall obtain greater freedom in the pursuit of higher values. On this ground people who abhor the idea of a political dictatorship often clamor for a dictator in the economic field.

The arguments used appeal to our best instincts and often attract the finest minds. If planning really did free us from the less important cares and so made it easier to render

97

our existence one of plain living and high thinking, who would wish to belittle such an ideal? If our economic activities really concerned only the inferior or even more sordid sides of life, of course we ought to endeavor by all means to find a way to relieve ourselves from the excessive care for material ends and, leaving them to be cared for by some piece of utilitarian machinery, set our minds free for the higher things of life.

Unfortunately, the assurance people derive from this belief that the power which is exercised over economic life is a power over matters of secondary importance only, and which makes them take lightly the threat to the freedom of our economic pursuits, is altogether unwarranted. It is largely a consequence of the erroneous belief that there are purely economic ends separate from the other ends of life. Yet, apart from the pathological case of the miser, there is no such thing. The ultimate ends of the activities of reasonable beings are never economic. Strictly speaking, there is no "economic motive" but only economic factors conditioning our striving for other ends. What in ordinary language is misleadingly called the "economic motive" means merely the desire for general opportunity, the desire for power to achieve unspecified ends.[1] If we strive for money, it is because it offers us the widest choice in enjoying the fruits of our efforts. Because in modern society it is through the limitation of our money incomes that we are made to feel the restrictions which our relative poverty still imposes upon us, many have come to hate money as the symbol of these restrictions. But this is to mistake for the cause the medium through which a force makes itself felt. It would be much truer to say that money is one of the greatest instruments of

1. Cf. Lionel Robbins, *The Economic Causes of War* (1939), Appendix.

freedom ever invented by man. It is money which in existing society opens an astounding range of choice to the poor man—a range greater than that which not many generations ago was open to the wealthy. We shall better understand the significance of this service of money if we consider what it would really mean if, as so many socialists characteristically propose, the "pecuniary motive" were largely displaced by "noneconomic incentives." If all rewards, instead of being offered in money, were offered in the form of public distinctions or privileges, positions of power over other men, or better housing or better food, opportunities for travel or education, this would merely mean that the recipient would no longer be allowed to choose and that whoever fixed the reward determined not only its size but also the particular form in which it should be enjoyed.

Once we realize that there is no separate economic motive and that an economic gain or economic loss is merely a gain or a loss where it is still in our power to decide which of our needs or desires shall be affected, it is also easier to see the important kernel of truth in the general belief that economic matters affect only the less important ends of life and to understand the contempt in which "merely" economic considerations are often held. In a sense this is quite justified in a market economy—but only in such a free economy. So long as we can freely dispose over our income and all our possessions, economic loss will always deprive us only of what we regard as the least important of the desires we were able to satisfy. A "merely" economic loss is thus one whose effect we can still make fall on our less important needs, while when we say that the value of something we have lost is much greater than its economic value, or that it cannot even be estimated in economic terms, this means that we must bear the loss where it falls. And similarly with an economic gain. Economic changes, in other words, usually affect only the fringe, the "margin," of our needs. There are many things which are more important than anything which economic gains or losses are likely to affect, which for us stand high above the amenities and even above many of the necessities of life which are affected by the economic ups and downs. Compared with them, the "filthy lucre," the question whether we are economically somewhat worse or better off, seems of little importance. This makes many people believe that anything which, like economic planning, affects only our economic interests cannot seriously interfere with the more basic values of life.

This, however, is an erroneous conclusion. Economic values are less important to us than many things precisely because in economic matters we are free to decide what to us is more, and what less, important. Or, as we might say, because in the present society it is *we* who have to solve the economic problems of our lives. To be controlled in our economic pursuits means to be always controlled unless we declare our specific purpose. Or, since when we declare our specific purpose we shall also have to get it approved, we should really be controlled in everything.

The question raised by economic planning is, therefore, not merely whether we shall be able to satisfy what we regard as our more or less important needs in the way we prefer. It is whether it shall be we who decide what is more, and what is less, important for us, or whether this is to be decided by the planner. Economic planning would not affect merely those of our marginal needs that we have in mind when we speak contemptuously about the merely economic. It would, in effect, mean that we as individuals should no longer be allowed to decide what we regard as marginal.

The authority directing all economic activity would control not merely the part of our lives which is concerned with inferior things; it would control the allocation of the limited means for all our ends. And whoever controls all economic activity controls the means for all our ends and must therefore decide which are to be satisfied and which not. This is really the crux of the matter. Economic control is not merely control of a sector of human life which can be separated from the rest; it is the control of the means for all our ends. And whoever has sole control of the means must also determine which ends are to be served, which values are to be rated higher and which lower—in short, what men should believe and strive for. Central planning means that the economic problem is to be solved by the community instead of by the individual; but this involves that it must also be the community, or rather its representatives, who must decide the relative importance of the different needs.

The so-called economic freedom which the planners promise us means precisely that we are to be relieved of the necessity of solving our own economic problems and that the bitter choices which this often involves are to be made for us. Since under modern conditions we are for almost everything dependent on means which our fellow-men provide, economic planning would involve direction of almost the whole of our life. There is hardly an aspect of it, from our primary needs to our relations with our family and friends, from the nature of our work to the use of our leisure, over which the planner would not exercise his "conscious control."[2]

2. The extent of the control over all life that economic control confers is nowhere better illustrated than in the field of foreign exchanges. Nothing would at first seem to affect private life less than a state control of the dealings in foreign exchange, and most people will regard its introduction with

The power of the planner over our private lives would be no less complete if he chose not to exercise it by direct control of our consumption. Although a planned society would probably to some extent employ rationing and similar devices, the power of the planner over our private lives does not depend on this and would be hardly less effective if the consumer were nominally free to spend his income as he pleased. The source of this power over all consumption which in a planned society the authority would possess would be its control over production.

Our freedom of choice in a competitive society rests on the fact that, if one person refuses to satisfy our wishes, we can turn to another. But if we face a monopolist we are at his mercy. And an authority directing the whole economic system would be the most powerful monopolist conceivable. While we need probably not be afraid that such an authority would exploit this power in the manner in which a private monopolist would do so, while its purpose would presumably not be the extortion of maximum financial gain, it would have complete power to decide what we are to be given and on what terms. It would not only decide what commodities and services were to be available and in what quantities; it would be able to direct their distribution be-

---

complete indifference. Yet the experience of most Continental countries has taught thoughtful people to regard this step as the decisive advance on the path to totalitarianism and the suppression of individual liberty. It is, in fact, the complete delivery of the individual to the tyranny of the state, the final suppression of all means of escape—not merely for the rich but for everybody. Once the individual is no longer free to travel, no longer free to buy foreign books or journals, once all the means of foreign contact can be restricted to those of whom official opinion approves or for whom it is regarded as necessary, the effective control of opinion is much greater than that ever exercised by any of the absolutist governments of the seventeenth and eighteenth centuries.

tween districts and groups and could, if it wished, discrimi-
nate between persons to any degree it liked. If we remember
why planning is advocated by most people, can there be
much doubt that this power would be used for the ends of
which the authority approves and to prevent the pursuits of
ends which it disapproves?

The power conferred by the control of production and
prices is almost unlimited. In a competitive society the prices
we have to pay for a thing, the rate at which we can get one
thing for another, depend on the quantities of other things
of which by taking one, we deprive the other members of
society. This price is not determined by the conscious will of
anybody. And if one way of achieving our ends proves too
expensive for us, we are free to try other ways. The obstacles
in our path are not due to someone's disapproving of our
ends but to the fact that the same means are also wanted
elsewhere. In a directed economy, where the authority
watches over the ends pursued, it is certain that it would use
its powers to assist some ends and to prevent the realization
of others. Not our own view, but somebody else's, of what we
ought to like or dislike would determine what we should get.
And since the authority would have the power to thwart any
efforts to elude its guidance, it would control what we consume almost as effectively as if it directly told us how to
spend our income.

Not only in our capacity as consumers, however, and not
even mainly in that capacity, would the will of the authority
shape and "guide" our daily lives. It would do so even more
in our position as producers. These two aspects of our lives
cannot be separated; and as for most of us the time we spend
at our work is a large part of our whole lives, and as our job
usually also determines the place where and the people

among whom we live, some freedom in choosing our work is, probably, even more important for our happiness than freedom to spend our income during the hours of leisure.

No doubt it is true that even in the best of worlds this freedom will be very limited. Few people ever have an abundance of choice of occupation. But what matters is that we have some choice, that we are not absolutely tied to a particular job which has been chosen for us, or which we may have chosen in the past, and that if one position becomes quite intolerable, or if we set our heart on another, there is almost always a way for the able, some sacrifice at the price of which he may achieve his goal. Nothing makes conditions more unbearable than the knowledge that no effort of ours can change them; and even if we should never have the strength of mind to make the necessary sacrifice, the knowledge that we could escape if we only strove hard enough makes many otherwise intolerable positions bearable.

This is not to say that in this respect all is for the best in our present world, or has been so in the most liberal past, and that there is not much that could be done to improve the opportunities of choice open to the people. Here as elsewhere the state can do a great deal to help the spreading of knowledge and information and to assist mobility. But the point is that the kind of state action which really would increase opportunity is almost precisely the opposite of the "planning" which is now generally advocated and practiced. Most planners, it is true, promise that in the new planned world free choice of occupation will be scrupulously preserved or even increased. But there they promise more than they can possibly fulfil. If they want to plan, they must control the entry into the different trades and occupations, or the terms of remuneration, or both. In almost all known instances of planning, the establishment of such controls and restrictions was among the first measures taken. If such control were universally practiced and exercised by a single planning authority, one needs little imagination to see what would become of the "free choice of occupation" promised. The "freedom of choice" would be purely fictitious, a mere promise to practice no discrimination where in the nature of the case discrimination must be practiced, and where all one could hope would be that the selection would be made on what the authority believed to be objective grounds.

There would be little difference if the planning authority confined itself to fixing the terms of employment and tried to regulate numbers by adjusting these terms. By prescribing the remuneration, it would no less effectively bar groups of people from entering many trades than by specifically excluding them. A rather plain girl who badly wants to become a saleswoman, a weakly boy who has set his heart on a job where his weakness handicaps him, as well as in general the apparently less able or less suitable are not necessarily excluded in a competitive society; if they value the position sufficiently they will frequently be able to get a start by a financial sacrifice and will later make good through qualities which at first are not so obvious. But when the authority fixes the remunerations for a whole category and the selection among the candidates is made by an objective test, the strength of their desire for the job will count for very little. The person whose qualifications are not of the standard type, or whose temperament is not of the ordinary kind, will no longer be able to come to special arrangements with an employer whose dispositions will fit in with his special needs: the person who prefers irregular hours or even a happy-go-lucky existence with a small and perhaps uncertain income to a regular routine will no longer have the choice. Conditions will be without exception what in some measure they inevitably are in a large organization—or rather worse, because there will be no possibility of escape. We shall no longer be free to be rational or efficient only when and where we think it worth while; we shall all have to conform to the standards which the planning authority must fix in order to simplify its task. To make this immense task manageable, it will have to reduce the diversity of human capacities and inclinations to a few categories of readily interchangeable units and deliberately to disregard minor personal differences.

Although the professed aim of planning would be that man should cease to be a mere means, in fact—since it would be impossible to take account in the plan of individual likes and dislikes—the individual would more than ever become a mere means, to be used by the authority in the service of such abstractions as the "social welfare" or the "good of the community."

That in a competitive society most things can be had at a price—though it is often a cruelly high price we have to pay—is a fact the importance of which can hardly be overrated. The alternative is not, however, complete freedom of choice, but orders and prohibitions which must be obeyed and, in the last resort, the favor of the mighty.

It is significant of the confusion prevailing on all these subjects that it should have become a cause for reproach that in a competitive society almost everything can be had at a price. If the people who protest against having the higher values of life brought into the "cash nexus" really mean that we should not be allowed to sacrifice our lesser needs in order to preserve the higher values, and that the choice should be made for us, this demand must be regarded as rather

peculiar and scarcely testifies to great respect for the dignity
of the individual. That life and health, beauty and virtue,
honor and peace of mind, can often be preserved only at
considerable material cost, and that somebody must make
the choice, is as undeniable as that we all are sometimes not
prepared to make the material sacrifices necessary to protect
those higher values against all injury.

To take only one example: We could, of course, reduce
casualties by automobile accidents to zero if we were willing
to bear the cost—if in no other way—by abolishing auto-
mobiles. And the same is true of thousands of other instances in which we are constantly risking life and health and
all the fine values of the spirit, of ourselves and of our
fellow-men, to further what we at the same time contemptuously describe as our material comfort. Nor can it be otherwise, since all our ends compete for the same means; and
we could not strive for anything but these absolute values if
they were on no account to be endangered.

That people should wish to be relieved of the bitter
choice which hard facts often impose upon them is not surprising. But few want to be relieved through having the
choice made for them by others. People just wish that the
choice should not be necessary at all. And they are only too
ready to believe that the choice is not really necessary, that it
is imposed upon them merely by the particular economic
system under which we live. What they resent is, in truth,
that there is an economic problem.

In their wishful belief that there is really no longer an
economic problem people have been confirmed by irresponsible talk about "potential plenty"—which, if it were a fact,
would indeed mean that there is no economic problem
which makes the choice inevitable. But although this snare

108

has served socialist propaganda under various names as long as socialism has existed, it is still as palpably untrue as it was when it was first used over a hundred years ago. In all this time not one of the many people who have used it has produced a workable plan of how production could be increased so as to abolish even in western Europe what we regard as poverty—not to speak of the world as a whole. The reader may take it that whoever talks about potential plenty is either dishonest or does not know what he is talking about.[3] Yet it is this false hope as much as anything which drives us along the road to planning.

While the popular movement still profits by this false belief, the claim that a planned economy would produce a substantially larger output than the competitive system is being progressively abandoned by most students of the problem. Even a good many economists with socialist views who have seriously studied the problems of central planning are now

3. To justify these strong words, the following conclusions may be quoted at which Colin Clark, one of the best known among the younger economic statisticians and a man of undoubted progressive views and a strictly scientific outlook, has arrived in his *Conditions of Economic Progress* (1940): The "oft-repeated phrases about poverty in the midst of plenty, and the problems of production having already been solved if only we understood the problem of distribution, turn out to be the most untruthful of all modern clichés. . . . The under-utilisation of productive capacity is a question of considerable importance only in the U.S.A., though in certain years also it has been of some importance in Great Britain, Germany and France, but for most of the world it is entirely subsidiary to the more important fact that, with productive resources fully employed, they can produce so little. The age of plenty will still be a long while in coming. . . . If preventable unemployment were eliminated throughout the trade cycle, this would mean a distinct improvement in the standard of living of the population of the U.S.A., but from the standpoint of the world as a whole it would only make a small contribution towards the much greater problem of raising the real income of the bulk of the world population to anything like a civilised standard" (pp. 3–4).

content to hope that a planned society will equal the efficiency of a competitive system; they advocate planning no
longer because of its superior productivity but because it will
enable us to secure a more just and equitable distribution of
wealth. This is, indeed, the only argument for planning
which can be seriously pressed. It is indisputable that if we
want to secure a distribution of wealth which conforms to
some predetermined standard, if we want consciously to decide who is to have what, we must plan the whole economic
system. But the question remains whether the price we
should have to pay for the realization of somebody's ideal of
justice is not bound to be more discontent and more oppression than was ever caused by the much-abused free play of
economic forces.

We should be seriously deceiving ourselves if for these
apprehensions we sought comfort in the consideration that
the adoption of central planning would merely mean a return, after a brief spell of a free economy, to the ties and
regulations which have governed economic activity through
most ages, and that therefore the infringements of personal
liberty need not be greater than they were before the age of
laissez faire. This is a dangerous illusion. Even during the
periods of European history when the regimentation of economic life went furthest, it amounted to little more than the
creation of a general and semipermanent framework of
rules within which the individual preserved a wide free
sphere. The apparatus of control then available would not
have been adequate to impose more than very general directions. And even where the control was most complete it extended only to those activities of a person through which he
took part in the social division of labor. In the much wider

sphere in which he then still lived on his own products, he was free to act as he chose.

The situation is now entirely different. During the liberal era the progressive division of labor has created a situation where almost every one of our activities is part of a social process. This is a development which we cannot reverse, since it is only because of it that we can maintain the vastly increased population at anything like present standards. But, in consequence, the substitution of central planning for competition would require central direction of a much greater part of our lives than was ever attempted before. It could not stop at what we regard as our economic activities, because we are now for almost every part of our lives dependent on somebody else's economic activities.[4] The passion for the "collective satisfaction of our needs," with which our socialists have so well prepared the way for totalitarianism, and which wants us to take our pleasures as well as our necessities at the appointed time and in the prescribed form, is, of course, partly intended as a means of political education. But it is also the result of the exigencies of planning, which consists essentially in depriving us of choice, in order to give us whatever fits best into the plan and that at a time determined by the plan.

It is often said that political freedom is meaningless without economic freedom. This is true enough, but in a sense almost opposite from that in which the phrase is used by our planners. The economic freedom which is the prerequisite of any other freedom cannot be the freedom from economic

4. It is no accident that in the totalitarian countries, be it Russia or Germany or Italy, the question of how to organize the people's leisure has become a problem of planning. The Germans have even invented for this problem the horrible and self-contradictory name of *Freizeitgestaltung* (literally: the shaping of the use made of the people's free time), as if it were still "free time" when it has to be spent in the way ordained by authority.

care which the socialists promise us and which can be obtained only by relieving the individual at the same time of the necessity and of the power of choice; it must be the freedom of our economic activity which, with the right of choice, inevitably also carries the risk and the responsibility of that right.

8
Who, Whom?

The finest opportunity ever given to the world was thrown away
because the passion of equality made vain the hope for freedom.
—LORD ACTON

I T IS significant that one of the commonest objections to
competition is that it is "blind." It is not irrelevant to
recall that to the ancients blindness was an attribute of
their deity of justice. Although competition and justice may
have little else in common, it is as much a commendation of
competition as of justice that it is no respecter of persons.
That it is impossible to foretell who will be the lucky ones or
whom disaster will strike, that rewards and penalties are not
shared out according to somebody's views about the merits
or demerits of different people but depend on their capacity
and their luck, is as important as that, in framing legal rules,
we should not be able to predict which particular person will
gain and which will lose by their application. And this is
nonetheless true, because in competition chance and good
luck are often as important as skill and foresight in determining the fate of different people.

The choice open to us is not between a system in which
everybody will get what he deserves according to some
absolute and universal standard of right, and one where the
individual shares are determined partly by accident or good
or ill chance, but between a system where it is the will of a
few persons that decides who is to get what, and one where
it depends at least partly on the ability and enterprise of the
people concerned and partly on unforeseeable circum-

stances. This is no less relevant because in a system of free enterprise chances are not equal, since such a system is necessarily based on private property and (though perhaps not with the same necessity) on inheritance, with the differences in opportunity which these create. There is, indeed, a strong case for reducing this inequality of opportunity as far as congenital differences permit and as it is possible to do so without destroying the impersonal character of the process by which everybody has to take his chance and no person's view about what is right and desirable overrules that of others.

The fact that the opportunities open to the poor in a competitive society are much more restricted than those open to the rich does not make it less true that in such a society the poor are much more free than a person commanding much greater material comfort in a different type of society. Although under competition the probability that a man who starts poor will reach great wealth is much smaller than is true of the man who has inherited property, it is not only possible for the former, but the competitive system is the only one where it depends solely on him and not on the favors of the mighty, and where nobody can prevent a man from attempting to achieve this result. It is only because we have forgotten what unfreedom means that we often overlook the patent fact that in every real sense a badly paid unskilled worker in this country has more freedom to shape his life than many a small entrepreneur in Germany or a much better paid engineer or manager in Russia. Whether it is a question of changing his job or the place where he lives, of professing certain views or of spending his leisure in a particular manner, although sometimes the price he may have to pay for following his inclinations may be high, and to many appear too high, there are no absolute impediments, no dangers to bodily security and freedom, that confine him by brute force to the task and the environment to which a superior has assigned him.

That the ideal of justice of most socialists would be satisfied if merely private income from property were abolished and the differences between the earned incomes of different people remained what they are now is true.[1] What these people forget is that, in transferring all property in the means of production to the state, they put the state in a position whereby its action must in effect decide all other incomes. The power thus given to the state and the demand that the state should use it to "plan" means nothing else than that it should use it in full awareness of all these effects.

To believe that the power which is thus conferred on the state is merely transferred to it from others is erroneous. It is a power which is newly created and which in a competitive society nobody possesses. So long as property is divided among many owners, none of them acting independently

1. It is probable that we habitually overestimate the extent to which inequality of incomes is mainly caused by income derived from property, and therefore the extent to which the major inequalities would be abolished by abolishing income from property. What little information we have about the distribution of incomes in Soviet Russia does not suggest that the inequalities are substantially smaller there than in a capitalist society. Max Eastman (*The End of Socialism in Russia* [1937], pp. 30–34) gives some information from official Russian sources which suggest that the difference between the highest and the lowest salaries paid in Russia is of the same order of magnitude (about 50 to 1) as in the United States; and Leon Trotsky, according to an article quoted by James Burnham (*The Managerial Revolution* [1941], p. 43), estimated as late as 1939 that "the upper 11 or 12 per cent of the Soviet population now receives approximately 50 per cent of the national income. This differentiation is sharper than in the United States, where the upper 10 per cent of the population receives approximately 35 per cent of the national income."

has exclusive power to determine the income and position of particular people—nobody is tied to any one property owner except by the fact that he may offer better terms than anybody else.

What our generation has forgotten is that the system of private property is the most important guaranty of freedom, not only for those who own property, but scarcely less for those who do not. It is only because the control of the means of production is divided among many people acting independently that nobody has complete power over us, that we as individuals can decide what to do with ourselves. If all the means of production were vested in a single hand, whether it be nominally that of "society" as a whole or that of a dictator, whoever exercises this control has complete power over us.

Who can seriously doubt that a member of a small racial or religious minority will be freer with no property so long as fellow-members of his community have property and are therefore able to employ him, than he would be if private property were abolished and he became owner of a nominal share in the communal property. Or that the power which a multiple millionaire, who may be my neighbor and perhaps my employer, has over me is very much less than that which the smallest *fonctionnaire* possesses who wields the coercive power of the state and on whose discretion it depends whether and how I am to be allowed to live or to work? And who will deny that a world in which the wealthy are powerful is still a better world than one in which only the already powerful can acquire wealth?

It is pathetic, yet at the same time encouraging, to find as prominent an old communist as Max Eastman rediscovering this truth:

"It seems obvious to me now—though I have been slow, I must say, in coming to the conclusion—that the institution of private property is one of the main things that have given man that limited amount of free and equalness that Marx hoped to render infinite by abolishing this institution. Strangely enough Marx was the first to see this. He is the one who informed us, looking backwards, that the evolution of private capitalism with its free market had been a precondition for the evolution of all our democratic freedoms. It never occurred to him, looking forward, that if this was so, these other freedoms might disappear with the abolition of the free market."[2]

It is sometimes said, in answer to such apprehensions, that there is no reason why the planner should determine the incomes of individuals. The social and political difficulties involved in deciding the shares of different people in the national income are so obvious that even the most inveterate planner may well hesitate before he charges any authority with this task. Probably everybody who realizes what it involves would prefer to confine planning to production, to use it only to secure a "rational organization of industry," leaving the distribution of incomes as far as possible to impersonal forces. Although it is impossible to direct industry without exercising some influence on distribution, and although no planner will wish to leave distribution entirely to the forces of the market, they would probably all prefer to confine themselves to seeing that this distribution conforms to certain general rules of equity and fairness, that extreme inequalities are avoided, and that the relation between the

2. Max Eastman in the *Reader's Digest*, July, 1941, p. 39.

remuneration of the major classes is just, without undertaking the responsibility for the position of particular people within their class or for the gradations and differentiations between smaller groups and individuals.

We have already seen that the close interdependence of all economic phenomena makes it difficult to stop planning just where we wish and that, once the free working of the market is impeded beyond a certain degree, the planner will be forced to extend his controls until they become all-comprehensive. These economic considerations, which explain why it is impossible to stop deliberate control just where we should wish, are strongly reinforced by certain social or political tendencies whose strength makes itself increasingly felt as planning extends.

Once it becomes increasingly true, and is generally recognized, that the position of the individual is determined not by impersonal forces, not as a result of the competitive effort of many, but by the deliberate decision of authority, the attitude of the people toward their position in the social order necessarily changes. There will always exist inequalities which will appear unjust to those who suffer from them, disappointments which will appear unmerited, and strokes of misfortune which those hit have not deserved. But when these things occur in a society which is consciously directed, the way in which people will react will be very different from what it is when they are nobody's conscious choice.

Inequality is undoubtedly more readily borne, and affects the dignity of the person much less, if it is determined by impersonal forces than when it is due to design. In a competitive society it is no slight to a person, no offense to his dignity, to be told by any particular firm that it has no need for his services or that it cannot offer him a better job. It is true that in periods of prolonged mass unemployment the effect on many may be very similar. But there are other and better methods to prevent that scourge than central direction. But the unemployment or the loss of income which will always affect some in any society is certainly less degrading if it is the result of misfortune and not deliberately imposed by authority. However bitter the experience, it would be very much worse in a planned society. There individuals will have to decide not whether a person is needed for a particular job but whether he is of use for anything, and how useful he is. His position in life must be assigned to him by somebody else.

While people will submit to suffering which may hit anyone, they will not so easily submit to suffering which is the result of the decision of authority. It may be bad to be just a cog in an impersonal machine; but it is infinitely worse if we can no longer leave it, if we are tied to our place and to the superiors who have been chosen for us. Dissatisfaction of everybody with his lot will inevitably grow with the consciousness that it is the result of deliberate human decision.

Once government has embarked upon planning for the sake of justice, it cannot refuse responsibility for anybody's fate or position. In a planned society we shall all know that we are better or worse off than others, not because of circumstances which nobody controls, and which it is impossible to foresee with certainty, but because some authority wills it. And all our efforts directed toward improving our position will have to aim, not at foreseeing and preparing as well as we can for the circumstances over which we have no control, but at influencing in our favor the authority which has all the power. The nightmare of English nineteenth-century political thinkers, the state in which "no avenue to wealth and honor would exist save through the government,"[3] would be realized in a completeness which they never imagined—though familiar enough in some countries which have since passed to totalitarianism.

As soon as the state takes upon itself the task of planning the whole economic life, the problem of the due station of the different individuals and groups must indeed inevitably become the central political problem. As the coercive power of the state will alone decide who is to have what, the only power worth having will be a share in the exercise of this directing power. There will be no economic or social questions that would not be political questions in the sense that their solution will depend exclusively on who wields the coercive power, on whose are the views that will prevail on all occasions.

I believe it was Lenin himself who introduced to Russia the famous phrase "who, whom?"—during the early years of Soviet rule the byword in which the people summed up the universal problem of a socialist society.[4] Who plans whom, who directs and dominates whom, who assigns to other people their station in life, and who is to have his due allotted by others? These become necessarily the central issues to be decided solely by the supreme power.

More recently an American student of politics has enlarged upon Lenin's phrase and asserted that the problem of all government is "who gets what, when, and how." In a way this is not untrue. That all government affects the relative position of different people and that there is under any system scarcely an aspect of our lives which may not be affected by government action is certainly true. In so far as

3. The actual words are those of the young Disraeli.
4. Cf. M. Muggeridge, *Winter in Moscow* (1934); Arthur Feiler, *The Experiment of Bolshevism* (1930).

government does anything at all, its action will always have some effect on "who gets what, when, and how."

There are, however, two fundamental distinctions to be made. First, particular measures may be taken without the possibility of knowing how they will affect particular individuals and therefore without aiming at such particular effects. This point we have already discussed. Second, it is the extent of the activities of the government which decides whether everything that any person gets any time depends on the government, or whether its influence is confined to whether some people will get some things in some way at some time. Here lies the whole difference between a free and a totalitarian system.

The contrast between a liberal and a totally planned system is characteristically illustrated by the common complaints of Nazis and socialists of the "artificial separations of economics and politics" and by their equally common demand for the dominance of politics over economics. These phrases presumably mean not only that economic forces are now allowed to work for ends which are not part of the policy of the government but also that economic power can be used independently of government direction and for ends of which the government may not approve. But the alternative is not merely that there should be only one power but that this single power, the ruling group, should have control over all human ends and particularly that it should have complete power over the position of each individual in society.

That a government which undertakes to direct economic activity will have to use its power to realize somebody's ideal of distributive justice is certain. But how can and how will it use that power? By what principles will it or ought it to be guided? Is there a definite answer to the innumerable questions of relative merits that will arise and that will have to be solved deliberately? Is there a scale of values, on which reasonable people can be expected to agree, which would justify a new hierarchical order of society and is likely to satisfy the demands for justice?

There is only one general principle, one simple rule which would indeed provide a definite answer to all these questions: equality, complete and absolute equality of all individuals in all those points which are subject to human control. If this were generally regarded as desirable (quite apart from the question whether it would be practicable, i.e., whether it would provide adequate incentives), it would give the vague idea of distributive justice a clear meaning and would give the planner definite guidance. But nothing is further from the truth than that people in general regard mechanical equality of this kind as desirable. No socialist movement which aimed at complete equality has ever gained substantial support. What socialism promised was not an absolutely equal, but a more just and more equal, distribution. Not equality in the absolute sense but "greater equality" is the only goal which is seriously aimed at.

Though these two ideals sound very similar, they are as different as possible as far as our problem is concerned. While absolute equality would clearly determine the planner's task, the desire for greater equality is merely negative, no more than an expression of dislike of the present state of affairs; and so long as we are not prepared to say that every move in the direction toward complete equality is desirable, it answers scarcely any of the questions the planner will have to decide.

This is not a quibble about words. We face here a crucial issue which the similarity of the terms used is likely to conceal. While agreement on complete equality would answer all the problems of merit the planner must answer, the formula of the approach to greater equality answers practically none. Its content is hardly more definite than the phrases "common good" or "social welfare." It does not free us from the necessity of deciding in every particular instance between the merits of particular individuals or groups, and it gives us no help in that decision. All it tells us in effect is to take from the rich as much as we can. But, when it comes to the distribution of the spoils, the problem is the same as if the formula of "greater equality" had never been conceived.

Most people find it difficult to admit that we do not possess moral standards which would enable us to settle these questions—if not perfectly, at least to greater general satisfaction than is done by the competitive system. Have we not all some idea of what is a "just price" or a "fair wage"? Can we not rely on the strong sense of fairness of the people? And even if we do not now agree fully on what is just or fair in a particular case, would popular ideas not soon consolidate into more definite standards if people were given an opportunity to see their ideals realized?

Unfortunately, there is little ground for such hopes. What standards we have are derived from the competitive regime we have known and would necessarily disappear soon after the disappearance of competition. What we mean by a just price, or a fair wage is either the customary price or wage, the return which past experience has made people expect, or the price or wage that would exist if there were no monopolistic exploitation. The only important exception

to this used to be the claim of the workers to the "full produce of their labor," to which so much of socialist doctrine
traces back. But there are few socialists today who believe
that in a socialist society the output of each industry would
be entirely shared by the workers of that industry; for this
would mean that workers in industries using a great deal of
capital would have a much larger income than those in industries using little capital, which most socialists would regard as very unjust. And it is now fairly generally agreed
that this particular claim was based on an erroneous interpretation of the facts. But once the claim of the individual
worker to the whole of "his" product is disallowed, and the
whole of the return from capital is to be divided among all
workers, the problem of how to divide it raises the same basic issue.

What the "just price" of a particular commodity or the
"fair" remuneration for a particular service is might conceiv-
ably be determined objectively if the quantities needed were
independently fixed. If these were given irrespective of cost,
the planner might try to find what price or wage is necessary
to bring forth this supply. But the planner must also decide
how much is to be produced of each kind of goods, and, in
so doing, he determines what will be the just price or fair
wage to pay. If the planner decides that fewer architects or
watchmakers are wanted and that the need can be met by
those who are willing to stay in the trade at a lower remuneration, the "fair" wage will be lower. In deciding the relative importance of the different ends, the planner also decides the relative importance of the different groups and
persons. As he is not supposed to treat the people merely as
a means, he must take account of these effects and consciously balance the importance of the different ends against
the effects of his decision. This means, however, that he will

necessarily exercise direct control over the conditions of the different people.

This applies to the relative position of individuals no less than to that of the different occupational groups. We are in general far too likely to think of incomes within a given trade or profession as more or less uniform. But the differences between the incomes, not only of the most and the least successful doctor or architect, writer or movie actor, boxer or jockey, but also of the more and the less successful plumber or market gardener, grocer or tailor, are as great as those between the propertied and the propertyless classes. And although, no doubt, there would be some attempt at standardization by creating categories, the necessity of discrimination between individuals would remain the same, whether it were exercised by fixing their individual incomes or by allocating them to particular categories.

We need say no more about the likelihood of men in a free society submitting to such control—or about their remaining free if they submitted. On the whole question, what John Stuart Mill wrote nearly a hundred years ago remains equally true today:

"A fixed rule, like that of equality, might be acquiesced in, and so might chance, or an external necessity; but that a handful of human beings should weigh everybody in the balance, and give more to one and less to another at their sole pleasure and judgement, would not be borne unless from persons believed to be more than men, and backed by supernatural terrors."[5]

These difficulties need not lead to open clashes so long as socialism is merely the aspiration of a limited and fairly ho-

5. *Principles of Political Economy,* Book I, chap. ii, par. 4.

mogeneous group. They come to the surface only when a socialist policy is actually attempted with the support of the many different groups which together compose the majority of a people. Then it soon becomes the one burning question which of the different sets of ideals shall be imposed upon all by making the whole resources of the country serve it. It is because successful planning requires the creation of a common view on the essential values that the restriction of our freedom with regard to material things touches so directly on our spiritual freedom.

Socialists, the cultivated parents of the barbarous offspring they have produced, traditionally hope to solve this problem by education. But what does education mean in this respect? Surely we have learned that knowledge cannot create new ethical values, that no amount of learning will lead people to hold the same views on the moral issues which a conscious ordering of all social relations raises. It is not rational conviction but the acceptance of a creed which is required to justify a particular plan. And, indeed, socialists everywhere were the first to recognize that the task they had set themselves required the general acceptance of a common Weltanschauung, of a definite set of values. It was in these efforts to produce a mass movement supported by such a single world view that the socialists first created most of the instruments of indoctrination of which Nazis and Fascists have made such effective use.

In Germany and Italy the Nazis and Fascists did, indeed, not have much to invent. The usages of the new political movements which pervaded all aspects of life had in both countries already been introduced by the socialists. The idea of a political party which embraces all activities of the individual from the cradle to the grave, which claims to guide his views on everything, and which delights in making all problems questions of party Weltanschauung, was first put into practice by the socialists. An Austrian socialist writer, speaking of the socialist movement of his country, reports with pride that it was its "characteristic feature that it created special organizations for every field of activities of workers and employees."[6]

Though the Austrian socialists may have gone further in this respect than others, the situation was not very different elsewhere. It was not the Fascists but the socialists who began to collect children from the tenderest age into political organizations to make sure that they grew up as good proletarians. It was not the Fascists but the socialists who first thought of organizing sports and games, football and hiking, in party clubs where the members would not be infected by other views. It was the socialists who first insisted that the party member should distinguish himself from others by the modes of greeting and forms of address. It was they who by their organization of "cells" and devices for the permanent supervision of private life created the prototype of the totalitarian party. *Balilla* and *Hitlerjugend, Dopolavoro* and *Kraft durch Freude,* political uniforms and military party formations, are all little more than imitations of older socialist institutions.[7]

So long as the socialist movement in a country is closely bound up with the interests of a particular group, usually the more highly skilled industrial workers, the problem of creating a common view on the desirable status of the different members of society is comparatively simple. The movement is immediately concerned with the status of one par-

6. G. Wieser, *Ein Staat stirbt, Oesterreich 1934–1938* (Paris, 1938), p. 41.
7. The political "book clubs" in England provide a not unimportant parallel.

ticular group, and its aim is to raise that status relatively to other groups. The character of the problem changes, however, as in the course of the progressive advance toward socialism it becomes more and more evident to everyone that his income and general position are determined by the coercive apparatus of the state, that he can maintain or improve his position only as a member of an organized group capable of influencing or controlling the state machine in his interest.

In the tug-of-war between the various pressure groups which arises at this stage, it is by no means necessary that the interests of the poorest and most numerous groups should prevail. Nor is it necessarily an advantage for the older socialist parties, who avowedly represented the interests of a particular group, to have been the first in the field and to have designed their whole ideology to appeal to the manual workers in industry. Their very success, and their insistence on the acceptance of the whole creed, is bound to create a powerful countermovement—not by the capitalists but by the very large and equally propertyless classes who find their relative status threatened by the advance of the élite of the industrial workers.

Socialist theory and socialist tactics, even where they have not been dominated by Marxist dogma, have been based everywhere on the idea of a division of society into two classes with common but mutually conflicting interests: capitalists and industrial workers. Socialism counted on a rapid disappearance of the old middle class and completely disregarded the rise of a new middle class, the countless army of clerks and typists, administrative workers and schoolteachers, tradesmen and small officials, and the lower ranks of the professions. For a time these classes often provided many of the leaders of the labor movement. But as it became increasingly clear that the position of those classes was deteriorating relatively to that of the industrial workers, the ideals which guided the latter lost much of their appeal to the others. While they were all socialists in the sense that they disliked the capitalist system and wanted a deliberate sharing-out of wealth according to their ideas of justice, these ideas proved to be very different from those embodied in the practice of the older socialist parties.

The means which the old socialist parties had successfully employed to secure the support of one occupational group— the raising of their relative economic position—cannot be used to secure the support of all. There are bound to arise rival socialist movements that appeal to the support of those whose relative position is worsened. There is a great deal of truth in the often heard statement that fascism and National Socialism are a sort of middle-class socialism—only that in Italy and Germany the supporters of these new movements were economically hardly a middle class any longer. It was to a large extent a revolt of a new underprivileged class against the labor aristocracy which the industrial labor movement had created.

There can be little doubt that no single economic factor has contributed more to help these movements than the envy of the unsuccessful professional man, the university-trained engineer or lawyer, and of the "white-collared proletariat" in general, of the engine driver or compositor and other members of the strongest trade-unions whose income was many times theirs. Nor can there be much doubt that in terms of money income the average member of the rank and file of the Nazi movement in its early years was poorer than the average trade-unionist or member of the older socialist party—a circumstance which only gained poignancy from the fact that the former had often seen better days and were frequently still living in surroundings which were the result of this past.

The expression "class struggle *à rebours*," current in Italy at the time of the rise of fascism, did point to a very important aspect of the movement. The conflict between the Fascist or National Socialist and the older socialist parties must, indeed, very largely be regarded as the kind of conflict which is bound to arise between rival socialist factions. There was no difference between them about the question of its being the will of the state which should assign to each person his proper place in society. But there were, as there always will be, most profound differences about what are the proper places of the different classes and groups.

The old socialist leaders, who had always regarded their parties as the natural spearhead of the future general movement toward socialism, found it difficult to understand that with every extension in the use of socialist methods the resentment of large poor classes should turn against them. But while the old socialist parties, or the organized labor in particular industries, had usually not found it unduly difficult to come to an understanding for joint action with the employers in their particular industries, very large classes were left out in the cold. To them, and not without some justification, the more prosperous sections of the labor movement seemed to belong to the exploiting rather than to the exploited class.[8]

The resentment of the lower middle class, from which

8. It is now twelve years since one of the leading European socialist intellectuals, Hendrick de Man (who has since consistently developed further and made his peace with the Nazis), observed that "for the first time since the beginning of socialism, anti-capitalist resentments are turning against the socialist movement" (*Sozialismus und National-Faszismus* [Potsdam, 1931], p. 6).

fascism and National Socialism recruited so large a proportion of their supporters, was intensified by the fact that their
education and training had in many instances made them
aspire to directing positions and that they regarded themselves as entitled to be members of the directing class. While
the younger generation, out of that contempt for profit-
making fostered by socialist teaching, spurned independent
positions which involved risk and flocked in ever increasing
numbers into salaried positions which promised security,
they demanded a place yielding them the income and power
to which in their opinion their training entitled them. While
they believed in an organized society, they expected a place
in that society very different from that which society ruled
by labor seemed to offer. They were quite ready to take over
the methods of the older socialism but intended to employ
them in the service of a different class. The movement was
able to attract all those who, while they agreed on the desirability of the state controlling all economic activity, disagreed
with the ends for which the aristocracy of the industrial
workers used their political strength.

The new socialist movement started with several tactical
advantages. Labor socialism had grown in a democratic and
liberal world, adapting its tactics to it and taking over many
of the ideals of liberalism. Its protagonists still believed that
the creation of socialism as such would solve all problems.
Fascism and National Socialism, on the other hand, grew
out of the experience of an increasingly regulated society's
awakening to the fact that democratic and international socialism was aiming at incompatible ideals. Their tactics were
developed in a world already dominated by socialist policy
and the problems it creates. They had no illusions about the
possibility of a democratic solution of problems which require more agreement among people than can reasonably

be expected. They had no illusions about the capacity of reason to decide all the questions of the relative importance of the wants of different men or groups which planning inevitably raises, or about the formula of equality providing an answer. They knew that the strongest group which rallied enough supporters in favor of a new hierarchical order of society, and which frankly promised privileges to the classes to which it appealed, was likely to obtain the support of all those who were disappointed because they had been promised equality but found that they had merely furthered the interest of a particular class. Above all, they were successful because they offered a theory, or Weltanschauung, which seemed to justify the privileges they promised to their supporters.

9
Security and Freedom

The whole of society will have become a single office and a single factory with equality of work and equality of pay.
—LENIN (1917)

In a country where the sole employer is the State, opposition means death by slow starvation. The old principle: who does not work shall not eat, has been replaced by a new one: who does not obey shall not eat.
—LEON TROTSKY (1937)

LIKE the spurious "economic freedom," and with more justice, economic security is often represented as an indispensable condition of real liberty. In a sense this is both true and important. Independence of mind or strength of character is rarely found among those who cannot be confident that they will make their way by their own effort. Yet the idea of economic security is no less vague and ambiguous than most other terms in this field; and because of this the general approval given to the demand for security may become a danger to liberty. Indeed, when security is understood in too absolute a sense, the general striving for it, far from increasing the chances of freedom, becomes the gravest threat to it.

It will be well to contrast at the outset the two kinds of security: the limited one, which can be achieved for all, and which is therefore no privilege but a legitimate object of desire; and absolute security, which in a free society cannot be achieved for all and which ought not to be given as a privilege—except in a few special instances such as that of the judges, where complete independence is of paramount importance. These two kinds of security are, first, security against severe physical privation, the certainty of a given minimum of sustenance for all; and, second, the security of a given standard of life, or of the relative position which one person or group enjoys compared with others; or, as we may put it briefly, the security of minimum income and the security of the particular income a person is thought to deserve. We shall presently see that this distinction largely coincides with the distinction between the security which can be provided for all outside of and supplementary to the market system and the security which can be provided only for some and only by controlling or abolishing the market.

There is no reason why in a society which has reached the general level of wealth which ours has attained the first kind of security should not be guaranteed to all without endangering general freedom. There are difficult questions about the precise standard which should thus be assured; there is particularly the important question whether those who thus rely on the community should indefinitely enjoy all the same liberties as the rest.[1] An incautious handling of these questions might well cause serious and perhaps even dangerous political problems; but there can be no doubt that some minimum of food, shelter, and clothing, sufficient to preserve health and the capacity to work, can be assured to everybody. Indeed, for a considerable part of the population of England this sort of security has long been achieved.

Nor is there any reason why the state should not assist the individuals in providing for those common hazards of life against which, because of their uncertainty, few individuals

1. There are also serious problems of international relations which arise if mere citizenship of a country confers the right to a standard of living higher than elsewhere and which ought not to be dismissed too lightly.

can make adequate provision. Where, as in the case of sickness and accident, neither the desire to avoid such calamities nor the efforts to overcome their consequences are as a rule weakened by the provision of assistance—where, in short, we deal with genuinely insurable risks—the case for the state's helping to organize a comprehensive system of social insurance is very strong. There are many points of detail where those wishing to preserve the competitive system and those wishing to supercede it by something different will disagree on the details of such schemes; and it is possible under the name of social insurance to introduce measures which tend to make competition more or less ineffective. But there is no incompatibility in principle between the state's providing greater security in this way and the preservation of individual freedom. To the same category belongs also the increase of security through the state's rendering assistance to the victims of such "acts of God" as earthquakes and floods. Wherever communal action can mitigate disasters against which the individual can neither attempt to guard himself nor make provision for the consequences, such communal action should undoubtedly be taken.

There is, finally, the supremely important problem of combating general fluctuations of economic activity and the recurrent waves of large-scale unemployment which accompany them. This is, of course, one of the gravest and most pressing problems of our time. But, though its solution will require much planning in the good sense, it does not—or at least need not—require that special kind of planning which according to its advocates is to replace the market. Many economists hope, indeed, that the ultimate remedy may be found in the field of monetary policy, which would involve nothing incompatible even with nineteenth-century liberalism. Others, it is true, believe that real success can be ex-

pected only from the skilful timing of public works undertaken on a very large scale. This might lead to much more
serious restrictions of the competitive sphere, and, in ex-
perimenting in this direction, we shall have carefully to
watch our step if we are to avoid making all economic activity progressively more dependent on the direction and
volume of government expenditure. But this is neither the
only nor, in my opinion, the most promising way of meeting
the gravest threat to economic security. In any case, the very
necessary efforts to secure protection against these fluctuations do not lead to the kind of planning which constitutes
such a threat to our freedom.

The planning for security which has such an insidious
effect on liberty is that for security of a different kind. It is
planning designed to protect individuals or groups against
diminutions of their income, which although in no way deserved yet in a competitive society occur daily, against losses
imposing severe hardships having no moral justification yet
inseparable from the competitive system. This demand for
security is thus another form of the demand for a just remuneration—a remuneration commensurate with the subjective merits and not with the objective results of a man's
efforts. This kind of security or justice seems irreconcilable
with freedom to choose one's employment.

In any system which for the distribution of men between
the different trades and occupations relies on their own
choice it is necessary that the remuneration in these trades
should correspond to their usefulness to the other members
of society, even if this should stand in no relation to subjective merit. Although the results achieved will often be commensurate with efforts and intentions, this cannot always be
true in any form of society. It will particularly not be true in

the many instances where the usefulness of some trade or special skill is changed by circumstances which could not be foreseen. We all know the tragic plight of the highly trained man whose hard-learned skill has suddenly lost its value because of some invention which greatly benefits the rest of society. The history of the last hundred years is full of instances of this kind, some of them affecting hundreds of thousands of people at a time.

That anyone should suffer a great diminution of his income and bitter disappointment of all his hopes through no fault of his own, and despite hard work and exceptional skill, undoubtedly offends our sense of justice. The demands of those who suffer in this way, for state interference on their behalf to safeguard their legitimate expectations, are certain to receive popular sympathy and support. The general approval of these demands has had the effect that governments everywhere have taken action, not merely to protect the people so threatened from severe hardship and privation, but to secure to them the continued receipt of their former income and to shelter them from the vicissitudes of the market.[2]

Certainty of a given income can, however, not be given to all if any freedom in the choice of one's occupation is to be allowed. And, if it is provided for some, it becomes a privilege at the expense of others whose security is thereby necessarily diminished. That security of an invariable income can be provided for all only by the abolition of all freedom in the choice of one's employment is easily shown. Yet, although such a general guaranty of legitimate expectation is

2. Very interesting suggestions of how these hardships might be mitigated within a liberal society have been put forward by Professor W. H. Hutt in a book which will repay careful study (*Plan for Reconstruction* [1942]).

often regarded as the ideal to be aimed at, it is not a thing which is seriously attempted. What is constantly being done is to grant this kind of security piecemeal, to this group and to that, with the result that for those who are left out in the cold the insecurity constantly increases. No wonder that in consequence the value attached to the privilege of security constantly increases, the demand for it becomes more and more urgent, until in the end no price, not even that of liberty, appears too high.

If those whose usefulness is reduced by circumstances which they could neither foresee nor control were to be protected against undeserved loss, and those whose usefulness has been increased in the same way were prevented from making an unmerited gain, remuneration would soon cease to have any relation to actual usefulness. It would depend on the views held by some authority about what a person ought to have done, what he ought to have foreseen, and how good or bad his intentions were. Such decisions could not but be to a large extent arbitrary. The application of this principle would necessarily bring it about that people doing the same work would receive different remuneration. The differences in remuneration would then no longer present an adequate inducement to people to make the changes which are socially desirable, and it would not even be possible for the individuals affected to judge whether a particular change is worth the trouble it causes.

But if the changes in the distribution of men between different employments, which are constantly necessary in any society, can no longer be brought about by pecuniary "rewards" and "penalties" (which have no necessary connection with subjective merit), they must be brought about by direct orders. When a person's income is guaranteed, he can neither be allowed to stay in his job merely because he likes it nor to choose what other work he would like to do. As it is not he who makes the gain or suffers the loss dependent on his moving or not moving, the choice must be made for him by those who control the distribution of the available income.

The problem of adequate incentives which arises here is commonly discussed as if it were a problem mainly of the willingness of people to do their best. But this, although important, is not the whole, nor even the most important, aspect of the problem. It is not merely that if we want people to give their best we must make it worth while for them. What is more important is that if we want to leave them the choice, if they are to be able to judge what they ought to do, they must be given some readily intelligible yardstick by which to measure the social importance of the different occupations. Even with the best will in the world it would be impossible for anyone intelligently to choose between various alternatives if the advantages they offered him stood in no relation to their usefulness to society. To know whether as the result of a change a man ought to leave a trade and an environment which he has come to like, and exchange it for another, it is necessary that the changed relative value of these occupations to society should find expression in the remunerations they offer.

The problem is, of course, even more important because in the world as it is men are, in fact, not likely to give their best for long periods unless their own interests are directly involved. At least for great numbers some external pressure is needed if they are to give their best. The problem of incentives in this sense is a very real one, both in the sphere of ordinary labor and in those of the managerial activities. The application of the engineering technique to a whole nation—and this is what planning means—"raises problems

SECURITY AND FREEDOM

of discipline which are hard to solve," as has been well described by an American engineer with great experience in government planning, who has clearly seen the problem.

"In order to do an engineering job," he explains, "there ought to be surrounding the work a comparatively large area of unplanned economic action. There should be a place from which workers can be drawn, and when a worker is fired he should vanish from the job and from the pay-roll. In the absence of such a free reservoir discipline cannot be maintained without corporal punishment, as with slave labor.[3]

In the sphere of executive work the problem of sanctions for negligence arises in a different but no less serious form. It has been well said that, while the last resort of a competitive economy is the bailiff, the ultimate sanction of a planned economy is the hangman.[4] The powers the manager of any plant will have to be given will still be considerable. But no more than in the case of the worker can the manager's position and income in a planned system be made to depend merely on the success or failure of the work under his direction. As neither the risk nor the gain is his, it cannot be his personal judgment, but whether he does what he ought to have done according to some established rule, which must decide. A mistake he "ought" to have avoided is not his own affair; it is a crime against the community and must be treated as such. While so long as he keeps to the safe path of objectively ascertainable duty he may be surer of his income than the capitalist entrepreneur, the danger which threatens him in case of real failure is worse than bankruptcy. He may be economically secure so long as he satisfies

3. D. C. Coyle, "The Twilight of National Planning," *Harper's Magazine*, October, 1935, p. 558.
4. W. Roepke, *Die Gesellschaftskrisis der Gegenwart* (Zurich, 1942), p. 172.

his superiors, but this security is bought at the price of the safety of freedom and life.

The conflict with which we have to deal is, indeed, a quite fundamental one between two irreconcilable types of social organization, which, from the most characteristic forms in which they appear, have often been described as the commercial and the military type of society. The terms were, perhaps, unfortunate, because they direct attention to unessentials and make it difficult to see that we face a real alternative and that there is no third possibility. Either both the choice and the risk rest with the individual or he is relieved of both. The army does, indeed, in many ways represent the closest approach familiar to us to the second type of organization, where work and worker alike are allotted by authority and where, if the available means are scanty, everybody is alike put on short-commons. This is the only system in which the individual can be conceded full economic security and through the extension of which to the whole of society it can be achieved for all its members. This security is, however, inseparable from the restrictions on liberty and the hierarchical order of military life—it is the security of the barracks.

It is possible, of course, to organize sections of an otherwise free society on this principle, and there is no reason why this form of life, with its necessary restrictions on individual liberty, should not be open to those who prefer it. Indeed, some voluntary labor service on military lines might well be the best form for the state to provide the certainty of an opportunity for work and a minimum income for all. That proposals of this sort have in the past proved so little acceptable is due to the fact that those who are willing to surrender their freedom for security have always demanded that if they give up their full freedom it should also be taken from those not prepared to do so. For this claim it is difficult to find a justification.

The military type of organization as we know it gives us, however, only a very inadequate picture of what it would be like if it were extended to the whole of society. So long as only a part of society is organized on military lines, the unfreedom of the members of the military organization is mitigated by the fact that there is still a free sphere to which they can move if the restrictions become too irksome. If we want to form a picture of what society would be like if, according to the ideal which has seduced so many socialists, it was organized as a single great factory, we have to look to ancient Sparta, or to contemporary Germany, which, after moving for two or three generations in this direction, has now so nearly reached it.

In a society used to freedom it is unlikely that many people would be ready deliberately to purchase security at this price. But the polities which are now followed everywhere, which hand out the privilege of security, now to this group and now to that, are nevertheless rapidly creating conditions in which the striving for security tends to become stronger than the love of freedom. The reason for this is that with every grant of complete security to one group the insecurity of the rest necessarily increases. If you guarantee to some a fixed part of a variable cake, the share left to the rest is bound to fluctuate proportionally more than the size of the whole. And the essential element of security which the competitive system offers, the great variety of opportunities, is more and more reduced.

Within the market system, security can be granted to particular groups only by the kind of planning known as restrictionism (which includes, however, almost all the planning which is actually practiced!). "Control," i.e., limitation of output so that prices will secure an "adequate" return, is the only way in which in a market economy producers can be guaranteed a certain income. But this necessarily involves a reduction of opportunities open to others. If the producer, be he entrepreneur or worker, is to be protected against underbidding by outsiders, it means that others who are worse off are precluded from sharing in the relatively greater prosperity of the controlled industries. Every restriction on the freedom of entry into a trade reduces the security of all those outside it. And, as the number of those whose income is secured in this manner increases, the field of alternative opportunities which are open to anyone who suffers a loss of income is restricted; and for those unfavorably affected by any change the chance of avoiding a fatal diminution of their income is correspondingly diminished. And if, as has become increasingly true, in each trade in which conditions improve, the members are allowed to exclude others in order to secure to themselves the full gain in the form of higher wages or profits, those in the trades where demand has fallen have nowhere to go, and every change becomes the cause of large unemployment. There can be little doubt that it is largely a consequence of the striving for security by these means in the last decades that unemployment and thus insecurity for large sections of the population has so much increased.

In England and America such restrictions, especially those affecting the intermediate strata of society, have assumed important dimensions only in comparatively recent times, and we have scarcely yet realized their full consequences. The utter hopelessness of the position of those who, in a society which has thus grown rigid, are left outside the range of sheltered occupation, and the magnitude of the gulf which separates them from the fortunate possessors of jobs for whom protection against competition has made it unnecessary to budge ever so little to make room for those without, can be appreciated only by those who have experienced it. It is not a question of the fortunate ones' giving up their places, but merely that they should share in the common misfortune by some reduction of their incomes, or frequently even merely by some sacrifice of their prospects of improvement. The protection of their "standard of life," of the "fair price," or the "professional income" to which they regard themselves as entitled, and in the protection of which they receive the support of the state, precludes this. In consequence, instead of prices, wages, and individual incomes, it is now employment and production which have become subject to violent fluctuations. There has never been a worse and more cruel exploitation of one class by another than that of the weaker or less fortunate members of a group of producers by the well-established which has been made possible by the "regulation" of competition. Few catch-words have done so much harm as the ideal of a "stabilization" of particular prices (or wages), which, while securing the income of some, makes the position of the rest more and more precarious.

Thus, the more we try to provide full security by interfering with the market system, the greater the insecurity becomes; and, what is worse, the greater becomes the contrast between the security of those to whom it is granted as a privilege and the ever increasing insecurity of the underprivileged. And the more security becomes a privilege, and the greater the danger to those excluded from it, the higher will security be prized. As the number of the privileged increases and the difference between their security and the insecurity of the others increases, a completely new set of social values gradually arises. It is no longer independence but security which gives rank and status, the certain right to a pension more than confidence in his making good which makes a young man eligible for marriage, while insecurity becomes the dreaded state of the pariah in which those who in their youth have been refused admission to the haven of a salaried position remain for life.

The general endeavor to achieve security by restrictive measures, tolerated or supported by the state, has in the course of time produced a progressive transformation of society—a transformation in which, as in so many other ways, Germany has led and the other countries have followed. This development has been hastened by another effect of socialist teaching, the deliberate disparagement of all activities involving economic risk and the moral opprobrium cast on the gains which make risks worth taking but which only few can win. We cannot blame our young men when they prefer the safe, salaried position to the risk of enterprise after they have heard from their earliest youth the former described as the superior, more unselfish and disinterested occupation. The younger generation of today has grown up in a world in which in school and press the spirit of commercial enterprise has been represented as disreputable and the making of profit as immoral, where to employ a hundred people is represented as exploitation but to command the same number as honorable. Older people may regard this as an exaggeration of the present state of affairs, but the daily experience of the university teacher leaves little doubt that, as a result of anticapitalist propaganda, values have already altered far in advance of the change in institutions which has so far taken place. The question is whether, by changing our institutions to satisfy the new demands, we shall not unwittingly destroy values which we still rate higher.

The change in the structure of society involved in the victory of the ideal of security over that of independence cannot be better illustrated than by a comparison of what ten or twenty years ago could still be regarded as the English and the German type of society. However great the influence of the army may have been in the latter country, it is a grave mistake to ascribe what the Englishman regarded as the "military" character of German society mainly to that influence. The difference went much deeper than could be explained on that ground, and the peculiar attribute of German society existed no less in circles in which the properly military influence was negligible than in those in which it was strong. It was not so much that at almost all times a larger part of the German people was organized for war than was true in other countries, but that the same type of organization was employed for so many other purposes, which gave German society its peculiar character. It was that a larger part of the civil life of Germany than of any other country was deliberately organized from the top, that so large a proportion of her people did not regard themselves as independent but as appointed functionaries, which gave her social structure its peculiar character. Germany had, as the Germans themselves boasted, for long been a *Beamtenstaat* in which not only in the civil service proper but in almost all spheres of life income and status were assigned and guaranteed by some authority.

While it is doubtful whether the spirit of freedom can anywhere be extirpated by force, it is not certain that any people would successfully withstand the process by which it was slowly smothered in Germany. Where distinction and rank are achieved almost exclusively by becoming a salaried servant of the state, where to do one's assigned duty is regarded as more laudable than to choose one's own field of usefulness, where all pursuits that do not give a recognized place in the official hierarchy or a claim to a fixed income are regarded as inferior and even somewhat disreputable, it is too much to expect that many will long prefer freedom to security. And where the alternative to security in a dependent position is a most precarious position, in which one is despised alike for success and for failure, only few will resist the temptation of safety at the price of freedom. Once things have gone so far, liberty indeed becomes almost a mockery, since it can be purchased only by the sacrifice of most of the good things of this earth. In this state it is little surprising that more and more people should come to feel that without economic security liberty is "not worth having" and that they are willing to sacrifice their liberty for security. But it is disquieting to find Professor Harold Laski employing the very same argument which has perhaps done more than any other to induce the German people to sacrifice their liberty.[5]

There can be no question that adequate security against severe privation, and the reduction of the avoidable causes of misdirected effort and consequent disappointment, will have to be one of the main goals of policy. But if these endeavors are to be successful and are not to destroy individual freedom, security must be provided outside the market and competition be left to function unobstructed. Some security is essential if freedom is to be preserved, because most men

5. H. J. Laski, *Liberty in the Modern State* (Pelican ed., 1937), p. 51: "Those who know the normal life of the poor, its haunting sense of impending disaster, its fitful search for beauty which perpetually eludes, will realise well enough that, without economic security, liberty is not worth having."

are willing to bear the risk which freedom inevitably involves only so long as that risk is not too great. But while this is a truth of which we must never lose sight, nothing is more fatal than the present fashion among intellectual leaders of extolling security at the expense of freedom. It is essential that we should re-learn frankly to face the fact that freedom can be had only at a price and that as individuals we must be prepared to make severe material sacrifices to preserve our liberty. If we want to retain this, we must regain the conviction on which the rule of liberty in the Anglo-Saxon countries has been based and which Benjamin Franklin expressed in a phrase, applicable to us in our lives as individuals no less than as nations: "Those who would give up essential liberty to purchase a little temporary safety deserve neither liberty nor safety."

10
Why the Worst Get on Top

*Power tends to corrupt, and absolute power
corrupts absolutely*
—LORD ACTON

WE MUST now examine a belief from which many who regard the advent of totalitarianism as inevitable derive consolation and which seriously weakens the resistance of many others who would oppose it with all their might if they fully apprehended its nature. It is the belief that the most repellent features of the totalitarian regimes are due to the historical accident that they were established by groups of blackguards and thugs. Surely, it is argued, if in Germany the creation of a totalitarian regime brought the Streichers and Killingers, the Leys and Heines, the Himmlers and Heydrichs to power, this may prove the viciousness of the German character but not that the rise of such people is the necessary consequence of a totalitarian system. Why should it not be possible that the same sort of system, if it be necessary to achieve important ends, be run by decent people for the good of the community as a whole?

We must not deceive ourselves into believing that all good people must be democrats or will necessarily wish to have a share in the government. Many, no doubt, would rather intrust it to somebody whom they think more competent. Although this might be unwise, there is nothing bad or dishonorable in approving a dictatorship of the good. Totalitarianism, we can already hear it argued, is a powerful system alike for good and evil, and the purpose for which it will be used depends entirely on the dictators. And those who think that it is not the system which we need fear, but the danger that it might be run by bad men, might even be tempted to forestall this danger by seeing that it is established in time by good men.

No doubt an American or English "Fascist" system would greatly differ from the Italian or German models; no doubt, if the transition were effected without violence, we might expect to get a better type of leader. And, if I had to live under a Fascist system, I have no doubt that I would rather live under one run by Englishmen or Americans than under one run by anybody else. Yet all this does not mean that, judged on our present standards, our Fascist system would in the end prove so very different or much less intolerable than its prototypes. There are strong reasons for believing that what to us appear the worst features of the existing totalitarian systems are not accidental by-products but phenomena which totalitarianism is certain sooner or later to produce. Just as the democratic statesman who sets out to plan economic life will soon be confronted with the alternative of either assuming dictatorial powers or abandoning his plans, so the totalitarian dictator would soon have to choose between disregard of ordinary morals and failure. It is for this reason that the unscrupulous and uninhibited are likely to be more successful in a society tending toward totalitarianism. Who does not see this has not yet grasped the full width of the gulf which separates totalitarianism from a liberal regime, the utter difference between the whole moral atmosphere under collectivism and the essentially individualist Western civilization.

The "moral basis of collectivism" has, of course, been much debated in the past; but what concerns us here is not its moral basis but its moral results. The usual discussions of the ethical aspects of collectivism refer to the question whether collectivism is demanded by existing moral convictions; or what moral convictions would be required if collectivism is to produce the hoped-for results. Our question, however, is what moral views will be produced by a collectivist organization of society, or what views are likely to rule it. The interaction between morals and institutions may well have the effect that the ethics produced by collectivism will be altogether different from the moral ideals that lead to the demand for collectivism. While we are likely to think that, since the desire for a collectivist system springs from high moral motives, such a system must be the breeding-ground for the highest virtues, there is, in fact, no reason why any system should necessarily enhance those attitudes which serve the purpose for which it was designed. The ruling moral views will depend partly on the qualities that will lead individuals to success in a collectivist or totalitarian system and partly on the requirements of the totalitarian machinery.

We must here return for a moment to the position which precedes the suppression of democratic institutions and the creation of a totalitarian regime. In this stage it is the general demand for quick and determined government action that is the dominating element in the situation, dissatisfaction with the slow and cumbersome course of democratic procedure which makes action for action's sake the goal. It is then the man or the party who seems strong and resolute enough "to get things done" who exercises the greatest appeal. "Strong" in this sense means not merely a numerical majority—it is the ineffectiveness of parliamentary majorities with which people are dissatisfied. What they will seek is somebody with such solid support as to inspire confidence that he can carry out whatever he wants. It is here that the new type of party, organized on military lines, comes in.

In the Central European countries the socialist parties had familiarized the masses with political organizations of a semi-military character designed to absorb as much as possible of the private life of the members. All that was wanted to give one group overwhelming power was to carry the same principle somewhat further, to seek strength not in the assured votes of huge numbers at occasional elections but in the absolute and unreserved support of a smaller but more thoroughly organized body. The chance of imposing a totalitarian regime on a whole people depends on the leader's first collecting round him a group which is prepared voluntarily to submit to that totalitarian discipline which they are to impose by force upon the rest.

Although the socialist parties had the strength to get anything if they had cared to use force, they were reluctant to do so. They had, without knowing it, set themselves a task which only the ruthless ready to disregard the barriers of accepted morals can execute.

That socialism can be put into practice only by methods which most socialists disapprove is, of course, a lesson learned by many social reformers in the past. The old socialist parties were inhibited by their democratic ideals; they did not possess the ruthlessness required for the performance of their chosen task. It is characteristic that both in Germany and in Italy the success of fascism was preceded by the refusal of the socialist parties to take over the responsibilities of government. They were unwilling wholeheartedly to employ the methods to which they had pointed the way. They still hoped for the miracle of a majority's agreeing on a particular plan for the organization of the whole of society; others had already learned the lesson that in a planned society the question can no longer be on what do a majority of the people agree but what the largest single group is whose members agree sufficiently to make unified direction of all affairs possible; or, if no such group large enough to enforce its views exists, how it can be created and who will succeed in creating it.

There are three main reasons why such a numerous and strong group with fairly homogeneous views is not likely to be formed by the best but rather by the worst elements of any society. By our standards the principles on which such a group would be selected will be almost entirely negative.

In the first instance, it is probably true that, in general, the higher the education and intelligence of individuals become, the more their views and tastes are differentiated and the less likely they are to agree on a particular hierarchy of values. It is a corollary of this that if we wish to find a high degree of uniformity and similarity of outlook, we have to descend to the regions of lower moral and intellectual standards where the more primitive and "common" instincts and tastes prevail. This does not mean that the majority of people have low moral standards; it merely means that the largest group of people whose values are very similar are the people with low standards. It is, as it were, the lowest common denominator which unites the largest number of people. If a numerous group is needed, strong enough to impose their views on the values of life on all the rest, it will never be those with highly differentiated and developed tastes—it will be those who form the "mass" in the derogatory sense of the term, the least original and independent, who will be able to put the weight of their numbers behind their particular ideals.

If, however, a political dictator had to rely entirely on those whose uncomplicated and primitive instincts happen to be very similar, their number would scarcely give sufficient weight to their endeavors. He will have to increase their numbers by converting more to the same simple creed.

Here comes in the second negative principle of selection: he will be able to obtain the support of all the docile and gullible, who have no strong convictions of their own but are prepared to accept a ready-made system of values if it is only drummed into their ears sufficiently loudly and frequently. It will be those whose vague and imperfectly formed ideas are easily swayed and whose passions and emotions are readily aroused who will thus swell the ranks of the totalitarian party.

It is in connection with the deliberate effort of the skilful demagogue to weld together a closely coherent and homogeneous body of supporters that the third and perhaps most important negative element of selection enters. It seems to be almost a law of human nature that it is easier for people to agree on a negative program—on the hatred of an enemy, on the envy of those better off—than on any positive task. The contrast between the "we" and the "they," the common fight against those outside the group, seems to be an essential ingredient in any creed which will solidly knit together a group for common action. It is consequently always employed by those who seek, not merely support of a policy, but the unreserved allegiance of huge masses. From their point of view it has the great advantage of leaving them greater freedom of action than almost any positive program. The enemy, whether he be internal, like the "Jew" or the "kulak," or external, seems to be an indispensable requisite in the armory of a totalitarian leader.

That in Germany it was the Jew who became the enemy until his place was taken by the "plutocracies" was no less result of the anticapitalist resentment on which the whole movement was based than the selection of the kulak in Russia. In Germany and Austria the Jew had come to be regarded as the representative of capitalism because a traditional dislike of large classes of the population for commercial pursuits had left these more readily accessible to a group that was practically excluded from the more highly esteemed occupations. It is the old story of the alien race's being admitted only to the less respected trades and then being hated still more for practicing them. The fact that German anti-Semitism and anti-capitalism spring from the same root is of great importance for the understanding of what has happened there, but this is rarely grasped by foreign observers.

To treat the universal tendency of collectivist policy to become nationalistic as due entirely to the necessity for securing unhesitating support would be to neglect another and no less important factor. It may, indeed, be questioned whether anyone can realistically conceive of a collectivist program other than in the service of a limited group, whether collectivism can exist in any form other than that of some kind of particularism, be it nationalism, racialism, or classism. The belief in the community of aims and interests with fellow-men seems to presuppose a greater degree of similarity of outlook and thought than exists between men merely as human beings. If the other members of one's group cannot all be personally known, they must at least be of the same kind as those around us, think and talk in the same way and about the same kind of things, in order that we may identify ourselves with them. Collectivism on a world scale seems to be unthinkable—except in the service of a small ruling élite. It would certainly raise not only technical but, above all, moral problems which none of our socialists is willing to face. If the English proletarian, for instance, is entitled to an equal share of the income now derived from his country's capital resources, and of the control of their use, because they are the result of exploitation, so on the same principle all the Indians would be entitled not only to the income from but also to the use of a proportional share of the British capital.

But what socialists seriously contemplate the equal division of existing capital resources among the people of the world? They all regard the capital as belonging not to humanity but to the nation—though even within the nation few would dare to advocate that the richer regions should be deprived of some of "their" capital equipment in order to help the poorer regions. What socialists proclaim as a duty toward the fellow-members of the existing states they are not prepared to grant to the foreigner. From a consistent collectivist point of view the claims of the "have-not" nations for a new division of the world are entirely justified—though, if consistently applied, those who demand it most loudly would lose by it almost as much as the richest nations. They are, therefore, careful not to base their claims on any equalitarian principles but on their pretended superior capacity to organize other peoples.

One of the inherent contradictions of the collectivist philosophy is that, while basing itself on the humanistic morals which individualism has developed, it is practicable only within a relatively small group. That socialism so long as it remains theoretical is internationalist, while as soon as it is put into practice, whether in Russia or in Germany, it becomes violently nationalist, is one of the reasons why "liberal socialism" as most people in the Western world imagine it is purely theoretical, while the practice of socialism is every-where totalitarian.[1] Collectivism has no room for the wide humanitarianism of liberalism but only for the narrow particularism of the totalitarian.

If the "community" or the state are prior to the individual, if they have ends of their own independent of and superior to those of the individuals, only those individuals who work for the same ends can be regarded as members of the community. It is a necessary consequence of this view that a person is respected only as a member of the group, that is, only if and in so far as he works for the recognized common ends, and that he derives his whole dignity only from this membership and not merely from being man. Indeed, the very concepts of humanity and therefore of any form of internationalism are entirely products of the individualistic view of man, and there can be no place for them in a collective system of thought.[2]

Apart from the basic fact that the community of collectivism can extend only as far as the unity of purpose of the individuals exists or can be created, several contributory factors strengthen the tendency of collectivism to become particularist and exclusive. Of these, one of the most important is that the desire of the individual to identify himself with a group is very frequently the result of a feeling of

1. Cf. now the instructive discussion in Franz Borkenau, *Socialism, National or International?* (1942).

2. It is entirely in the spirit of collectivism when Nietzsche makes his Zarathustra say:

"A thousand goals have existed hitherto, for a thousand people existed. But the fetter for the thousand necks is still lacking, the one goal is still lacking. Humanity has no goal yet.

"But tell me, I pray, my brethen; if the goal be lacking to humanity, is not humanity itself lacking?"

inferiority and that therefore his want will be satisfied only
if membership of the group confers some superiority over
outsiders. Sometimes, it seems, the very fact that these violent instincts which the individual knows he must curb
within the group can be given a free range in the collective
action toward the outsider, becomes a further inducement
for merging personality in that of the group. There is a
profound truth expressed in the title of Reinhold Niebuhr's
Moral Man and Immoral Society—however little we can follow him in the conclusions he draws from his thesis. There
is, indeed, as he says elsewhere, "an increasing tendency
among modern men to imagine themselves ethical because
they have delegated their vices to larger and larger groups."[3]
To act on behalf of a group seems to free people of many of
the moral restraints which control their behavior as individuals within the group.

The definitely antagonistic attitude which most planners
take toward internationalism is further explained by the fact
that in the existing world all outside contacts of a group are
obstacles to their effectively planning the sphere in which
they can attempt it. It is therefore no accident that, as the
editor of one of the most comprehensive collective studies
on planning has discovered to his chagrin, "most 'planners'
are militant nationalists."[4]

The nationalist and imperialist propensities of socialist
planners, much more common than is generally recognized,
are not always as flagrant as, for example, in the case of the
Webbs and some of the other early Fabians, with whom en-

3. Quoted from an article of Dr. Niebuhr's by E. H. Carr, *The Twenty
Years' Crisis* (1941), p. 203.

4. Findlay Mackenzie (ed.), *Planned Society, Yesterday, Today, Tomorrow: A
Symposium* (1937), p. xx.

thusiasm for planning was characteristically combined with the veneration for the large and powerful political units and a contempt for the small state. The historian Élie Halévy, speaking of the Webbs when he first knew them forty years ago, records that their socialism was profoundly antiliberal. "They did not hate the Tories, indeed they were extraordinarily lenient to them, but they had no mercy for Gladstonian Liberalism. It was the time of the Boer War and both the advanced liberals and the men who were beginning to form the Labour Party had generously sided with the Boers against British Imperialism, in the name of freedom and humanity. But the two Webbs and their friend, Bernard Shaw, stood apart. They were ostentatiously imperialistic. The independence of small nations might mean something to the liberal individualist. It meant nothing to collectivists like themselves. I can still hear Sidney Webb explaining to me that the future belonged to the great administrative nations, where the officials govern and the police keep order." And elsewhere Halévy quotes George Bernard Shaw, arguing, about the same time, that "the world is to the big and powerful states by necessity; and the little ones must come within their borders or be crushed out of existence."[5]

I have quoted at length these passages, which would not surprise one in a description of the German ancestors of National Socialism, because they provide so characteristic an example of that glorification of power which easily leads from socialism to nationalism and which profoundly affects the ethical views of all collectivists. So far as the rights of small nations are concerned, Marx and Engels were little better than most other consistent collectivists, and the views

5. Élie Halévy, *L'Ere des tyrannies* (Paris, 1938), p. 217, and *History of the English People,* Epilogue, I, 105–6.

occasionally expressed about Czechs or Poles resemble those of contemporary National Socialists.[6]

While to the great individualist social philosophers of the nineteenth century, to a Lord Acton or a Jacob Burckhardt, down to contemporary socialists, like Bertrand Russell, who have inherited the liberal tradition, power itself has always appeared the archevil, to the strict collectivist it is a goal in itself. It is not only, as Russell has so well described, that the desire to organize social life according to a unitary plan itself springs largely from a desire for power.[7] It is even more the outcome of the fact that, in order to achieve their end, collectivists must create power—power over men wielded by other men—of a magnitude never before known, and that their success will depend on the extent to which they achieve such power.

This remains true even though many liberal socialists are guided in their endeavors by the tragic illusion that by depriving private individuals of the power they possess in an individualist system, and by transferring this power to society, they can thereby extinguish power. What all those who argue in this manner overlook is that, by concentrating power so that it can be used in the service of a single plan, it is not merely transferred but infinitely heightened; that, by uniting in the hands of some single body power formerly exercised independently by many, an amount of power is created infinitely greater than any that existed before, so much more far-reaching as almost to be different in kind. It is entirely fallacious when it is sometimes argued that the great power

6. Cf. Karl Marx, *Revolution and Counter-revolution*, and Engels' letter to Marx, May 23, 1851.
7. Bertrand Russell, *The Scientific Outlook* (1931), p. 211.

exercised by a central planning board would be "no greater than the power collectively exercised by private boards of directors."[8] There is, in a competitive society, nobody who can exercise even a fraction of the power which a socialist planning board would possess, and if nobody can consciously use the power, it is just an abuse of words to assert that it rests with all the capitalists put together.[9] It is merely a play upon words to speak of the "power collectively exercised by private boards of directors" so long as they do not combine to concerted action—which would, of course, mean the end of competition and the creation of a planned economy. To split or decentralize power is necessarily to reduce the absolute amount of power, and the competitive system is the only system designed to minimize by decentralization the power exercised by man over man.

We have seen before how the separation of economic and political aims is an essential guaranty of individual freedom and how it is consequently attacked by all collectivists. To this we must now add that the "substitution of political for economic power" now so often demanded means necessarily the substitution of power from which there is no escape for a power which is always limited. What is called economic power, while it can be an instrument of coercion, is, in the hands of private individuals, never exclusive or complete power, never power over the whole life of a person. But

8. B. E. Lippincott, in his Introduction to Oscar Lange and F. M. Taylor, *On the Economic Theory of Socialism* (Minneapolis, 1938), p. 35.

9. We must not allow ourselves to be deceived by the fact that the word "power," apart from the sense in which it is used with respect to human beings, is also used in an impersonal (or rather anthropomorphic) sense for any determining cause. Of course, there will always be something that determines everything that happens, and in this sense the amount of power existing must always be the same. But this is not true of the power consciously wielded by human beings.

centralized as an instrument of political power it creates a degree of dependence scarcely distinguishable from slavery.

From the two central features of every collectivist system, the need for a commonly accepted system of ends of the group and the all-overriding desire to give to the group the maximum of power to achieve these ends, grows a definite system of morals, which on some points coincides and on others violently contrasts with ours—but differs from it in one point which makes it doubtful whether we can call it morals: that it does not leave the individual conscience free to apply its own rules and does not even know any general rules which the individual is required or allowed to observe in all circumstances. This makes collectivist morals so different from what we have known as morals that we find it difficult to discover any principle in them, which they nevertheless possess.

The difference of principle is very much the same as that which we have already considered in connection with the Rule of Law. Like formal law, the rules of individualist ethics, however unprecise they may be in many respects, are general and absolute; they prescribe or prohibit a general type of action irrespective of whether in the particular instance the ultimate purpose is good or bad. To cheat or steal, to torture or betray a confidence, is held to be bad, irrespective of whether or not in the particular instance any harm follows from it. Neither the fact that in a given instance nobody may be the worse for it, nor any high purpose for which such an act may have been committed, can alter the fact that it is bad. Though we may sometimes be forced to choose between different evils, they remain evils.

The principle that the end justifies the means in individualist ethics is regarded as the denial of all morals. In collectivist ethics it becomes necessarily the supreme rule; there is literally nothing which the consistent collectivist must not be prepared to do if it serves "the good of the whole," because the "good of the whole" is to him the only criterion of what ought to be done. The *raison d'état*, in which collectivist ethics has found its most explicit formulation, knows no other limit than that set by expediency—the suitability of the particular act for the end in view. And what the *raison d'état* affirms with respect to the relations between different countries applies equally to the relations between different individuals within the collectivist state. There can be no limit to what its citizen must be prepared to do, no act which his conscience must prevent him from committing, if it is necessary for an end which the community has set itself or which his superiors order him to achieve.

The absence of absolute formal rules in collectivist ethics does not, of course, mean that there are not some useful habits of the individual which a collectivist community will encourage and others which it will discourage. Quite the reverse; it will take a much greater interest in the individual's habits of life than an individualist community. To be a useful member of a collectivist society requires very definite qualities which must be strengthened by constant practice. The reason why we designate these qualities as "useful habits" and can hardly describe them as moral virtues is that the individual could never be allowed to put these rules above any definite orders or to let them become an obstacle to the achievement of any of the particular aims of his community. They only serve, as it were, to fill any gaps which direct orders or the designation of particular aims may leave, but they can never justify a conflict with the will of the authority.

The differences between the virtues which will continue

to be esteemed under a collectivist system and those which will disappear is well illustrated by a comparison of the virtues which even their worst enemies admit the Germans, or rather the "typical Prussian," to possess, and those of which they are commonly thought lacking and in which the English people, with some justification, used to pride themselves as excelling. Few people will deny that the Germans on the whole are industrious and disciplined, thorough and energetic to the degree of ruthlessness, conscientious and single-minded in any tasks they undertake; that they possess a strong sense of order, duty, and strict obedience to authority; and that they often show great readiness to make personal sacrifices and great courage in physical danger. All these make the German an efficient instrument in carrying out an assigned task, and they have accordingly been carefully nurtured in the old Prussian state and the new Prussian-dominated Reich. What the "typical German" is often thought to lack are the individualist virtues of tolerance and respect for other individuals and their opinions, of independence of mind and that uprightness of character and readiness to defend one's own convictions against a superior which the Germans themselves, usually conscious that they lack it, call *Zivilcourage,* of consideration for the weak and infirm, and of that healthy contempt and dislike of power which only an old tradition of personal liberty creates. Deficient they seem also in most of those little yet so important qualities which facilitate the intercourse between men in a free society: kindliness and a sense of humor, personal modesty, and respect for the privacy and belief in the good intentions of one's neighbor.

After what we have already said it will not cause surprise that these individualist virtues are at the same time eminently social virtues—virtues which smooth social contacts and which make control from above less necessary and at the same time more difficult. They are virtues which flourish wherever the individualist or commercial type of society has prevailed and which are missing according as the collectivist or military type of society predominates—a difference which is, or was, as noticeable between the various regions of Germany as it has now become of the views which rule in Germany and those characteristic of the West. Until recently, at least, in those parts of Germany which have been longest exposed to the civilizing forces of commerce, the old commercial towns of the south and west and the Hanse towns, the general moral concepts were probably much more akin to those of the Western people than to those which have now become dominant all over Germany.

It would, however, be highly unjust to regard the masses of the totalitarian people as devoid of moral fervor because they give unstinted support to a system which to us seems a denial of most moral values. For the great majority of them the opposite is probably true: the intensity of the moral emotions behind a movement like that of National Socialism or communism can probably be compared only to those of the great religious movements of history. Once you admit that the individual is merely a means to serve the ends of the higher entity called society or the nation, most of those features of totalitarian regimes which horrify us follow of necessity. From the collectivist standpoint intolerance and brutal suppression of dissent, the complete disregard of the life and happiness of the individual, are essential and unavoidable consequences of this basic premise, and the collectivist can admit this and at the same time claim that his system is superior to one in which the "selfish" interests of the individual are allowed to obstruct the full realization of the ends the community pursues. When German philosophers again and again represent the striving for personal happiness as itself immoral and only the fulfillment of an imposed duty as praiseworthy, they are perfectly sincere, however difficult this may be to understand for those who have been brought up in a different tradition.

Where there is one common all-overriding end, there is no room for any general morals or rules. To a limited extent we ourselves experience this in wartime. But even war and the greatest peril had led in the democratic countries only to a very moderate approach to totalitarianism, very little setting-aside of all other values in the service of a single purpose. But where a few specific ends dominate the whole of society, it is inevitable that occasionally cruelty may become a duty; that acts which revolt all our feeling, such as the shooting of hostages or the killing of the old or sick, should be treated as mere matters of expediency; that the compulsory uprooting and transportation of hundreds of thousands should become an instrument of policy approved by almost everybody except the victims; or that suggestions like that of a "conscription of women for breeding purposes" can be seriously contemplated. There is always in the eyes of the collectivist a greater goal which these acts serve and which to him justifies them because the pursuit of the common end of society can know no limits in any rights or values of any individual.

But while for the mass of the citizens of the totalitarian state it is often unselfish devotion to an ideal, although one that is repellent to us, which makes them approve and even perform such deeds, this cannot be pleaded for those who guide its policy. To be a useful assistant in the running of a totalitarian state, it is not enough that a man should be prepared to accept specious justification of vile deeds; he must himself be prepared actively to break every moral rule he has ever known if this seems necessary to achieve the end set for him. Since it is the supreme leader who alone determines the ends, his instruments must have no moral convictions of their own. They must, above all, be unreservedly committed to the person of the leader; but next to this the most important thing is that they should be completely unprincipled and literally capable of everything. They must have no ideals of their own which they want to realize; no ideas about right or wrong which might interfere with the intentions of the leader. There is thus in the positions of power little to attract those who hold moral beliefs of the kind which in the past have guided the European peoples, little which could compensate for the distastefulness of many of the particular tasks, and little opportunity to gratify any more idealistic desires, to recompense for the undeniable risk, the sacrifice of most of the pleasures of private life and of personal independence which the posts of great responsibility involve. The only tastes which are satisfied are the taste for power as such and the pleasure of being obeyed and of being part of a well-functioning and immensely powerful machine to which everything else must give way.

Yet while there is little that is likely to induce men who are good by our standards to aspire to leading positions in the totalitarian machine, and much to deter them, there will be special opportunities for the ruthless and unscrupulous. There will be jobs to be done about the badness of which taken by themselves nobody has any doubt, but which have to be done in the service of some higher end, and which have to be executed with the same expertness and efficiency as any others. And as there will be need for actions which are bad in themselves, and which all those still influenced by traditional morals will be reluctant to perform, the readiness to do bad things becomes a path to promotion and power.

The positions in a totalitarian society in which it is necessary to practice cruelty and intimidation, deliberate deception and spying, are numerous. Neither the Gestapo nor the administration of a concentration camp, neither the Ministry of Propaganda nor the S.A. or S.S. (or their Italian or Russian counterparts), are suitable places for the exercise of humanitarian feelings. Yet it is through positions like these that the road to the highest positions in the totalitarian state leads. It is only too true when a distinguished American economist concludes from a similar brief enumeration of the duties of the authorities of a collectivist state that "they would have to do these things whether they wanted to or not: and the probability of the people in power being individuals who would dislike the possession and exercise of power is on a level with the probability that an extremely tender-hearted person would get the job of whipping-master in a slave plantation." [10]

We cannot, however, exhaust this subject here. The problem of the selection of the leaders is closely bound up with the wide problem of selection according to the opinions held, or rather according to the readiness with which a person conforms to an ever changing set of doctrines. And this leads us to one of the most characteristic moral features of totalitarianism: its relation to, and its effect on, all the virtues falling under the general heading of truthfulness. This is so big a subject that it requires a separate chapter.

10. Professor Frank H. Knight in the *Journal of Political Economy*, December, 1938, p. 869.

11
The End of Truth

HE most effective way of making everybody serve the single system of ends toward which the social plan is directed is to make everybody believe in those ends. To make a totalitarian system function efficiently, it is not enough that everybody should be forced to work for the same ends. It is essential that the people should come to regard them as their own ends. Although the beliefs must be chosen for the people and imposed upon them, they must become their beliefs, a generally accepted creed which makes the individuals as far as possible act spontaneously in the way the planner wants. If the feeling of oppression in totalitarian countries is in general much less acute than most people in liberal countries imagine, this is because the totalitarian governments succeed to a high degree in making people think as they want them to.

This is, of course, brought about by the various forms of propaganda. Its technique is now so familiar that we need say little about it. The only point that needs to be stressed is that neither propaganda in itself nor the techniques employed are peculiar to totalitarianism and that what so completely changes its nature and effect in a totalitarian state is that all propaganda serves the same goal—that all the instruments of propaganda are co-ordinated to influence the individuals in the same direction and to produce the characteristic *Gleichschaltung* of all minds. As a result, the effect of propaganda in totalitarian countries is different not only in magnitude but in kind from that of the propaganda made for different ends by independent and competing agencies. If all the sources of current information are effectively under one single control, it is no longer a question of merely persuading the people of this or that. The skilful propagandist then has power to mold their minds in any direction he chooses, and even the most intelligent and independent people cannot entirely escape that influence if they are long isolated from all other sources of information.

While in the totalitarian states this status of propaganda gives it a unique power over the minds of the people, the peculiar moral effects arise not from the technique but from the object and scope of totalitarian propaganda. If it could be confined to indoctrinating the people with the whole system of values toward which the social effort is directed, propaganda would represent merely a particular manifestation of the characteristic features of collectivist morals which we have already considered. If its object were merely to teach the people a definite and comprehensive moral code, the problem would be solely whether this moral code is good or bad. We have seen that the moral code of a totalitarian society is not likely to appeal to us, that even the striving for equality by means of a directed economy can result only in an officially enforced inequality—an authoritarian determination of the status of each individual in the new hierarchial order—and that most of the humanitarian elements of our morals, the respect for human life, for the weak, and for the individual generally, will disappear. However repellent this may be to most people, and though it involves a change in moral standards, it is not necessarily entirely antimoral.

Some features of such a system may even appeal to the sternest moralists of a conservative tint and seem to them preferable to the softer standards of a liberal society.

The moral consequences of totalitarian propaganda which we must now consider are, however, of an even more profound kind. They are destructive of all morals because they undermine one of the foundations of all morals: the sense of and the respect for truth. From the nature of its task, totalitarian propaganda cannot confine itself to values, to questions of opinion and moral convictions in which the individual always will conform more or less to the views ruling his community, but must extend to questions of fact where human intelligence is involved in a different way. This is so, first, because, in order to induce people to accept the official values, these must be justified, or shown to be connected with the values already held by the people, which usually will involve assertions about causal connections between means and ends; and, second, because the distinction between ends and means, between the goal aimed at and the measures taken to achieve it, is in fact never so clear cut and definite as any general discussion of these problems is likely to suggest; and because, therefore, people must be brought to agree not only with the ultimate aims but also with the views about the facts and possibilities on which the particular measures are based.

We have seen that agreement on that complete ethical code, that all-comprehensive system of values which is implicit in an economic plan, does not exist in a free society but would have to be created. But we must not assume that the planner will approach his task aware of that need or that, even if he were aware of it, it would be possible to create such a comprehensive code in advance. He only finds out about the conflicts between different needs as he goes along, and he has to make his decisions as the necessity arises. The code of values guiding his decisions does not exist *in abstracto* before the decisions have to be made; it has to be created with the particular decisions. We have also seen how this inability to separate the general problem of values from the particular decisions makes it impossible that a democratic body, while unable to decide the technical details of a plan, should yet determine the values guiding it.

And while the planning authority will constantly have to decide issues on merits about which there exist no definite moral rules, it will have to justify its decisions to the people— or, at least, have somehow to make the people believe that they are the right decisions. Although those responsible for a decision may have been guided by no more than prejudice, some guiding principle will have to be stated publicly if the community is not merely passively to submit but actively to support the measure. The need to rationalize the likes and dislikes which, for lack of anything else, must guide the planner in many of his decisions, and the necessity of stating his reasons in a form in which they will appeal to as many people as possible, will force him to construct theories, i.e., assertions about the connections between facts, which then become an integral part of the governing doctrine.

This process of creating a "myth" to justify his action need not be conscious. The totalitarian leader may be guided merely by an instinctive dislike of the state of things he has found and a desire to create a new hierarchical order which conforms better to his conception of merit; he may merely know that he dislikes the Jews who seemed to be so successful in an order which did not provide a satisfactory place for him, and that he loves and admires the tall blond man, the "aristocratic" figure of the novels of his youth. So he will readily embrace theories which seem to provide a rational justification for the prejudices which he shares with many of his fellows. Thus a pseudo-scientific theory becomes part of the official creed which to a greater or lesser degree directs everybody's action. Or the widespread dislike of the industrial civilization and a romantic yearning for country life, together with a (probably erroneous) idea about the special value of country people as soldiers, provide the basis for another myth: *Blut und Boden* ("blood and soil"), expressing not merely ultimate values but a whole host of beliefs about cause and effect which, once they have become ideals directing the activity of the whole community, must not be questioned.

The need for such official doctrines as an instrument of directing and rallying the efforts of the people has been clearly foreseen by the various theoreticians of the totalitarian system. Plato's "noble lies" and Sorel's "myths" serve the same purpose as the racial doctrine of the Nazis or the theory of the corporative state of Mussolini. They are all necessarily based on particular views about facts which are then elaborated into scientific theories in order to justify a preconceived opinion.

The most effective way of making people accept the validity of the values they are to serve is to persuade them that they are really the same as those which they, or at least the best among them, have always held, but which were not properly understood or recognized before. The people are made to transfer their allegiance from the old gods to the new under the pretense that the new gods really are what their sound instinct had always told them but what before they had only dimly seen. And the most efficient technique to this end is to use the old words but change their meaning.

Few traits of totalitarian regimes are at the same time so confusing to the superficial observer and yet so characteristic of the whole intellectual climate as the complete perversion of language, the change of meaning of the words by which the ideals of the new regimes are expressed.

The worst sufferer in this respect is, of course, the word "liberty." It is a word used as freely in totalitarian states as elsewhere. Indeed, it could almost be said—and it should serve as a warning to us to be on our guard against all the tempters who promise us *New Liberties for Old*[1]—that wherever liberty as we understand it has been destroyed, this has almost always been done in the name of some new freedom promised to the people. Even among us we have "planners for freedom" who promise us a "collective freedom for the group," the nature of which may be gathered from the fact that its advocates find it necessary to assure us that "naturally the advent of planned freedom does not mean that all [*sic*] earlier forms of freedom must be abolished." Dr. Karl Mannheim, from whose work[2] these sentences are taken, at least warns us that "a conception of freedom modelled on the preceding age is an obstacle to any real understanding of the problem." But his use of the word "freedom" is as misleading as it is in the mouth of totalitarian politicians. Like their freedom, the "collective freedom" he offers us is not the freedom of the members of society but the unlimited freedom of the planner to do with society what he pleases.[3]

1. This is the title of a recent work by the historian Carl L. Becker.
2. *Man and Society in an Age of Reconstruction,* p. 377.
3. Peter Drucker (*The End of Economic Man,* p. 74) correctly observes that "the less freedom there is, the more there is talk of the 'new freedom.' Yet this new freedom is a mere word which covers the exact contradiction of all that Europe ever understood by freedom. . . . . The new freedom which is preached in Europe is, however, the right of the majority against the individual."

It is the confusion of freedom with power carried to the extreme.

In this particular case the perversion of the meaning of the word has, of course, been well prepared by a long line of German philosophers and, not least, by many of the theoreticians of socialism. But "freedom" or "liberty" are by no means the only words whose meaning has been changed into their opposites to make them serve as instruments of totalitarian propaganda. We have already seen how the same happens to "justice" and "law," "right" and "equality." The list could be extended until it includes almost all moral and political terms in general use.

If one has not one's self experienced this process, it is difficult to appreciate the magnitude of this change of the meaning of words, the confusion which it causes, and the barriers to any rational discussion which it creates. It has to be seen to be understood how, if one of two brothers embraces the new faith, after a short while he appears to speak a different language which makes any real communication between them impossible. And the confusion becomes worse because this change of meaning of the words describing political ideals is not a single event but a continuous process, a technique employed consciously or unconsciously to direct the people. Gradually, as this process continues, the whole language becomes despoiled, and words become empty shells deprived of any definite meaning, as capable of denoting one thing as its opposite and used solely for the emotional associations which still adhere to them.

It is not difficult to deprive the great majority of independent thought. But the minority who will retain an inclination to criticize must also be silenced. We have already seen why coercion cannot be confined to the acceptance of the ethical code underlying the plan according to which all social activity is directed. Since many parts of this code will never be explicitly stated, since many parts of the guiding scale of values will exist only implicitly in the plan, the plan itself in every detail, in fact every act of the government, must become sacrosanct and exempt from criticism. If the people are to support the common effort without hesitation, they must be convinced that not only the end aimed at but also the means chosen are the right ones. The official creed, to which adherence must be enforced, will therefore comprise all the views about facts on which the plan is based. Public criticism or even expressions of doubt must be suppressed because they tend to weaken public support. As the Webbs report of the position in every Russian enterprise: "Whilst the work is in progress, any public expression of doubt, or even fear that the plan will not be successful, is an act of disloyalty and even of treachery because of its possible effects on the will and on the efforts of the rest of the staff."[4] When the doubt or fear expressed concerns not the success of a particular enterprise but of the whole social plan, it must be treated even more as sabotage.

Facts and theories must thus become no less the object of an official doctrine than views about values. And the whole apparatus for spreading knowledge—the schools and the press, radio and motion picture—will be used exclusively to spread those views which, whether true or false, will strengthen the belief in the rightness of the decisions taken by the authority; and all information that might cause doubt or hesitation will be withheld. The probable effect on the

4. Sidney and Beatrice Webb, *Soviet Communism*, p. 1038.

people's loyalty to the system becomes the only criterion for deciding whether a particular piece of information is to be published or suppressed. The situation in a totalitarian state is permanently and in all fields the same that it is elsewhere in some fields in wartime. Everything which might cause doubt about the wisdom of the government or create discontent will be kept from the people. The basis of unfavorable comparisons with conditions elsewhere, the knowledge of possible alternatives to the course actually taken, information which might suggest failure on the part of the government to live up to its promises or to take advantage of opportunities to improve conditions—all will be suppressed. There is consequently no field where the systematic control of information will not be practiced and uniformity of views not enforced.

This applies even to fields apparently most remote from any political interests and particularly to all the sciences, even the most abstract. That in the disciplines dealing directly with human affairs and therefore most immediately affecting political views, such as history, law, or economics, the disinterested search for truth cannot be allowed in a totalitarian system, and the vindication of the official views becomes the sole object, is easily seen and has been amply confirmed by experience. These disciplines have, indeed, in all totalitarian countries become the most fertile factories of the official myths which the rulers use to guide the minds and wills of their subjects. It is not surprising that in these spheres even the pretense that they search for truth is abandoned and that the authorities decide what doctrines ought to be taught and published.

Totalitarian control of opinion extends, however, also to subjects which at first seem to have no political significance.

THE END OF TRUTH

Sometimes it is difficult to explain why particular doctrines should be officially proscribed or why others should be encouraged, and it is curious that these likes and dislikes are apparently somewhat similar in the different totalitarian systems. In particular, they all seem to have in common an intense dislike of the more abstract forms of thought— a dislike characteristically also shown by many of the collectivists among our scientists. Whether the theory of relativity is represented as a "Semitic attack on the foundation of Christian and Nordic physics" or opposed because it is "in conflict with dialectical materialism and Marxist dogma" comes very much to the same thing. Nor does it make much difference whether certain theorems of mathematical statistics are attacked because they "form part of the class struggle on the ideological frontier and are a product of the historical role of mathematics as the servant of the bourgeoisie," or whether the whole subject is condemned because "it provides no guaranty that it will serve the interest of the people." It seems that pure mathematics is no less a victim and that even the holding of particular views about the nature of continuity can be ascribed to "bourgeois prejudices." According to the Webbs, the *Journal for Marxist-Leninist Natural Sciences* has the following slogans: "We stand for Party in Mathematics. We stand for the purity of Marxist-Leninist theory in surgery." The situation seems to be very similar in Germany. The *Journal of the National-Socialist Association of Mathematicians* is full of "party in mathematics," and one of the best-known German physicists, the Nobel prizeman Lenard, has summed up his lifework under the title *German Physics in Four Volumes!*

It is entirely in keeping with the whole spirit of totalitarianism that it condemns any human activity done for its own sake and without ulterior purpose. Science for science' sake, art for art's sake, are equally abhorrent to the Nazis, our socialist intellectuals, and the communists. *Every* activity must derive its justification from a conscious social purpose. There must be no spontaneous, unguided activity, because it might produce results which cannot be foreseen and for which the plan does not provide. It might produce something new, undreamed of in the philosophy of the planner. The principle extends even to games and amusements. I leave it to the reader to guess whether it was in Germany or in Russia that chess-players were officially exhorted that "we must finish once and for all with the neutrality of chess. We must condemn once and for all the formula 'chess for the sake of chess' like the formula 'art for art's sake.'"

Incredible as some of these aberrations may appear, we must yet be on our guard not to dismiss them as mere accidental by-products which have nothing to do with the essential character of a planned or totalitarian system. They are not. They are a direct result of that same desire to see everything directed by a "unitary conception of the whole," of the need to uphold at all costs the views in the service of which people are asked to make constant sacrifices, and of the general idea that the knowledge and beliefs of the people are an instrument to be used for a single purpose. Once science has to serve, not truth, but the interests of a class, a community, or a state, the sole task of argument and discussion is to vindicate and to spread still further the beliefs by which the whole life of the community is directed. As the Nazi minister of justice has explained, the question which every new scientific theory must ask itself is: "Do I serve National Socialism for the greatest benefit of all?"

The word "truth" itself ceases to have its old meaning. It

describes no longer something to be found, with the individual conscience as the sole arbiter of whether in any particular instance the evidence (or the standing of those proclaiming it) warrants a belief; it becomes something to be laid down by authority, something which has to be believed in the interest of the unity of the organized effort and which may have to be altered as the exigencies of this organized effort require it.

The general intellectual climate which this produces, the spirit of complete cynicism as regards truth which it engenders, the loss of the sense of even the meaning of truth, the disappearance of the spirit of independent inquiry and of the belief in the power of rational conviction, the way in which differences of opinion in every branch of knowledge become political issues to be decided by authority, are all things which one must personally experience—no short description can convey their extent. Perhaps the most alarming fact is that contempt for intellectual liberty is not a thing which arises only once the totalitarian system is established but one which can be found everywhere among intellectuals who have embraced a collectivist faith and who are acclaimed as intellectual leaders even in countries still under a liberal regime. Not only is even the worst oppression condoned if it is committed in the name of socialism, and the creation of a totalitarian system openly advocated by people who pretend to speak for the scientists of liberal countries; intolerance, too, is openly extolled. Have we not recently seen a British scientific writer defend even Inquisition because in his opinion it "is beneficial to science when it protects a rising class"?[5] This view is, of course, practically in-

5. J. G. Crowther, *The Social Relations of Science* (1941), p. 333.

distinguishable from the views which led the Nazis to the persecution of men of science, the burning of scientific books, and the systematic eradication of the intelligentsia of the subjected people.

The desire to force upon the people a creed which is regarded as salutary for them is, of course, not a thing that is new or peculiar to our time. New, however, is the argument by which many of our intellectuals try to justify such attempts. There is no real freedom of thought in our society, so it is said, because the opinions and tastes of the masses are shaped by propaganda, by advertising, by the example of the upper classes, and by other environmental factors which inevitably force the thinking of the people into well-worn grooves. From this it is concluded that if the ideals and tastes of the great majority are always fashioned by circumstances which we can control, we ought to use this power deliberately to turn the thoughts of the people in what we think is a desirable direction.

Probably it is true enough that the great majority are rarely capable of thinking independently, that on most questions they accept views which they find ready-made, and that they will be equally content if born or coaxed into one set of beliefs or another. In any society freedom of thought will probably be of direct significance only for a small minority. But this does not mean that anyone is competent, or ought to have power, to select those to whom this freedom is to be reserved. It certainly does not justify the presumption of any group of people to claim the right to determine what people ought to think or believe. It shows a complete confusion of thought to suggest that, because under any sort of system the majority of people follow the lead of somebody, it makes no difference if everybody has to follow the same lead. To deprecate the value of intellectual freedom because it will never mean for everybody the same possibility of independent thought is completely to miss the reasons which give intellectual freedom its value. What is essential to make it serve its function as the prime mover of intellectual progress is not that everybody may be able to think or write anything but that any cause or idea may be argued by somebody. So long as dissent is not suppressed, there will always be some who will query the ideas ruling their contemporaries and put new ideas to the test of argument and propaganda.

This interaction of individuals, possessing different knowledge and different views, is what constitutes the life of thought. The growth of reason is a social process based on the existence of such differences. It is of its essence that its results cannot be predicted, that we cannot know which views will assist this growth and which will not—in short, that this growth cannot be governed by any views which we now possess without at the same time limiting it. To "plan" or "organize" the growth of mind, or, for that matter, progress in general, is a contradiction in terms. The idea that the human mind ought "consciously" to control its own development confuses individual reason, which alone can "consciously control" anything, with the interpersonal process to which its growth is due. By attempting to control it, we are merely setting bounds to its development and must sooner or later produce a stagnation of thought and a decline of reason.

The tragedy of collectivist thought is that, while it starts out to make reason supreme, it ends by destroying reason because it misconceives the process on which the growth of reason depends. It may indeed be said that it is the paradox of all collectivist doctrine and its demand for "conscious" control or "conscious" planning that they necessarily lead to the demand that the mind of some individual should rule supreme—while only the individualist approach to social phenomena makes us recognize the superindividual forces which guide the growth of reason. Individualism is thus an attitude of humility before this social process and of tolerance to other opinions and is the exact opposite of that intellectual *hubris* which is at the root of the demand for comprehensive direction of the social process.

12

The Socialist Roots of Naziism

All antiliberal forces are combining against
everything that is liberal.
—A. MOELLER VAN DEN BRUCK

I T IS a common mistake to regard National Socialism as
a mere revolt against reason, an irrational movement
without intellectual background. If that were so, the
movement would be much less dangerous than it is. But
nothing could be further from the truth or more misleading. The doctrines of National Socialism are the culmination
of a long evolution of thought, a process in which thinkers
who have had great influence far beyond the confines of
Germany have taken part. Whatever one may think of the
premises from which they started, it cannot be denied that
the men who produced the new doctrines were powerful
writers who left the impress of their ideas on the whole of
European thought. Their system was developed with ruthless consistency. Once one accepts the premises from which
it starts, there is no escape from its logic. It is simply collectivism freed from all traces of an individualist tradition
which might hamper its realization.

Though in this development German thinkers have taken
the lead, they were by no means alone. Thomas Carlyle
and Houston Stewart Chamberlain, Auguste Comte and
Georges Sorel, are as much a part of that continuous development as any Germans. The development of this strand of
thought within Germany has been well traced recently by
R. D. Butler in his study of *The Roots of National Socialism.*
But, although its persistence there through a hundred and

fifty years in almost unchanged and ever recurring form, which emerges from that study, is rather frightening, it is easy to exaggerate the importance these ideas had in Germany before 1914. They were only one strand of thought among a people then perhaps more varied in its views than any other. And they were on the whole represented by a small minority and held in as great contempt by the majority of Germans as they were in other countries.

What, then, caused these views held by a reactionary minority finally to gain the support of the great majority of Germans and practically the whole of Germany's youth? It was not merely the defeat, the suffering, and the wave of nationalism which led to their success. Still less was the cause, as so many people wish to believe, a capitalist reaction against the advance of socialism. On the contrary, the support which brought these ideas to power came precisely from the socialist camp. It was certainly not through the bourgeoisie, but rather through the absence of a strong bourgeoisie, that they were helped to power.

The doctrines which had guided the ruling elements in Germany for the past generation were opposed not to the socialism in Marxism but to the liberal elements contained in it, its internationalism and its democracy. And as it became increasingly clear that it was just these elements which formed obstacles to the realization of socialism, the socialists of the Left approached more and more to those of the Right. It was the union of the anticapitalist forces of the Right and of the Left, the fusion of radical and conservative socialism, which drove out from Germany everything that was liberal.

The connection between socialism and nationalism in Germany was close from the beginning. It is significant that the most important ancestors of National Socialism—Fichte,

Rodbertus, and Lassalle—are at the same time acknowledged fathers of socialism. While theoretical socialism in its
Marxist form was directing the German labor movement,
the authoritarian and nationalist element receded for a time
into the background. But not for long.[1] From 1914 onward
there arose from the ranks of Marxist socialism one teacher
after another who led, not the conservatives and reaction-
aries, but the hard-working laborer and idealist youth into
the National Socialist fold. It was only thereafter that the
tide of nationalist socialism attained major importance and
rapidly grew into the Hitlerian doctrine. The war hysteria
of 1914, which, just because of the German defeat, was
never fully cured, is the beginning of the modern development which produced National Socialism, and it was largely
with the assistance of old socialists that it rose during this
period.

Perhaps the first, and in some ways the most characteristic, representative of this development is the late Professor Werner Sombart, whose notorious *Händler und Helden*
("Merchants and Heroes") appeared in 1915. Sombart had
begun as a Marxian socialist and, as late as 1909, could assert
with pride that he had devoted the greater part of his life to
fighting for the ideas of Karl Marx. He had done as much
as any man to spread socialist ideas and anticapitalist resentment of varying shades throughout Germany; and if German thought became penetrated with Marxian elements in
a way that was true of no other country until the Russian
revolution, this was in a large measure due to Sombart. At

1. And only partially. In 1892 one of the leaders of the social-
democratic party, August Bebel, was able to tell Bismarck that "the Imperial
Chancellor can rest assured that German Social Democracy is a sort of pre-
paratory school for militarism"!

one time he was regarded as the outstanding representative of the persecuted socialist intelligentsia, unable, because of his radical views, to obtain a university chair. And even after the last war the influence, inside and outside Germany, of his work as a historian, which remained Marxist in approach after he had ceased to be a Marxist in politics, was most extensive and is particularly noticeable in the works of many of the English and American planners.

In his war book this old socialist welcomed the "German War" as the inevitable conflict between the commercial civilization of England and the heroic culture of Germany. His contempt for the "commercial" views of the English people, who had lost all warlike instincts, is unlimited. Nothing is more contemptible in his eyes than the universal striving after the happiness of the individual; and what he describes as the leading maxim of English morals: be just "that it may be well with thee and that thou mayest prolong thy days upon the land" is to him "the most infamous maxim which has ever been pronounced by a commercial mind." The "German idea of the state," as formulated by Fichte, Lassalle, and Rodbertus, is that the state is neither founded nor formed by individuals, nor an aggregate of individuals, nor is its purpose to serve any interest of individuals. It is a *Volksgemeinschaft* in which the individual has no rights but only duties. Claims of the individual are always an outcome of the commercial spirit. "The ideas of 1789"—liberty, equality, fraternity—are characteristically commercial ideas which have no other purpose but to secure certain advantages to individuals.

Before 1914 all the true German ideals of a heroic life were in deadly danger before the continuous advance of English commercial ideals, English comfort, and English sport.

The English people had not only themselves become completely corrupted, every trade-unionist being sunk in the "morass of comfort," but they had begun to infect all other peoples. Only the war had helped the Germans to remember that they were really a people of warriors, a people among whom all activities and particularly all economic activities were subordinated to military ends. Sombart knew that the Germans were held in contempt by other people because they regard war as sacred—but he glories in it. To regard war as inhuman and senseless is a product of commercial views. There is a life higher than the individual life, the life of the people and the life of the state, and it is the purpose of the individual to sacrifice himself for that higher life. War is to Sombart the consummation of the heroic view of life, and the war against England is the war against the opposite ideal, the commercial ideal of individual freedom and of English comfort, which in his eyes finds its most contemptible expression in—the safety razors found in the English trenches.

If Sombart's outburst was at the time too much even for most Germans, another German professor arrived at essentially the same ideas in a more moderate and more scholarly, but for that reason even more effective, form. Professor Johann Plenge was as great an authority on Marx as Sombart. His book on *Marx und Hegel* marks the beginning of the modern Hegel renaissance among Marxian scholars; and there can be no doubt about the genuinely socialist nature of the convictions with which he started. Among his numerous war publications the most important is a small but at the time widely discussed book with the significant title, *1789 and 1914: The Symbolic Years in the History of the Political*

Mind. It is devoted to the conflict between the "Ideas of 1789," the ideal of freedom, and the "Ideas of 1914," the ideal of organization.

Organization is to him, as to all socialists who derive their socialism from a crude application of scientific ideals to the problems of society, the essence of socialism. It was, as he rightly emphasizes, the root of the socialist movement at its inception in early nineteenth-century France. Marx and Marxism have betrayed this basic idea of socialism by their fanatic but utopian adherence to the abstract idea of freedom. Only now was the idea of organization again coming into its own, elsewhere, as witnessed by the work of H. G. Wells (by whose *Future in America* Professor Plenge was profoundly influenced, and whom he describes as one of the outstanding figures of modern socialism), but particularly in Germany, where it is best understood and most fully realized. The war between England and Germany is therefore really a conflict between two opposite principles. The "Economic World War" is the third great epoch of spiritual struggle in modern history. It is of equal importance with the Reformation and the bourgeois revolution of liberty. It is the struggle for the victory of the new forces born out of the advanced economic life of the nineteenth century: socialism and organization.

"Because in the sphere of ideas Germany was the most convinced exponent of all socialist dreams, and in the sphere of reality she was the most powerful architect of the most highly organized economic system.—In us is the twentieth century. However the war may end, we are the exemplary people. Our ideas will determine the aims of the life of humanity.—World History experiences at present the colossal spectacle that with us a new great ideal of life penetrates to final victory, while at the same time in England one of the World-Historical principles finally collapses."

The war economy created in Germany in 1914 "is the first realization of a socialist society and its spirit the first active, and not merely demanding, appearance of a socialist spirit. The needs of the war have established the socialist idea in German economic life, and thus the defense of our nation produced for humanity the idea of 1914, the idea of German organization, the people's community (*Volksgemeinschaft*) of national socialism. . . . Without our really noticing it the whole of our political life in state and industry has risen to a higher stage. State and economic life form a new unity. . . . The feeling of economic responsibility which characterizes the work of the civil servant pervades all private activity." The new German corporative constitution of economic life, which Professor Plenge admits is not yet ripe or complete, "is the highest form of life of the state which has ever been known on earth."

At first Professor Plenge still hoped to reconcile the ideal of liberty and the ideal of organization, although largely through the complete but voluntary submission of the individual to the whole. But these traces of liberal ideas soon disappear from his writings. By 1918 the union between socialism and ruthless power politics had become complete in his mind. Shortly before the end of the war he exhorted his compatriots in the socialist journal *Die Glocke* in the following manner:

"It is high time to recognize the fact that socialism must be power policy, because it is to be organization. Socialism has to win power: it must never blindly destroy power. And the most important and critical question for socialism in the time of war of peoples is necessarily this: what people is preeminently summoned to power, because it is the exemplary leader in the organization of peoples?"

And he forecast all the ideas which were finally to justify Hitler's New Order: "Just from the point of view of socialism, which is organization, is not an absolute right of self-determination of the peoples the right of individualistic economic anarchy? Are we willing to grant complete self-determination to the individual in economic life? Consistent socialism can accord to the people a right to incorporation only in accordance with the real distribution of forces historically determined."

The ideals which Plenge expressed so clearly were especially popular among, and perhaps even derive from, certain circles of German scientists and engineers who, precisely as is now so loudly demanded by their English and American counterparts, clamored for the centrally planned organization of all aspects of life. Leading among these was the famous chemist Wilhelm Ostwald, one of whose pronouncements on this point has achieved a certain celebrity. He is reported to have stated publicly that "Germany wants to organize Europe which up to now still lacks organization. I will explain to you now Germany's great secret: we, or perhaps the German race, have discovered the significance of organization. While the other nations still live under the regime of individualism, we have already achieved that of organization."

Ideas very similar to these were current in the offices of the German raw-material dictator, Walter Rathenau, who, although he would have shuddered had he realized the consequences of his totalitarian economics, yet deserves a considerable place in any fuller history of the growth of Nazi ideas. Through his writings he has probably, more than any

other man, determined the economic views of the generation which grew up in Germany during and immediately after the last war; and some of his closest collaborators were
later to form the backbone of the staff of Göring's Five-
Year Plan administration. Very similar also was much of the
teaching of another former Marxist, Friedrich Naumann,
whose *Mitteleuropa* reached probably the greatest circulation
of any war book in Germany.[2]

But it was left to an active socialist politician, a member
of the Left wing of the social-democratic party in the Reichstag, to develop these ideas most fully and to spread them
far and wide. Paul Lensch had already in earlier books described the war as "the flight of the English bourgeoisie before the advance of socialism" and explained how different
were the socialist ideal of freedom and the English conception. But only in his third and most successful war book, his
Three Years of World Revolution, were his characteristic ideas,
under the influence of Plenge, to achieve full development.[3]
Lensch bases his argument on an interesting and in many
respects accurate historical account of how the adoption of
protection by Bismarck had made possible in Germany a development toward that industrial concentration and carteli-
zation which, from his Marxist standpoint, represented a
higher state of industrial development.

"The result of Bismarck's decision of the year 1879 was
that Germany took on the role of the revolutionary; that is
to say, of a state whose position in relation to the rest of the

2. A good summary of Naumann's views, as characteristic of the
German combination of socialism and imperialism as any we quote in the
text, will be found in R. D. Butler, *The Roots of National Socialism* (1941),
pp. 203–9.
3. Paul Lensch, *Three Years of World Revolution,* with a Preface by J. E. M.
(London, 1918). The English translation of this work was made available,
still during the last war, by some far-seeing person.

world is that of a representative of a higher and more advanced economic system. Having realized this, we should perceive that *in the present World Revolution Germany represents the revolutionary, and her greatest antagonist, England, the counter-revolutionary side.* This fact proves how little the constitution of a country, whether it be liberal and republican or monarchic and autocratic, affects the question whether, from the point of view of historical development, that country is to be regarded as liberal or not. Or, to put it more plainly, our conceptions of Liberalism, Democracy, and so forth, are derived from the ideas of English Individualism, according to which a state with a weak government is a liberal state, and every restriction upon the freedom of the individual is conceived as the product of autocracy and militarism."

In Germany, the "historically appointed representative" of this higher form of economic life, "the struggle for socialism has been extraordinarily simplified, since all the prerequisite conditions of Socialism had already become established there. And hence it was necessarily a vital concern of any socialist party that Germany should triumphantly hold her own against her enemies, and thereby be able to fulfil her historic mission of revolutionizing the world. Hence the war of the Entente against Germany resembled the attempt of the lower bourgeoisie of the pre-capitalistic age to prevent the decline of their own class."

That organization of capital, Lensch continues, "which began unconsciously before the war, and which during the war has been continued consciously, will be systematically continued after the war. Not through any desire for any arts of organization nor yet because socialism has been recognized as a higher principle of social development. The classes who are today the practical pioneers of socialism are, in theory, its avowed opponents, or, at any rate, were so up to a short time ago. Socialism is coming, and in fact has to some extent already arrived, since we can no longer live without it."

The only people who still oppose this tendency are the liberals. "This class of people, who unconsciously reason from English standards, comprises the whole educated German bourgeoisie. Their political notions of 'freedom' and 'civic right,' of constitutionalism and parliamentarianism, are derived from that individualistic conception of the world, of which English Liberalism is a classical embodiment, and which was adopted, by the spokesmen of the German bourgeoisie in the fifties, sixties, and seventies of the nineteenth century. But these standards are old-fashioned and shattered, just as old-fashioned English Liberalism has been shattered by this war. What has to be done now is to get rid of these inherited political ideas and to assist the growth of a new conception of State and Society. In this sphere also Socialism must present a conscious and determined opposition to individualism. In this connection it is an astonishing fact that, in the so-called 'reactionary' Germany, the working classes have won for themselves a much more solid and powerful position in the life of the state than is the case either in England or in France."

Lensch follows this up with a consideration which again contains much truth and which deserves to be pondered:

"Since the Social Democrats, by the aid of this [universal] Suffrage, occupied every post which they could obtain in the Reichstag, the State Parliament, the municipal councils, the courts for the settlement of trade disputes, the sick funds, and so forth, they penetrated very deeply into the organism of the state; but the price which they had to pay for this was that the state, in its turn, exercised a profound influence upon the working classes. To be sure, as the result of strenuous socialistic labors for fifty years, the state is no longer the same as it was in the year 1867, when universal suffrage first came into operation; but then, Social Democracy, in its turn, is no longer the same as it was at the time. *The state has undergone a process of socialization, and Social Democracy has undergone a process of nationalization."*

Plenge and Lensch in turn have provided the leading ideas for the immediate masters of National Socialism, particularly Oswald Spengler and Arthur Moeller van den Bruck, to mention only the two best-known names.[4] Opinions may differ in how far the former can be regarded as a socialist. But that in his tract on *Prussianism and Socialism,* which appeared in 1920, he merely gave expression to ideas widely held by German socialists will now be evident. A few specimens of his argument will suffice. "Old Prussian spirit and socialist conviction, which today hate each other with the hatred of brothers, are one and the same." The representatives of Western civilization in Germany, the German liberals, are "the invisible English army which after the Battle of Jena, Napoleon left behind on German soil." To Spengler, men like Hardenberg and Humboldt and all the other liberal reformers were "English." But this "English" spirit will be turned out by the German revolution which began in 1914.

"The three last nations of the Occident have aimed at

4. The same applies to many others of the intellectual leaders of the generation which has produced naziism, such as Othmar Spann, Hans Freyer, Carl Schmitt, and Ernst Jünger. On these compare the interesting study by Aurel Kolnai, *The War against the West* (1938), which suffers, however, from the defect that, by confining itself to the postwar period when these ideals had already been taken over by the nationalists, it overlooks their socialist creators.

three forms of existence, represented by famous watch-
words: Freedom, Equality, Community. They appear in the
political forms of liberal Parliamentarianism, social Democracy, and authoritarian socialism.[5] . . . The German, more
correctly, Prussian, instinct is: the power belongs to the
whole. . . . Everyone is given his place. One commands or
obeys. This is, since the eighteenth century, authoritarian socialism, essentially illiberal and anti-democratic, in so far as
English Liberalism and French Democracy are meant. . . .
There are in Germany many hated and ill-reputed contrasts,
but liberalism alone is contemptible on German soil.

"The structure of the English nation is based on the distinction between rich and poor, that of the Prussian on that
between command and obedience. The meaning of class distinction is accordingly fundamentally different in the two
countries."

After pointing out the essential difference between the
English competitive system and the Prussian system of "economic administration" and after showing (consciously following Lensch) how since Bismarck the deliberate organization of economic activity had progressively assumed more
socialist forms, Spengler continues:

"In Prussia there existed a real state in the most ambitious
meaning of the word. There could be, strictly speaking, no
private persons. Everybody who lived within the system that
worked with the precision of a clockwork, was in some way
a link in it. The conduct of public business could therefore

5. This Spenglerian formula finds its echo in an often-quoted statement
of Schmitt, the leading Nazi expert on constitutional law, according to
which the evolution of government proceeds "in three dialectic stages: from
the *absolute* state of the seventeenth and eighteenth centuries through the
neutral state of the liberal nineteenth century to the *totalitarian* state in
which state and society are identical" (Carl Schmitt, *Der Hüter der Verfassung*
[Tübingen, 1931], p. 79).

not be in the hands of private people, as is supposed by Parliamentarianism. It was an *Amt* and the responsible politician was a civil servant, a servant of the whole."

The "Prussian idea" requires that everybody should become a state official—that all wages and salaries be fixed by the state. The administration of all property, in particular, becomes a salaried function. The state of the future will be a *Beamtenstaat*. But "the decisive question not only for Germany, but for the world, which must be solved *by* Germany *for* the world is: Is in the future trade to govern the state, or the state to govern trade? In the face of this question Prussianism and Socialism are the same. . . . Prussianism and Socialism combat the England in our midst."

It was only a step from this for the patron saint of National Socialism, Moeller van den Bruck, to proclaim World War I a war between liberalism and socialism: "We have lost the war against the West. Socialism has lost it against Liberalism."[6] As with Spengler, liberalism is, therefore, the archenemy. Moeller van den Bruck glories in the fact that "there are no liberals in Germany today; there are young revolutionaries: there are young conservatives. But who would be a liberal? . . . Liberalism is a philosophy of life from which German youth now turns with nausea, with wrath, with quite peculiar scorn, for there is none more foreign, more repugnant, more opposed to its philosophy. German youth today recognizes the liberal *as the archenemy*." Moeller van den Bruck's Third Reich was intended to give the Germans a socialism adapted to their nature and undefiled by Western liberal ideas. And so it did.

6. Arthur Moeller van den Bruck, *Sozialismus und Aussenpolitik* (1933), pp. 87, 90, and 100. The articles here reprinted, particularly the article on "Lenin and Keynes," which discusses most fully the contention discussed in the text, were first published between 1919 and 1923.

These writers were by no means isolated phenomena. As early as 1922 a detached observer could speak of a "peculiar and, on a first glance, surprising phenomenon" then to be observed in Germany: "The fight against the capitalistic order, according to this view, is a continuation of the war against the Entente with the weapons of the spirit and of economic organization, the way which leads to practical socialism, a return of the German people to their best and noblest traditions."[7]

Fight against liberalism in all its forms, liberalism that had defeated Germany, was the common idea which united socialists and conservatives in one common front. At first it was mainly in the German Youth Movement, almost entirely socialist in inspiration and outlook, where these ideas were most readily accepted and the fusion of socialism and nationalism completed. In the later twenties and until the advent to power of Hitler a circle of young men gathered round the journal *Die Tat* and, led by Ferdinand Fried, became the chief exponent of this tradition in the intellectual sphere. Fried's *Ende des Kapitalismus* is perhaps the most characteristic product of this group of *Edelnazis*, as they were known in Germany, and is particularly disquieting because of its resemblance to so much of the literature which we see in England and the United States today, where we can watch the same drawing-together of the socialists of the Left and the Right and nearly the same contempt of all that is liberal in the old sense. "Conservative Socialism" (and, in other circles, "Religious Socialism") was the slogan under

7. K. Pribram, "Deutscher Nationalismus und deutscher Sozialismus," *Archiv für Sozialwissenschaft und Sozialpolitik*, XLIX (1922), 298–99. The writer mentions as further examples the philosopher Max Scheler, preaching "the socialist world mission of Germany," and the Marxist K. Korsch, writing on the spirit of the new *Volksgemeinschaft*, as arguing in the same vein.

which a large number of writers prepared the atmosphere in which "National Socialism" succeeded. It is "conservative socialism" which is the dominant trend among us now. Had the war against the Western powers "with the weapons of the spirit and of economic organization" not almost succeeded before the real war began?

13

The Totalitarians in Our Midst

When authority presents itself in the guise of organization,
it develops charms fascinating enough to convert communities of
free people into totalitarian States.
—"THE TIMES" (LONDON)

P ROBABLY it is true that the very magnitude of the outrages committed by the totalitarian governments, instead of increasing the fear that such a system might one day arise in more enlightened countries, has rather strengthened the assurance that it cannot happen here. When we look to Nazi Germany, the gulf which separates us seems so immense that nothing that happens there can possess relevance for any possible development here. And the fact that the difference has steadily become greater seems to refute any suggestion that we may be moving in a similar direction. But let us not forget that fifteen years ago the possibility of such a thing's happening in Germany would have appeared just as fantastic, not only to nine-tenths of the Germans themselves, but also to the most hostile foreign observers (however wise they may now pretend to have been).

As suggested earlier in these pages, however, it is not the present Germany but the Germany of twenty or thirty years ago to which conditions in the democracies show an ever increasing resemblance. There are many features which were then regarded as "typically German" and which are now equally familiar in England, for instance, and many symptoms that point to a further development in the same direction. We have already mentioned the most significant—the increasing similarity between the economic views of the Right and Left and their common opposition to the liberalism that used to be the common basis of most English politics. We have the authority of Mr. Harold Nicolson for the statement that, during the last Conservative government, among the back-benchers of the Conservative party "the most gifted . . . were all socialists at heart";[1] and there can be little question that, as in the days of the Fabians, many socialists have more sympathy with the Conservatives than with the Liberals. There are many other features closely related to this. The increasing veneration for the state, the admiration of power, and of bigness for bigness' sake, the enthusiasm for "organization" of everything (we now call it "planning"), and that "inability to leave anything to the simple power of organic growth," which even von Treitschke deplored in the Germans sixty years ago, are all scarcely less marked in England now than they were in Germany.

How far in the last twenty years England has traveled on the German path is brought home to one with extraordinary vividness if one now reads some of the more serious discussions of the differences between British and German views on political and moral issues which appeared in England during the last war. It is probably true to say that then the British public had, in general, a truer appreciation of these differences than it has now; but while the people of England were then proud of their distinctive tradition, there are few of the political views then regarded as characteristically English of which the majority of her people do not now seem half-ashamed, if they do not positively repudiate them. It is scarcely an exaggeration to say that the more typically English a writer on political or social problems then appeared to the world, the more is he today forgotten in his own coun-

1. *Spectator,* April 12, 1940, p. 523.

try. Men like Lord Morley or Henry Sidgwick, Lord Acton or A. V. Dicey, who were then admired in the world at large as outstanding examples of the political wisdom of liberal England, are to the present generation largely obsolete Victorians. Perhaps nothing shows this change more clearly than that, while there is no lack of sympathetic treatment of Bismarck in contemporary English literature, the name of Gladstone is rarely mentioned by the younger generation without a sneer over his Victorian morality and naïve utopianism.

I wish I could in a few paragraphs adequately convey the alarming impression gained from the perusal of a few of the English works on the ideas dominating the Germany of the last war, where almost every word could be applied to the views most conspicuous in current English literature. I shall merely quote one brief passage by Lord Keynes, describing in 1915 the "nightmare" which he found expounded in a typical German work of that period: he describes how, according to a German author, "even in peace industrial life must remain mobilised. This is what he means by speaking of the 'militarisation of our industrial life' [the title of the work reviewed]. Individualism must come to an end absolutely. A system of regulations must be set up, the object of which is not the greater happiness of the individual (Professor Jaffé is not ashamed to say this in so many words), but the strengthening of the organised unity of the state for the object of attaining the maximum degree of efficiency (*Leistungsfähigkeit*), the influence of which on individual advantage is only indirect.—This hideous doctrine is enshrined in a sort of idealism. The nation will grow into a 'closed unity' and will become, in fact, what Plato declared it should be—'Der Mensch im Grossen.' In particular, the coming peace will bring with it a strengthening of the idea of State action in industry. . . . Foreign investment, emigration, the industrial policy which in recent years had regarded the whole world as a market, are too dangerous. The old order of industry, which is dying to-day, is based on Profit; and the new Germany of the twentieth-century Power without consideration of Profit is to make an end of that system of Capitalism, which came over from England one hundred years ago."[2] Except that no English author has yet to my knowledge dared openly to disparage individual happiness, is there a passage in this which is not mirrored in much of contemporary English literature?

And, undoubtedly, not merely the ideas which in Germany and elsewhere prepared totalitarianism but also many of the principles of totalitarianism itself are what exercises an increasing fascination in many other countries. Although few people, if anybody, in England would probably be ready to swallow totalitarianism whole, there are few single features which have not yet been advised by somebody or other. Indeed, there is scarcely a leaf out of Hitler's book which somebody or other in England or America has not recommended us to take and use for our own purposes. This applies particularly to many people who are undoubtedly Hitler's mortal enemies because of one special feature in his system. We should never forget that the anti-Semitism of Hitler has driven from his country, or turned into his enemies, many people who in every respect are confirmed totalitarians of the German type.[3]

2. *Economic Journal*, 1915, p. 450.
3. Especially when we consider the proportion of former socialists who have become Nazis it is important to remember that the true significance of this ratio is seen only if we compare it, not with the total number of former socialists, but with the number of those whose conversion would not in any

THE TOTALITARIANS IN OUR MIDST

No description in general terms can give an adequate idea of the similarity of much of current English political literature to the works which destroyed the belief in Western civilization in Germany and created the state of mind in which naziism could become successful. The similarity is even more one of the temper with which the problems are approached than of the specific arguments used—a similar readiness to break all cultural ties with the past and to stake everything on the success of a particular experiment. As was also true in Germany, most of the works which are preparing the way for a totalitarian course in the democracies are the product of sincere idealists and often of men of considerable intellectual distinction. So, although it is invidious to single out particular persons as illustrations where similar views are advocated by hundreds of others, I see no other way of demonstrating effectively how far this development has actually advanced. I shall deliberately choose as illustrations authors whose sincerity and disinterestedness are above suspicion. But though I hope in this way to show how the views from which totalitarianism springs are now rapidly spreading here, I stand little chance of conveying successfully the equally important similarity in the emotional atmosphere. An extensive investigation into all the subtle changes in thought and language would be necessary to make explicit

---

case have been prevented by their ancestry. In fact, one of the surprising features of the political emigration from Germany is the comparatively small number of refugees from the Left who are not "Jews" in the German sense of the term. How often do we not hear eulogies of the German system prefaced by some statement such as the following with which at a recent conference an enumeration of the "features of the totalitarian technique of economic mobilization which are worth thinking about" was introduced: "Herr Hitler is not my ideal—far from it. There are very pressing personal reasons why Herr Hitler should not be my ideal, but . . ."

what one readily enough recognizes as symptoms of a familiar development. Through meeting the kind of people who
talk about the necessity of opposing "big" ideas to "small"
ones and of replacing the old "static" or "partial" thinking
by the new "dynamic" or "global" way, one learns to recognize that what at first appears sheer nonsense is a sign of the
same intellectual attitude with whose manifestations we can
alone concern ourselves here.

My first examples are two works by a gifted scholar which
in the past few years have attracted much attention. There
are, perhaps, few other instances in contemporary English
literature where the influence of the specific German ideas
with which we are concerned is so marked as in Professor
E. H. Carr's books on the *Twenty Years' Crisis* and the *Conditions of Peace*.

In the first of these two books Professor Carr frankly con-
fessed himself an adherent of "the 'historical school' of realists [which] had its home in Germany and [whose] development can be traced through the great names of Hegel and
Marx." A realist, he explains, is one "who makes morality a
function of politics" and who "cannot logically accept any
standard of value save that of fact." This "realism" is con-
trasted, in truly German fashion, with the "utopian" thought
dating from the eighteenth century "which was essentially
individualist in that it made the human conscience the final
court of appeal." But the old morals with their "abstract
general principles" must disappear because "the empiricist
treats the concrete case on its individual merits." In other
words, nothing but expediency matters, and we are even
assured that "the rule *pacta sunt servanda* is not a moral principle." That without abstract general principles merit be-

comes solely a matter of arbitrary opinion and that international treaties, if they are not morally binding, have no meaning whatever does not seem to worry Professor Carr.

According to Professor Carr, indeed, although he does not explicitly say so, it appears that England fought the last war on the wrong side. Anyone who re-reads now the statements of British war aims of twenty-five years ago and compares them with Professor Carr's present views will readily see that what were then believed to be the German views are now those of Professor Carr, who would presumably argue that the different views then professed in this country were merely a product of British hypocrisy. How little difference he is able to see between the ideals held in this country and those practiced by present-day Germany is best illustrated by his assertion that "it is true that when a prominent National Socialist asserts that 'anything that benefits the German people is right, anything that harms them is wrong' he is merely propounding the same identification of national interest with universal right which has already been established for English-speaking countries by [President] Wilson, Professor Toynbee, Lord Cecil, and many others."

Since Professor Carr's books are devoted to international problems, it is mainly in that field that their characteristic tendency becomes apparent. But from the glimpses one gets of the character of the future society which he contemplates, it appears also to be quite on the totalitarian model. Sometimes one even wonders whether the resemblance is accidental or deliberate. Does Professor Carr, for example, realize, when he asserts that "we can no longer find much meaning in the distinction familiar to nineteenth-century thought between 'society' and 'state,'" that this is precisely the doctrine of Professor Carl Schmitt, the leading Nazi theoretician of totalitarianism and, in fact, the essence of the definition of totalitarianism which that author has given to that term which he himself had introduced? Or that the view that "the mass production of opinion is the corollary of the mass production of goods" and that, therefore, "the prejudice which the word propaganda still exerts in many minds today is closely parallel to the prejudice against control of industry and trade" is really an apology for a regimentation of opinion of the kind practiced by the Nazis?

In his more recent *Conditions of Peace* Professor Carr answers with an emphatic affirmative the question with which we concluded the last chapter:

"The victors lost the peace, and Soviet Russia and Germany won it, because the former continued to preach, and in part to apply, the once valid, but now disruptive ideals of the rights of nations and laissez faire capitalism, whereas the latter, consciously or unconsciously borne forward on the tide of the twentieth century, were striving to build up the world in larger units under centralized planning and control."

Professor Carr completely makes his own the German battle cry of the socialist revolution of the East against the liberal West in which Germany was the leader: "The revolution which began in the last war, which has been the driving force of every significant political movement in the last twenty years . . . a revolution against the predominant ideas of the nineteenth century: liberal democracy, national self-determination and laissez faire economics." As he himself rightly says, "it was almost inevitable that this challenge to nineteenth-century beliefs which she had never really shared should find in Germany one of its strongest protagonists." With all the fatalistic belief of every pseudo-historian since Hegel and Marx, this development is represented as inevitable: "We know the direction in which the world is moving, and we must bow to it or perish."

The conviction that this trend is inevitable is characteristically based on familiar economic fallacies—the presumed necessity of the general growth of monopolies in consequence of technological developments, the alleged "potential plenty," and all the other popular catchwords which appear in works of this kind. Professor Carr is not an economist, and his economic argument generally will not bear serious examination. But neither this nor his belief characteristically held at the same time, that the importance of the economic factor in social life is rapidly decreasing, prevents him from basing on economic arguments all his predictions about the inevitable developments or from presenting as his main demands for the future "the reinterpretation in predominantly economic terms of the democratic ideals of 'equality' and 'liberty'"!

Professor Carr's contempt for all the ideas of liberal economists (which he insists on calling nineteenth-century ideas, though he knows that Germany "had never really shared" them and had already in the nineteenth century practiced most of the principles he now advocates) is as profound as that of any of the German writers quoted in the last chapter. He even takes over the German thesis, originated by Friedrich List, that free trade was a policy dictated solely by, and appropriate only to, the special interests of England in the nineteenth century. Now, however, "the artificial production of some degree of autarchy is a necessary condition of orderly social existence." To bring about a "return to a more dispersed and generalized world trade . . . . by a 'removal of trade barriers' or by a resuscitation of the laissez faire principles of the nineteenth century" is "unthinkable." The future belongs to *Grossraumwirtschaft* of the

German kind: "The result which we desire can be won only by a deliberate reorganization of European life such as Hitler has undertaken"!

After all this one is hardly surprised to find a characteristic section headed "The Moral Functions of War," in which Professor Carr condescendingly pities "the well-meaning people (especially in English-speaking countries) who, steeped in the nineteenth-century tradition, persist in regarding war as senseless and devoid of purpose," and rejoices in the "sense of meaning and purpose" which war, "the most powerful instrument of social solidarity," creates. This is all very familiar—but it was not in the works of English scholars that one expected to find these views.

Possibly we have not yet given enough attention to one feature of the intellectual development in Germany during the last hundred years which is now in an almost identical form making its appearance in the English-speaking countries: the scientists' agitating for a "scientific" organization of society. The ideal of a society organized "through and through" from the top has in Germany been considerably furthered by the quite unique influence which her scientific and technological specialists were allowed to exercise on the formation of social and political opinions. Few people remember that in the modern history of Germany the political professors have played a role comparable to that of the political lawyers in France.[4] The influence of these scientist-politicians was of late years not often on the side of liberty: the "intolerance of reason" so frequently conspicuous in the scientific specialist, the impatience with the ways of the ordinary man so characteristic of the expert, and the contempt

4. Cf. Franz Schnabel, *Deutsche Geschichte im neunzehnten Jahrhundert,* II (1933), 204.

for anything which was not consciously organized by superior minds according to a scientific blueprint were phenomena familiar in German public life for generations before they became of significance in England. And perhaps no other country provides a better illustration of the effects on a nation of a general and thorough shift of the greater part of its educational system from the "humanities" to the "realities" than Germany between 1840 and 1940.[5]

The way in which, in the end, with few exceptions, her scholars and scientists put themselves readily at the service of the new rulers is one of the most depressing and shameful spectacles in the whole history of the rise of National Socialism.[6] It is well known that particularly the scientists and engineers, who had so loudly claimed to be the leaders on the march to a new and better world, submitted more readily than almost any other class to the new tyranny.[7]

5. I believe it was the author of *Leviathan* who first suggested that the teaching of the classics should be suppressed, because it instilled a dangerous spirit of liberty!

6. The servility of the scientists to the powers-that-be appeared early in Germany, hand in hand with the great development of state-organized science, which today is the subject of so much eulogy abroad. One of the most famous of German scientists, the physiologist, Emil du Bois-Reymond, was not ashamed, in an oration delivered in 1870 in his double capacity of rector of the University of Berlin and president of the Prussian Academy of Science, to proclaim that "we, the University of Berlin, quartered opposite the King's palace, are, by the deed of our foundation, the intellectual bodyguard of the House of Hohenzollern" (*A Speech on the German War* [London, 1870], p. 31.—It is remarkable that Du Bois-Reymond should have thought it advisable to issue an English edition of this oration.)

7. It will suffice to quote one foreign witness: R. A. Brady, in his study of *The Spirit and Structure of German Fascism,* concludes his detailed account of the development in the German academic world with the statement that "the scientist, per se, is hence, perhaps, the most easily used and 'coordinated' of all the especially trained people in modern society. The Nazis, to be true, fired a good many University professors, and dismissed a good many scientists from research laboratories. But the professors were primar-

The role which the intellectuals played in the totalitarian transformation of society was prophetically foreseen in another country by Julien Benda, whose *Trahison des clercs* assumes new significance when one now re-reads it, fifteen years after it has been written. There is particularly one passage in that work which deserves to be well pondered and kept in mind when we come to consider certain examples of the excursions of British scientists into politics. It is the passage in which M. Benda speaks of the "superstition of science held to be competent in all domains, including that of morality; a superstition which, I repeat, is an acquisition of the nineteenth century. It remains to discover whether those who brandish this doctrine believe in it or whether they simply want to give the prestige of a scientific appearance to passions of their hearts, which they perfectly know are nothing but passions. It is to be noted that the dogma that history is obedient to scientific laws is preached especially by partisans of arbitrary authority. This is quite natural, since it eliminates the two realities they most hate, i.e., human liberty and the historical action of the individual."

We have already had occasion to mention one English product of this kind, a work in which, on a Marxist background, all the characteristic idiosyncrasies of the totalitarian intellectual, a hatred of almost everything which distinguishes West-

---

ily among the social sciences where there was more common awareness of and a more persistent criticism of the Nazi programmes, and not among the natural sciences where thinking is supposed to be most rigorous. Those dismissed in this latter field were primarily Jewish or exceptions to the generalisations made above, because of the equally uncritical acceptance of beliefs running contrary to Nazi views.—Consequently the Nazis were able to 'co-ordinate' scholars and scientists with relative ease, and hence to throw behind their elaborate propaganda the seeming weight of the bulk of German learned opinion and support."

ern civilization since the Renaissance, is combined with an approval of the methods of Inquisition. We do not wish to consider here such an extreme case and shall take a work which is more representative and which has achieved considerable publicity. C. H. Waddington's little book under the characteristic title, *The Scientific Attitude,* is as good an example as any of a class of literature which is actively sponsored by the influential British weekly *Nature* and which combines claims for greater political power for the scientists with an ardent advocacy of wholesale "planning." Though not quite so outspoken in his contempt for freedom as Mr. Crowther, Dr. Waddington is hardly more reassuring. He differs from most of the writers of the same kind in that he clearly sees and even emphasizes that the tendencies he describes and supports inevitably lead to a totalitarian system. Yet apparently this appears to him preferable to what he describes as "the present ferocious monkey-house civilization."

Dr. Waddington's claim that the scientist is qualified to run a totalitarian society is based mainly on his thesis that "science can pass ethical judgment on human behavior"—a claim to the elaboration of which by Dr. Waddington *Nature* has given considerable publicity. It is, of course, a thesis which has long been familiar to the German scientist-politicians and which has justly been singled out by J. Benda. For an illustration of what this means we do not need to go outside Dr. Waddington's book. Freedom, he explains, "is a very troublesome concept for the scientist to discuss, partly because he is not convinced that, in the last analysis, there is such a thing." Nevertheless, we are told that "science recognizes" this and that kind of freedom, but "the freedom to be odd and unlike one's neighbor is not . . . . a scientific value." Apparently the "harlot humanities," about which Dr. Waddington has to say many uncomplimentary things, have gravely misled us in teaching us tolerance!

That when it comes to social and economic questions this book on the "scientific attitude" is anything but scientific is what one has learned to expect of this kind of literature. We find again all the familiar clichés and baseless generalizations about "potential plenty" and the inevitable tendency toward monopoly, though the "best authorities" quoted in support of these contentions prove on examination to be mostly political tracts of questionable scientific standing, while the serious studies of the same problems are conspicuously neglected.

As in almost all works of this type, Dr. Waddington's convictions are largely determined by his belief in "inevitable historical tendencies" which science is presumed to have discovered and which he derives from "the profound scientific philosophy" of Marxism, whose basic notions are "almost, if not quite, identical with those underlying the scientific approach to nature" and which his "competence to judge" tells Dr. Waddington are an advance on anything which has gone before. Thus Dr. Waddington, though he finds it "difficult to deny that England now is a worse country to live in than it was" in 1913, looks forward to an economic system which "will be centralized and totalitarian in the sense that all aspects of the economic development of large regions are consciously planned as an integrated whole." And for his facile optimism that in this totalitarian system freedom of thought will be preserved, his "scientific attitude" has no better counsel than the conviction that "there must be very valuable evidence about questions which one does not need to be an expert to understand," such as, for example, whether it is possible "to continue totalitarianism with freedom of thought."

A fuller survey of the various tendencies toward totalitarianism in England would have to give considerable attention to the various attempts to create some kind of middle-class socialism bearing, no doubt unknown to their authors, an alarming resemblance to similar developments in pre-Hitler Germany.[8] If we were concerned here with political movements proper, we should have to consider such new organizations as the "Forward-March" or "Common-Wealth" movement of Sir Richard Acland, the author of *Unser Kampf,* or the activities of the "1941 Committee" of Mr. J. B. Priestley, at one time associated with the former. But, though it would be unwise to disregard the symptomatic significance of such phenomena as these, they can hardly yet be counted as important political forces. Apart from the intellectual influences which we have illustrated by two instances, the impetus of the movement toward totalitarianism comes mainly from the two great vested interests: organized capital and organized labor. Probably the greatest menace of all is the fact that the policies of these two most powerful groups point in the same direction.

They do this through their common, and often concerted, support of the monopolistic organization of industry; and it is this tendency which is the great immediate danger. While there is no reason to believe that this movement

8. Another element which after this war is likely to strengthen the tendencies in this direction will be some of the men who during the war have tasted the powers of coercive control and will find it difficult to reconcile themselves with the humbler roles they will then have to play. Though after the last war men of this kind were not so numerous as they will probably be in the future, they exercised even then a not inconsiderable influence on the economic policy of this country. It was in the company of some of these men that as long as ten or twelve years ago I first experienced in this country the then still unusual sensation of being suddenly transported into what I had learned to regard as a thoroughly "German" intellectual atmosphere.

is inevitable, there can be little doubt that if we continue on the path we have been treading, it will lead us to totalitarianism.

This movement is, of course, deliberately planned mainly by the capitalist organizers of monopolies, and they are thus one of the main sources of this danger. Their responsibility is not altered by the fact that their aim is not a totalitarian system but rather a sort of corporative society in which the organized industries would appear as semi-independent and self-governing "estates." But they are as shortsighted as were their German colleagues in believing that they will be allowed not only to create but also for any length of time to run such a system. The decisions which the managers of such an organized industry would constantly have to make are not decisions which any society will long leave to private individuals. A state which allows such enormous aggregations of power to grow up cannot afford to let this power rest entirely in private control. Nor is the belief any less illusory that in such conditions the entrepreneurs will be long allowed to enjoy the favored position which in a competitive society is justified by the fact that, of the many who take the risks, only a few achieve the success the chances of which make the risk worth taking. It is not surprising that entrepreneurs should like to enjoy both the high income which in a competitive society the successful ones among them gain and the security of the civil servant. So long as a large sector of private industry exists side by side with the government-run industry, great industrial talent is likely to command high salaries even in fairly secure positions. But while the entrepreneurs may well see their expectations borne out during a transition stage, it will not be long before they will find, as their German colleagues did, that they are no longer masters but will in every respect have to be satisfied with

whatever power and emoluments the government will con-
cede them.

Unless the argument of this book has been completely
misunderstood, the author will not be suspected of any tenderness toward the capitalists if he stresses here that it would
nevertheless be a mistake to put the blame for the modern
movement toward monopoly exclusively or mainly on that
class. Their propensity in this direction is neither new nor
would it by itself be likely to become a formidable power.
The fatal development was that they have succeeded in en-
listing the support of an ever increasing number of other
groups and, with their help, in obtaining the support of the
state.

In some measure the monopolists have gained this support either by letting other groups participate in their gains
or, and perhaps even more frequently, by persuading them
that the formation of monopolies was in the public interest.
But the change in public opinion, which through its influence on legislation and judicature[9] has been the most important factor to make this development possible, is more than
anything the result of the propaganda against competition
by the Left. Very frequently even measures aimed against
the monopolists in fact serve only to strengthen the power
of monopoly. Every raid on the gains of monopoly, be it in
the interest of particular groups or of the state as a whole,
tends to create new vested interests which will help to bolster
up monopoly. A system in which large privileged groups
profit from the gains of monopoly may be politically much
more dangerous, and monopoly in such a system certainly is
much more powerful, than in one where the profits go to a
limited few. But though it should be clear that, for example,

9. Cf. on this the instructive article by W. Arthur Lewis, "Monopoly and
the Law," *Modern Law Review,* Vol. VI, No. 3 (April, 1943).

the higher wages which the monopolist is in a position to pay
are just as much the result of exploitation as his own profit,
and are just as certain to make poorer not only all the consumers but still more all other wage-earners, not merely
those who benefit from it but the public generally nowadays
accept the ability to pay higher wages as a legitimate argument in favor of monopoly.[10]

There is serious reason for doubt whether even in those
cases where monopoly is inevitable the best way of controlling it is to put it in the hands of the state. If only a single
industry were in question, this might well be so. But, when
we have to deal with many different monopolistic industries,
there is much to be said for leaving them in different private
hands rather than combining them under the single control
of the state. Even if railways, road and air transport, or the
supply of gas and electricity were all inevitably monopolies,
the consumer is unquestionably in a much stronger position
so long as they remain separate monopolies than when they
are "co-ordinated" by a central control. Private monopoly is
scarcely ever complete and even more rarely of long duration or able to disregard potential competition. But a state
monopoly is always a state-protected monopoly—protected
against both potential competition and effective criticism. It
means in most instances that a temporary monopoly is given
the power to secure its position for all time—a power almost
certain to be used. Where the power which ought to check

10. Even more surprising, perhaps, is the remarkable tenderness which
many socialists are likely to show toward the *rentier* bondholders to whom
monopolist organization of industry frequently guarantees secure incomes.
That their blind enmity to profits should lead people to represent effortless
fixed income as socially or ethically more desirable than profits, and to accept even monopoly to secure such a guaranteed income to, for example,
railway bondholders, is one of the most extraordinary symptoms of the perversion of values which has taken place during the last generation.

and control monopoly becomes interested in sheltering and defending its appointees, where for the government to remedy an abuse is to admit responsibility for it, and where criticism of the actions of monopoly means criticism of the government, there is little hope of monopoly becoming the servant of the community. A state which is entangled in all directions in the running of monopolistic enterprise, while it would possess crushing power over the individual, would yet be a weak state in so far as its freedom in formulating policy is concerned. The machinery of monopoly becomes identical with the machinery of the state, and the state itself becomes more and more identified with the interests of those who run things than with the interests of the people in general.

The probability is that wherever monopoly is really inevitable the plan which used to be preferred by Americans, of a strong state control over private monopolies, if consistently pursued, offers a better chance of satisfactory results than state management. This would at least seem to be so where the state enforces a stringent price control which leaves no room for extraordinary profits in which others than the monopolists can participate. Even if this should have the effect (as it sometimes had with American public utilities) that the services of the monopolistic industries would become less satisfactory than they might be, this would be a small price to pay for an effective check on the powers of monopoly. Personally, I should much prefer to have to put up with some such inefficiency than have organized monopoly control my ways of life. Such a method of dealing with monopoly, which would rapidly make the position of the monopolist the least eligible among entrepreneurial positions, would also do as much as anything to reduce monopoly to the spheres where it is inevitable and to stimulate the invention of substitutes which can be provided competitively. Only make the position of the monopolist once more that of the whipping boy of economic policy, and you will be surprised how quickly most of the abler entrepreneurs will rediscover their taste for the bracing air of competition!

The problem of monopoly would not be difficult as it is if it were only the capitalist monopolist whom we have to fight. But, as has already been said, monopoly has become the danger that it is, not through the efforts of a few interested capitalists, but through the support they have obtained from those whom they have let share in their gains, and from the many more whom they have persuaded that in supporting monopoly they assist in the creation of a more just and or-derly society. The fatal turning-point in the modern devel-opment was when the great movement which can serve its original ends only by fighting all privilege, the labor move-ment, came under the influence of anti-competition doc-trines and became itself entangled in the strife for privilege. The recent growth of monopoly is largely the result of a deliberate collaboration of organized capital and organized labor where the privileged groups of labor share in the mo-nopoly profits at the expense of the community and particu-larly at the expense of the poorest, those employed in the less-well-organized industries and the unemployed.

It is one of the saddest spectacles of our time to see a great democratic movement support a policy which must lead to the destruction of democracy and which meanwhile can benefit only a minority of the masses who support it. Yet it is this support from the Left of the tendencies toward mo-nopoly which make them so irresistible and the prospects of the future so dark. So long as labor continues to assist in the destruction of the only order under which at least some degree of independence and freedom has been secured to every worker, there is indeed little hope for the future. The labor leaders who now proclaim so loudly that they have "done once and for all with the mad competitive system"[11] are proclaiming the doom of the freedom of the individual. There is no other possibility than either the order governed by the impersonal discipline of the market or that directed by the will of a few individuals; and those who are out to destroy the first are wittingly or unwittingly helping to create the second. Even though some workmen will perhaps be better fed, and all will no doubt be more uniformly dressed in that new order, it is permissible to doubt whether the majority of English workmen will in the end thank the intellectuals among their leaders who have presented them with a socialist doctrine which endangers their personal freedom.

To anyone who is familiar with the history of the major Continental countries in the last twenty-five years, the study of the recent program of the Labour party in England, now committed to the creation of a "planned society," is a most depressing experience. To "any attempt to restore traditional Britain" there is opposed a scheme which not only in general outline but also in detail and even wording is indistinguishable from the socialist dreams which dominated German discussion twenty-five years ago. Not only demands, like those of the resolution, adopted on Professor Laski's motion, which requires the retention in peacetime of the "measures of government control needed for mobilizing the national resources in war" but all the characteristic catch-

11. Professor H. J. Laski, in his address to the Forty-first Annual Labour Party Conference, London, May 26, 1942 (*Report*, p. 111). It deserves to be noted that, according to Professor Laski, it is "this mad competitive system which spells poverty for all peoples, and war as outcome of that poverty"—a curious reading of the history of the last hundred and fifty years.

words, such as the "balanced economy," which Professor Laski now demands for Great Britain, or the "community consumption" toward which production is to be centrally directed, are bodily taken over from the German ideology.

Twenty-five years ago there was perhaps still some excuse for holding the naïve belief that "a planned society can be a far more free society than the competitive laissez faire order it has come to replace." [12] But to find it once more held after twenty-five years of experience and the re-examination of the old beliefs to which this experience has led, and at a time when we are fighting the results of those very doctrines, is tragic beyond words. That the great party which in Parliament and public opinion has largely taken the place of the progressive parties of the past should have ranged itself with what, in the light of all past development, must be regarded as a reactionary movement, is the decisive change which has taken place in our time and the source of the mortal danger to everything a liberal must value. That the advances of the past should be threatened by the traditionalist forces of the Right is a phenomenon of all ages which need not alarm us. But if the place of the opposition, in public discussion as well as in Parliament, should become lastingly the monopoly of a second reactionary party, there would, indeed, be no hope left.

12. *The Old World and the New Society: An Interim Report of the National Executive of the British Labour Party on the Problems of Reconstruction,* pp. 12 and 16.

14
Material Conditions and Ideal Ends

Is it just or reasonable, that most voices against the main end
of government should enslave the less number that would be free?
More just it is, doubtless, if it come to force, that a less number
compel a greater to retain, which can be no wrong to them, their
liberty, than that a greater number, for the pleasure of their
baseness, compel a less most injuriously to be their fellow slaves.
They who seek nothing but their own just liberty, have always
the right to win it, whenever they have the power, be the
voices never so numerous that oppose it.
—JOHN MILTON

OUR generation likes to flatter itself that it attaches
less weight to economic considerations than did its
parents or grandparents. The "End of Economic
Man" bids fair to become one of the governing myths of our
age. Before we accept this claim, or treat the change as
praiseworthy, we must inquire a little further how far it is
true. When we consider the claims for social reconstruction
which are most strongly pressed, it appears that they are
almost all economic in character: we have seen already that
the "reinterpretation in economic terms" of the political
ideals of the past, of liberty, equality, and security, is one of
the main demands of people who at the same time proclaim
the end of economic man. Nor can there be much doubt that
in their beliefs and aspirations men are today more than
ever before governed by economic doctrines, by the carefully fostered belief in the irrationality of our economic system, by the false assertions about "potential plenty," pseudo-
theories about the inevitable trend toward monopoly, and

the impression created by certain much-advertised occurrences such as the destruction of stocks of raw materials or the suppression of inventions, for which competition is blamed, though they are precisely the sort of thing which could not happen under competition and which are made possible only by monopoly and usually by government-aided monopoly.[1]

In a different sense, however, it is no doubt true that our generation is less willing to listen to economic considerations than was true of its predecessors. It is most decidedly unwilling to sacrifice any of its demands to what are called economic arguments; it is impatient and intolerant of all restraints on their immediate ambitions and unwilling to bow to economic necessities. It is not any contempt for material welfare, or even any diminished desire for it, but, on the contrary, a refusal to recognize any obstacles, any conflict with other aims which might impede the fulfilment of their own desires, which distinguishes our generation. Economophobia would be a more correct description of this attitude than the doubly misleading "End of Economic Man," which suggests a change from a state of affairs which has never existed in a direction in which we are not moving. Man has come to hate, and to revolt against, the impersonal forces to which in the past he submitted, even though they have often frustrated his individual efforts.

---

1. The frequent use that is made of the occasional destruction of wheat, coffee, etc., as an argument against competition is a good illustration of the intellectual dishonesty of much of this argument, since a little reflection will show that in a competitive market no owner of such stocks can gain by their destruction. The case of the alleged suppression of useful patents is more complicated and cannot be adequately discussed in a note; but the conditions in which it would be profitable to put into cold storage a patent *which in the social interest ought to be used* are so exceptional that it is more than doubtful whether this has happened in any important instance.

MATERIAL CONDITIONS AND IDEAL ENDS

This revolt is an instance of a much more general phenomenon, a new unwillingness to submit to any rule or necessity the rationale of which man does not understand; it makes itself felt in many fields of life, particularly in that of morals; and it is often a commendable attitude. But there are fields where this craving for intelligibility cannot be fully satisfied and where at the same time a refusal to submit to anything we cannot understand must lead to the destruction of our civilization. Though it is natural that, as the world around us becomes more complex, our resistance grows against the forces which, without our understanding them, constantly interfere with individual hopes and plans, it is just in these circumstances that it becomes less and less possible for anyone fully to understand these forces. A complex civilization like ours is necessarily based on the individual's adjusting himself to changes whose cause and nature he cannot understand: why he should have more or less, why he should have to move to another occupation, why some things he wants should become more difficult to get than others, will always be connected with such a multitude of circumstances that no single mind will be able to grasp them; or, even worse, those affected will put all the blame on an obvious immediate and avoidable cause, while the more complex interrelationships which determine the change remain inevitably hidden to them. Even the director of a completely planned society, if he wanted to give an adequate explanation to anyone why he has to be directed to a different job, or why his remuneration has to be changed, could not fully do so without explaining and vindicating his whole plan—which means, of course, that it could not be explained to more than a few.

It was men's submission to the impersonal forces of the market that in the past has made possible the growth of a civilization which without this could not have developed; it is by thus submitting that we are every day helping to build something that is greater than any one of us can fully comprehend. It does not matter whether men in the past did submit from beliefs which some now regard as superstitious: from a religious spirit of humility or an exaggerated respect for the crude teachings of the early economists. The crucial point is that it is infinitely more difficult rationally to comprehend the necessity of submitting to forces whose operation we cannot follow in detail than to do so out of the humble awe which religion, or even the respect for the doctrines of economics, did inspire. It may, indeed, be the case that infinitely more intelligence on the part of everybody would be needed than anybody now possesses, if we were even merely to maintain our present complex civilization without anyone's having to do things of which he does not comprehend the necessity. The refusal to yield to forces which we neither understand nor can recognize as the conscious decisions of an intelligent being is the product of an incomplete and therefore erroneous rationalism. It is incomplete because it fails to comprehend that the co-ordination of the multifarious individual efforts in a complex society must take account of facts no individual can completely survey. And it fails to see that, unless this complex society is to be destroyed, the only alternative to submission to the impersonal and seemingly irrational forces of the market is submission to an equally uncontrollable and therefore arbitrary power of other men. In his anxiety to escape the irksome restraints which he now feels, man does not realize that the new authoritarian restraints which will have to be deliberately imposed in their stead will be even more painful.

Those who argue that we have to an astounding degree learned to master the forces of nature but are sadly behind

in making successful use of the possibilities of social collaboration are quite right so far as this statement goes. But they
are mistaken when they carry the comparison further and
argue that we must learn to master the forces of society in
the same manner in which we have learned to master the
forces of nature. This is not only the path to totalitarianism
but the path to the destruction of our civilization and a certain way to block future progress. Those who demand it
show by their very demands that they have not yet compre-
hended the extent to which the mere preservation of what
we have so far achieved depends on the co-ordination of
individual efforts by impersonal forces.

We must now return briefly to the crucial point—that individual freedom cannot be reconciled with the supremacy
of one single purpose to which the whole society must be
entirely and permanently subordinated. The only exception
to the rule that a free society must not be subjected to a
single purpose is war and other temporary disasters when
subordination of almost everything to the immediate and
pressing need is the price at which we preserve our freedom in the long run. This explains also why so many of the
fashionable phrases about doing for the purposes of peace
what we have learned to do for the purposes of war are so
very misleading: it is sensible temporarily to sacrifice freedom in order to make it more secure in the future; but the
same cannot be said for a system proposed as a permanent
arrangement.

That no single purpose must be allowed in peace to have
absolute preference over all others applies even to the one
aim which everybody now agrees comes in the front rank:
the conquest of unemployment. There can be no doubt that
this must be the goal of our greatest endeavor; even so, it

does not mean that such an aim should be allowed to dominate us to the exclusion of everything else, that, as the glib phrase runs, it must be accomplished "at any price." It is, in fact, in this field that the fascination of vague but popular phrases like "full employment" may well lead to extremely shortsighted measures, and where the categorical and irresponsible "it must be done at all cost" of the single-minded idealist is likely to do the greatest harm.

It is of very great importance that we should approach with open eyes the task which in this field we shall have to face after the war and that we should clearly realize what we may hope to achieve. One of the dominant features of the immediate postwar situation will be that the special needs of war have drawn hundreds of thousands of men and women into specialized jobs where during the war they have been able to earn relatively high wages. There will, in many instances, be no possibility of employing the same numbers in these particular trades. There will be an urgent need for the transfer of large numbers to other jobs, and many of them will find that the work they can then get is less favorably remunerated than was true of their war job. Even retraining, which certainly ought to be provided on a liberal scale, cannot entirely overcome this problem. There will still be many people who, if they are to be paid according to what their services will then be worth to society, would under any system have to be content with a lowering of their material position relative to that of others.

If, then, the trade unions successfully resist any lowering of the wages of the particular groups in question, there will be only two alternatives open: either coercion will have to be used (i.e., certain individuals will have to be selected for compulsory transfer to other and relatively less well paid positions) or those who can no longer be employed at the relatively high wages they have earned during the war must be allowed to remain unemployed until they are willing to accept work at a relatively lower wage. This is a problem which would arise in a socialist society no less than in any other; and the great majority of workmen would probably be just as little inclined to guarantee in perpetuity their present wages to those who were drawn into specially well-paid employments because of the special need of war. A socialist society would certainly use coercion in this position. The point that is relevant for us is that if we are determined not to allow unemployment at any price, and are not willing to use coercion, we shall be driven to all sorts of desperate expedients, none of which can bring any lasting relief and all of which will seriously interfere with the most productive use of our resources. It should be specially noted that monetary policy cannot provide a real cure for this difficulty except by a general and considerable inflation, sufficient to raise all other wages and prices relatively to those which cannot be lowered, and that even this would bring about the desired result only by effecting in a concealed and underhand fashion that reduction of real wages which could not be brought about directly. Yet to raise all other wages and incomes to an extent sufficient to adjust the position of the group in question would involve an inflationary expansion on such a scale that the disturbances, hardships, and injustices caused would be much greater than those to be cured.

This problem, which will arise in a particularly acute form after the war, is one which will always be with us so long as the economic system has to adopt itself to continuous changes. There will always be a possible maximum of employment in the short run which can be achieved by giving all people employment where they happen to be and which can be achieved by monetary expansion. But not only can

this maximum be maintained solely by progressive inflationary expansion and with the effect of holding up those redis-
tributions of labor between industries made necessary by the
changed circumstances, and which so long as workmen are
free to choose their jobs will always come about only with
some delays and thereby cause some unemployment: to aim
always at the maximum of employment achievable by monetary means is a policy which is certain in the end to defeat its
own purposes. It tends to lower the productivity of labor
and thereby constantly increases the proportion of the
working population which can be kept employed at present
wages only by artificial means.

There is little doubt that after the war wisdom in the
management of our economic affairs will be even more important than before and that the fate of our civilization will
ultimately depend on how we solve the economic problems
we shall then face. The British, at least, will at first be poor,
very poor indeed—and the problem of regaining and improving former standards may in fact prove for Great Britain more difficult than for many other countries. If they act
wisely, there is little question that by hard work and by de-
voting a considerable part of their efforts to overhauling and
renewing their industrial apparatus and organization, they
will in the course of a few years be able to return to and even
surpass the level they had reached. But this presupposes
that they will be satisfied to consume currently no more than
is possible without impairing the task of reconstruction, that
no exaggerated hopes create irresistible claims for more
than this, and that they regard it as more important to use
their resources in the best manner and for the purposes
which contribute most to well-being than that we should use

all their resources somehow.[2] Perhaps no less important is that they should not, by shortsighted attempts to cure poverty by a redistribution instead of by an increase in our income, so depress large classes as to turn them into determined enemies of the existing political order. It should never be forgotten that the one decisive factor in the rise of totalitarianism on the Continent, which is yet absent in England and America, is the existence of a large recently dispossessed middle class.

Our hopes of avoiding the fate which threatens must indeed to a large extent rest on the prospect that we can resume rapid economic progress which, however low we may have to start, will continue to carry us upward; and the main condition for such progress is that we should all be ready to adapt ourselves quickly to a very much changed world, that no considerations for the accustomed standard of particular groups must be allowed to obstruct this adaptation, and that we learn once more to turn all our resources to wherever they contribute most to make us all richer. The adjustments that will be needed if we are to recover and surpass our former standards will be greater than any similar adjustments we had to make in the past; and only if every one of us is ready individually to obey the necessities of this readjustment shall we be able to get through a difficult pe-

2. This is perhaps the place to emphasize that, however much one may wish a speedy return to a free economy, this cannot mean the removal at one stroke of most of the wartime restrictions. Nothing would discredit the system of free enterprise more than the acute, though probably short-lived, dislocation and instability such an attempt would produce. The problem is at what kind of system we should aim in the process of demobilization, not whether the wartime system should be transformed into more permanent arrangements by a carefully thought-out policy of gradual relaxation of controls, which may have to extend over several years.

riod as free men who can choose their own way of life. Let a uniform minimum be secured to everybody by all means; but let us admit at the same time that with this assurance of a basic minimum all claims for a privileged security of particular classes must lapse, that all excuses disappear for allowing groups to exclude newcomers from sharing their relative prosperity in order to maintain a special standard of their own.

It may sound noble to say, "Damn economics, let us build up a decent world"—but it is, in fact, merely irresponsible. With our world as it is, with everyone convinced that the material conditions here or there must be improved, our only chance of building a decent world is that we can continue to improve the general level of wealth. The one thing modern democracy will not bear without cracking is the necessity of a substantial lowering of the standards of living in peacetime or even prolonged stationariness of its economic conditions.

People who admit that present political trends constitute a serious threat to our economic prospects, and through their economic effects endanger much higher values, are yet likely to deceive themselves that we are making material sacrifices to gain ideal ends. It is, however, more than doubtful whether a fifty years' approach toward collectivism has raised our moral standards, or whether the change has not rather been in the opposite direction. Though we are in the habit of priding ourselves on our more sensitive social conscience, it is by no means clear that this is justified by the practice of our individual conduct. On the negative side, in its indignation about the inequities of the existing social order, our generation probably surpasses most of its predecessors. But the effect of that movement on our positive standards in the proper field of morals, individual conduct, and on the seriousness with which we uphold moral principles against the expediencies and exigencies of social machinery, is a very different matter.

Issues in this field have become so confused that it is necessary to go back to fundamentals. What our generation is in danger of forgetting is not only that morals are of necessity a phenomenon of individual conduct but also that they can exist only in the sphere in which the individual is free to decide for himself and is called upon voluntarily to sacrifice personal advantage to the observance of a moral rule. Outside the sphere of individual responsibility there is neither goodness nor badness, neither opportunity for moral merit nor the chance of proving one's conviction by sacrificing one's desires to what one thinks right. Only where we ourselves are responsible for our own interests and are free to sacrifice them has our decision moral value. We are neither entitled to be unselfish at someone else's expense nor is there any merit in being unselfish if we have no choice. The members of a society who in all respects are *made* to do the good thing have no title to praise. As Milton said: "If every action which is good or evil in a man of ripe years were under pittance and prescription and compulsion, what were virtue but a name, what praise should then be due to well-doing, what gramercy to be sober, just, or continent?"

Freedom to order our own conduct in the sphere where material circumstances force a choice upon us, and responsibility for the arrangement of our own life according to our own conscience, is the air in which alone moral sense grows and in which moral values are daily re-created in the free decision of the individual. Responsibility, not to a superior, but to one's conscience, the awareness of a duty not exacted by compulsion, the necessity to decide which of the things one values are to be sacrificed to others, and to bear the consequences of one's own decision, are the very essence of any morals which deserve the name.

That in this sphere of individual conduct the effect of collectivism has been almost entirely destructive is both inevitable and undeniable. A movement whose main promise is the relief from responsibility[3] cannot but be antimoral in its effect, however lofty the ideals to which it owes its birth. Can there be much doubt that the feeling of personal obligation to remedy inequities, where our individual power permits, has been weakened rather than strengthened, that both the willingness to bear responsibility and the consciousness that it is our own individual duty to know how to choose have been perceptibly impaired? There is all the difference between demanding that a desirable state of affairs should be brought about by the authorities, or even being willing to submit provided everyone else is made to do the same, and the readiness to do what one thinks right one's self at the sacrifice of one's own desires and perhaps in the face of hostile public opinion. There is much to suggest that we have in fact become more tolerant toward particular abuses and

3. This becomes more and more clearly expressed as socialism approaches totalitarianism, and in England is most explicitly stated in the program of that latest and most totalitarian form of English socialism, Sir Richard Acland's "Common-Wealth" movement. The main feature of the new order he promises is that in it the community will "say to the individual 'Don't *you* bother about the business of getting your *own* living.'" In consequence, of course, "it must be the community as a whole which must decide whether or not a man shall be employed upon our resources, and how and when and in what manner he shall work," and that the community will have "to run camps for shirkers in very tolerable conditions." Is it surprising that the author discovers that Hitler "has stumbled across (or has needed to make use of) a small part, or perhaps one should say one particular aspect of, what will ultimately be required of humanity" (Sir Richard Acland, Bt., *The Forward March* [1941], pp. 127, 126, 135, and 32)?

much more indifferent to inequities in individual cases, since we have fixed our eyes on an entirely different system in which the state will set everything right. It may even be, as has been suggested, that the passion for collective action is a way in which we now without compunction collectively indulge in that selfishness which as individuals we had learned a little to restrain.

It is true that the virtues which are less esteemed and practiced now—independence, self-reliance, and the willingness to bear risks, the readiness to back one's conviction against a majority, and the willingness to voluntary cooperation with one's neighbors—are essentially those on which the working of an individualist society rests. Collectivism has nothing to put in their place, and in so far as it has destroyed them it has left a void filled by nothing but the demand for obedience and the compulsion of the individual to do what is collectively decided to be good. The periodical election of representatives, to which the moral choice of the individual tends to be more and more reduced, is not an occasion on which his moral values are tested or where he has constantly to reassert and prove the order of his values and to testify to the sincerity of his profession by the sacrifice of those of his values he rates lower to those he puts higher.

As the rules of conduct evolved by individuals are the source from which collective political action derives what moral standards it possesses, it would indeed be surprising if the relaxation of the standards of individual conduct were accompanied by a raising of the standards of social action. That there have been great changes is clear. Every generation, of course, puts some values higher and some lower than its predecessors. Which, however, are the aims which take a lower place now, which are the values which we are now warned may have to give way if they come into conflict with others? Which kind of values figure less prominently in the picture of the future held out to us by the popular writers and speakers than they did in the dreams and hopes of our fathers?

It is certainly not material comfort, certainly not a rise in our standard of living or the assurance of a certain status in society which ranks lower. Is there a popular writer or speaker who dares to suggest to the masses that they might have to make sacrifices of their material prospects for the enhancement of an ideal end? Is it not, in fact, entirely the other way round? Are not the things which we are more and more frequently taught to regard as "nineteenth-century illusions" all moral values—liberty and independence, truth and intellectual honesty, peace and democracy, and the respect for the individual *qua* man instead of merely as the member of an organized group?

What are the fixed poles now which are regarded as sacrosanct, which no reformer dare touch, since they are treated as the immutable boundaries which must be respected in any plan for the future? They are no longer the liberty of the individual, his freedom of movement, and scarcely that of speech. They are the protected standards of this or that group, their "right" to exclude others from providing their fellowmen with what they need. Discrimination between members and nonmembers of closed groups, not to speak of nationals of different countries, is accepted more and more as a matter of course; injustices inflicted on individuals by government action in the interest of a group are disregarded with an indifference hardly distinguishable from callousness; and the grossest violations of the most elementary rights of the individual, such as are involved in the compulsory transfer of populations, are more and more often countenanced even by supposed liberals.

All this surely indicates that our moral sense has been blunted rather than sharpened. When we are reminded, as more and more frequently happens, that one cannot make omelettes without breaking eggs, the eggs which are broken are almost all of the kind which a generation or two ago were regarded as the essential bases of civilized life. And what atrocities committed by powers with whose professed principles they sympathize have not been readily condoned by many of our so-called "liberals"?

There is one aspect of the change in moral values brought about by the advance of collectivism which at the present time provides special food for thought. It is that the virtues which are held less and less in esteem and which consequently become rarer are precisely those on which Anglo-Saxons justly prided themselves and in which they were generally recognized to excel. The virtues these people possessed—in a higher degree than most other people, excepting only a few of the smaller nations, like the Swiss and the Dutch—were independence and self-reliance, individual initiative and local responsibility, the successful reliance on voluntary activity, noninterference with one's neighbor and tolerance of the different and queer, respect for custom and tradition, and a healthy suspicion of power and authority. Almost all the traditions and institutions in which democratic moral genius has found its most characteristic expression, and which in turn have molded the national character and the whole moral climate of England and America, are those which the progress of collectivism and its inherently centralistic tendencies are progressively destroying.

A foreign background is sometimes helpful in seeing more clearly to what circumstances the peculiar excellencies of the moral atmosphere of a nation are due. And if one who, whatever the law may say, must forever remain a foreigner, may be allowed to say so, it is one of the most disheartening spectacles of our time to see to what extent some of the most precious things which England, for example, has given to the world are now held in contempt in England herself. The English hardly know to what degree they differ from most other people in that they all, irrespective of party, hold to a greater or less extent the ideas which in their most pronounced form are known as liberalism. Compared with most other peoples only twenty years ago almost all Englishmen were liberals—however much they may have differed from party liberalism. And even today the English conservative or socialist, no less than the liberal, if he travels abroad, though he may find the ideas and writings of Carlyle or Disraeli, of the Webbs or H. G. Wells, exceedingly popular in circles with which he has little in common, among Nazis and other totalitarians, if he finds an intellectual island where the tradition of Macaulay and Gladstone, of J. S. Mill or John Morley, lives, will find kindred spirits who "talk the same language" as himself—however much he himself may differ from the ideals for which these men specifically stood.

Nowhere is the loss of the belief in the specific values of British civilization more manifest, and nowhere has it had a more paralyzing effect on the pursuit of our immediate great purpose, than in the fatuous ineffectiveness of most British propaganda. The first prerequisite for success in propaganda directed to other people is the proud acknowledgment of the characteristic values and distinguishing traits for which the country attempting it is known to the other peoples. The main cause of the ineffectiveness of British propaganda is that those directing it seem to have lost their own belief in the peculiar values of English civilization or to be completely ignorant of the main points on which it differs from that of other people. The Left intelligentsia, indeed, have so long worshiped foreign gods that they seem to have become almost incapable of seeing any good in the characteristic English institutions and traditions. That the moral values on which most of them pride themselves are largely the product of the institutions they are out to destroy, these socialists cannot, of course, admit. And this attitude is unfortunately not confined to avowed socialists. Though one must hope that this is not true of the less vocal but more numerous cultivated Englishmen, if one were to judge by the ideas which find expression in current political discussion and propaganda, the Englishmen who not only "the language speak that Shakespeare spake" but also "the faith and morals hold that Milton held" seem to have almost vanished.[4]

To believe, however, that the kind of propaganda produced by this attitude can have the desired effect on our enemies and particularly on the Germans, is a fatal blunder. The Germans know England and America, not well, perhaps, yet sufficiently to know what are the characteristic traditional values of democratic life, and what for the last two or three generations has increasingly separated the minds of the countries. If we wish to convince them, not only of our sincerity, but also that we have to offer a real alternative to the way they have gone, it will not be by concessions to their system of thought. We shall not delude them with a stale

4. Though the subject of this chapter has already invited more than one reference to Milton, it is difficult to resist the temptation to add here one more quotation, a very familiar one, though one, it seems, which nowadays nobody but a foreigner would dare to cite: "Let not England forget her precedence of teaching nations how to live." It is, perhaps, significant that our generation has seen a host of American and English detractors of Milton—and that the first of them, Ezra Pound, was during this war broadcasting from Italy!

reproduction of the ideas of their fathers which we have borrowed from them—be it state socialism, *Realpolitik*, "scientific" planning, or corporativism. We shall not persuade them by following them half the way which leads to totalitarianism. If the democracies themselves abandon the supreme ideal of the freedom and happiness of the individual, if they implicitly admit that their civilization is not worth preserving, and that they know nothing better than to follow the path along which the Germans have led, they have indeed nothing to offer. To the Germans all these are merely belated admissions that the liberals have been wrong all the way through and that they themselves are leading the way to a new and better world, however appalling the period of transition may be. The Germans know that what they still regard as the British and American traditions and their own new ideals are fundamentally opposed and irreconcilable views of life. They might be convinced that the way they have chosen was wrong—but nothing will ever convince them that the British or Americans will be better guides on the German path.

Least of all will that type of propaganda appeal to those Germans on whose help we must ultimately count in rebuilding Europe because their values are nearest to our own. For experience has made them wiser and sadder men: they have learned that neither good intentions nor efficiency of organization can preserve decency in a system in which personal freedom and individual responsibility are destroyed. What the German and Italian who have learned the lesson want above all is protection against the monster state—not grandiose schemes for organization on a colossal scale, but opportunity peacefully and in freedom to build up once more their own little worlds. It is not because they believe that to be ordered about by British or Americans is preferable to being ordered about by the Prussians, but because they believe that in a world where democratic ideals have been victorious they will be less ordered about and left in peace to pursue their own concerns, that we can hope for support from some of the nationals of the enemy countries.

If we are to succeed in the war of ideologies and to win over the decent elements in the enemy countries, we must, first of all, regain the belief in the traditional values for which we have stood in the past and must have the moral courage stoutly to defend the ideals which our enemies attack. Not by shamefaced apologies and by assurances that we are rapidly reforming, not by explaining that we are seeking some compromise between the traditional liberal values and the new totalitarian ideas, shall we win confidence and support. Not the latest improvements we may have effected in our social institutions, which count but little compared with the basic differences of two opposed ways of life, but our unwavering faith in those traditions which have made England and America countries of free and upright, tolerant and independent, people is the thing that counts.

15

The Prospects
of International Order

*Of all checks on democracy, federation has been the most
efficacious and the most congenial. . . . The federal system
limits and restrains the sovereign power by dividing it and by
assigning to Government only certain defined rights.
It is the only method of curbing not only the majority
but the power of the whole people.*
—LORD ACTON

IN NO other field has the world yet paid so dearly for the abandonment of nineteenth-century liberalism as in the field where the retreat began: in international relations. Yet only a small part of the lesson which experience ought to have taught us has been learned. Perhaps even more than elsewhere current notions of what is desirable and practicable are here still of a kind which may well produce the opposite of what they promise.

The part of the lesson of the recent past which is slowly and gradually being appreciated is that many kinds of economic planning, conducted independently on a national scale, are bound in their aggregate effect to be harmful even from a purely economic point of view and, in addition, to produce serious international friction. That there is little hope of international order or lasting peace so long as every country is free to employ whatever measures it thinks desirable in its own immediate interest, however damaging they may be to others, needs little emphasis now. Many kinds of economic planning are indeed practicable only if the planning authority can effectively shut out all extraneous influences; the result of such planning is therefore inevitably the piling-up of restrictions on the movements of men and goods.

Less obvious but by no means less real are the dangers to peace arising out of the artificially fostered economic solidarity of all the inhabitants of any one country and from the new blocs of opposed interests created by planning on a national scale. It is neither necessary nor desirable that national boundaries should mark sharp differences in standards of living, that membership of a national group should entitle to a share in a cake altogether different from that in which members of other groups share. If the resources of different nations are treated as exclusive properties of these nations as wholes, if international economic relations, instead of being relations between individuals, become increasingly relations between whole nations organized as trading bodies, they inevitably become the source of friction and envy between whole nations. It is one of the most fatal illusions that, by substituting negotiations between states or organized groups for competition for markets or for raw materials, international friction would be reduced. This would merely put a contest of force in the place of what can only metaphorically be called the "struggle" of competition and would transfer to powerful and armed states, subject to no superior law, the rivalries which between individuals had to be decided without recourse to force. Economic transactions between national bodies who are at the same time the supreme judges of their own behavior, who bow to no superior law, and whose representatives cannot be bound by any considerations but the immediate interest of their respective nations, must end in clashes of power.[1]

1. On all these and on the following points, which can be touched upon

If we were to make no better use of victory than to countenance existing trends in this direction, only too visible before 1939, we might indeed find that we have defeated National Socialism merely to create a world of many national socialisms, differing in detail, but all equally totalitarian, nationalistic, and in recurrent conflict with each other. The Germans would appear as the disturbers of peace, as they already do to some people,[2] merely because they were the first to take the path along which all the others were ultimately to follow.

Those who at least partly realize these dangers usually draw the conclusion that economic planning must be done "internationally," i.e., by some supernational authority. But though this would avert some of the obvious dangers raised by planning on a national scale, it seems that those who advocate such ambitious schemes have little conception of the even greater difficulties and dangers which their proposal create. The problems raised by a conscious direction of economic affairs on a national scale inevitably assume even greater dimensions when the same is attempted internationally. The conflict between planning and freedom cannot but become more serious as the similarity of standards and values among those submitted to a unitary plan diminishes. There need be little difficulty in planning the economic life of a family, comparatively little in a small community. But, as the scale increases, the amount of agreement on the order of ends decreases and the necessity to rely on force and compulsion grows. In a small community common views on the

only very briefly, see Professor Lionel Robbins' *Economic Planning and International Order* (1937), *passim*.

2. See particularly the significant book by James Burnham, *The Managerial Revolution* (1941).

relative importance of the main tasks, agreed standards of value, will exist on a great many subjects. But their number will become less and less the wider we throw the net; and, as there is less community of views, the necessity to rely on force and coercion increases.

The people of any one country may easily be persuaded to make a sacrifice in order to assist what they regard as "their" iron industry or "their" agriculture, or in order that in their country nobody should sink below a certain level. So long as it is a question of helping people whose habits of life and ways of thinking are familiar to us, of correcting the distribution of incomes among, or the working conditions of, people we can well imagine and whose views on their appropriate status are fundamentally similar to ours, we are usually ready to make some sacrifices. But one has only to visualize the problems raised by economic planning of even an area such as western Europe to see that the moral bases for such an undertaking are completely lacking. Who imagines that there exist any common ideals of distributive justice such as will make the Norwegian fisherman consent to forego the prospect of economic improvement in order to help his Portuguese fellow, or the Dutch worker to pay more for his bicycle to help the Coventry mechanic, or the French peasant to pay more taxes to assist the industrialization of Italy?

If most people are not willing to see the difficulty, this is mainly because, consciously or unconsciously, they assume that it will be they who will settle these questions for the others, and because they are convinced of their own capacity to do this justly and equitably. The English people, for instance, perhaps even more than others, begin to realize what such schemes mean only when it is presented to them that they might be a minority in the planning authority and that the main lines of the future economic development of Great Britain might be determined by a non-British majority. How many people in England would be prepared to submit to the decision of an international authority, however democratically constituted, which had power to decree that the development of the Spanish iron industry must have precedence over similar development in South Wales, that the optical industry had better be concentrated in Germany to the exclusion of Great Britain, or that only fully refined gasoline should be imported to Great Britain and all the industries connected with refining reserved for the producer countries?

To imagine that the economic life of a vast area comprising many different people can be directed or planned by democratic procedure betrays a complete lack of awareness of the problems such planning would raise. Planning on an international scale, even more than is true on a national scale, cannot be anything but a naked rule of force, an imposition by a small group on all the rest of that sort of standard and employment which the planners think suitable for the rest. If anything is certain, it is that *Grossraumwirtschaft* of the kind at which the Germans have been aiming can be successfully realized only by a master-race, a *Herrenvolk*, ruthlessly imposing its aims and ideas on the rest. It is a mistake to regard the brutality and the disregard of all the wishes and ideals of the smaller people shown by the Germans simply as a sign of their special wickedness; it is the nature of the task they have assumed which makes these things inevitable. To undertake the direction of the economic life of people with widely divergent ideals and values is to assume responsibilities which commit one to the use of force; it is to assume a position where the best intentions cannot prevent one from being forced to act in a way which to some of those affected must appear highly immoral.[3]

This is true even if we assume the dominant power to be as idealistic and unselfish as we can possibly conceive. But how small is the likelihood that it will be unselfish, and how great are the temptations! I believe the standards of decency and fairness, particularly with regard to international affairs, to be as high, if not higher, in England than in any other country. Yet even now we can hear people in England arguing that victory must be used to create conditions in which British industry will be able to utilize to the full the particular equipment which it has built up during the war, that the reconstruction of Europe must be so directed as to fit in with the special requirements of the industries of England, and to secure to everybody in the country the kind of employment for which he thinks himself most fit. The alarming thing about these suggestions is not that they are made but that they are made in all innocence and regarded as a matter of course by decent people who are completely unaware of the moral enormity which the use of force for such purposes involves.[4]

3. The experience in the colonial sphere, of Great Britain as much as of any other, has amply shown that even the mild forms of planning which Englishmen know as colonial development involve, whether they wish it or not, the imposition of certain values and ideals on those whom they try to assist. It is, indeed, this experience which has made even the most internationally minded of colonial experts so very skeptical of the practicability of an "international" administration of colonies.

4. If anyone should still fail to see the difficulties, or cherish the belief that with a little good will they can all be overcome, it will help if he tries to follow the implications of central direction of economic activity applied on a world scale. Can there be much doubt that this would mean a more or less conscious endeavor to secure the dominance of the white man, and would rightly be so regarded by all other races? Until I find a sane person

Perhaps the most powerful agent in creating the belief in the possibility of a single central direction by democratic means of the economic life of many different peoples is the fatal delusion that if the decisions were left to the "people," the community of interest of the working classes would readily overcome the differences which exist between the ruling classes. There is every reason to expect that with world planning the clash of economic interests which arises now about the economic policy of any one nation would in fact appear in even fiercer form as a clash of interests between whole peoples which could be decided only by force. On the questions which an international planning authority would have to decide, the interests and opinions of the working classes of the different people will inevitably be as much in conflict, and there will be even less of a commonly accepted basis for an equitable settlement than there is with respect to different classes in any one country. To the worker in a poor country the demand of his more fortunate colleague to be protected against his low-wage competition by minimum-wage legislation, supposedly in his interest, is frequently no more than a means to deprive him of his only chance to better his conditions by overcoming natural disadvantages by working at wages lower than his fellows in other countries. And to him the fact that he has to give the product of ten hours of his labor for the product of five hours of the man elsewhere who is better equipped with ma-

---

who seriously believes that the European races will voluntarily submit to their standard of life and rate of progress being determined by a world parliament, I cannot regard such plans as anything but absurd. But this does unfortunately not preclude that particular measures, which could be justified only if the principle of world direction were a feasible ideal, are seriously advocated.

chinery is as much "exploitation" as that practiced by any capitalist.

It is fairly certain that in a planned international system the wealthier and therefore most powerful nations would to a very much greater degree than in a free economy become the object of hatred and envy of the poorer ones: and the latter, rightly or wrongly, would all be convinced that their position could be improved much more quickly if they were only free to do what they wished. Indeed, if it comes to be regarded as the duty of the international authority to bring about distributive justice between the different peoples, it is no more than a consistent and inevitable development of socialist doctrine that class strife would become a struggle between the working classes of the different countries.

There is at present a great deal of muddleheaded talk about "planning to equalize standards of life." It is instructive to consider in a little more detail one of these proposals to see what precisely it involves. The area for which at the present moment our planners are particularly fond of drawing up such schemes is the Danube Basin and southeastern Europe. There can be no doubt about the urgent need for amelioration of economic conditions in this region, from humanitarian and economic considerations as well as in the interest of the future peace of Europe, nor that this can be achieved only in a political setting different from that of the past. But this is not the same thing as to wish to see economic life in this region directed according to a single master-plan, to foster the development of the different industries according to a schedule laid down beforehand in a way which makes the success of local initiative dependent on being approved by the central authority and being incorporated in its plan. One cannot, for example, create a kind of Tennessee Valley Authority for the Danube Basin without thereby determining beforehand for many years to come the relative rate of progress of the different races inhabiting this area or without subordinating all their individual aspirations and wishes to this task.

Planning of this kind must of necessity begin by fixing an order of priorities of the different claims. To plan for the deliberate equalization of standards of living means that the different claims must be ranked according to merit, that some must be given precedence over others, and that the latter must wait their turn—even though those whose interests are thus relegated may be convinced, not only of their better right, but also of their ability to reach their goal sooner if they were only given freedom to act on their own devices. There exists no basis which allows us to decide whether the claims of the poor Rumanian peasant are more or less urgent than those of the still poorer Albanian, or the needs of the Slovakian mountain shepherd greater than those of his Slovenian colleague. But if the raising of their standards of life is to be effected according to a unitary plan, somebody must deliberately balance the merits of all these claims and decide between them. And once such a plan is put into execution, all the resources of the planned area must serve that plan—there can be no exemption for those who feel they could do better for themselves. Once their claim has been given a lower rank, they will have to work for the prior satisfaction of the needs of those who have been given preference.

In such a state of affairs *everybody* will rightly feel that he is worse off than he might be if some other plan had been adopted and that it is the decision and the might of the dominant powers which have condemned him to a place less favorable than he thinks is due to him. To attempt such a thing in a region peopled by small nations, each of which believes equally fervently in its own superiority over the others, is to undertake a task which can be performed only by the use of force. What it would amount to in practice is that the decisions and power of the large nations would have to settle whether the standards of the Macedonian or the Bulgarian peasant should be raised faster, whether the Czech or the Hungarian miner should more rapidly approach Western standards. It does not need much knowledge of human nature, and certainly only a little knowledge of the people of Central Europe, to see that, whatever the decision imposed, there will be many, probably a majority, to whom the particular order chosen will appear supreme injustice and that their common hatred will soon turn against the power which, however disinterestedly, in fact decides their fate.

Though there are no doubt many people who honestly believe that if they were allowed to handle the job they would be able to settle all those problems justly and impartially, and who would be genuinely surprised to find suspicion and hatred turning against them, they would probably be the first to apply force when those whom they mean to benefit prove recalcitrant, and to show themselves quite ruthless in coercing people in what is presumed to be their own interests. What these dangerous idealists do not see is that where the assumption of a moral responsibility involves that one's moral views should by force be made to prevail over those dominant in other communities, the assumption of such responsibility may place one in a position in which it becomes impossible to act morally. To impose such an impossible moral task on the victorious nations is a certain way morally to corrupt and discredit them.

By all means let us assist the poorer people as much as we can in their own efforts to build up their lives and to raise their standards of living. An international authority can be very just and contribute enormously to economic prosperity if it merely keeps order and creates conditions in which the people can develop their own life; but it is impossible to be just or to let people live their own life if the central authority doles out raw materials and allocates markets, if every spontaneous effort has to be "approved" and nothing can be done without the sanction of the central authority.

After the discussions in earlier chapters it is hardly necessary to stress that these difficulties cannot be met by conferring on the various international authorities "merely" specific economic powers. The belief that this is a practical solution rests on the fallacy that economic planning is merely a technical task, which can be solved in a strictly objective manner by experts, and that the really vital things would still be left in the hands of the political authorities. Any international economic authority, not subject to a superior political power, even if strictly confined to a particular field, could easily exercise the most tyrannical and irresponsible power imaginable. Exclusive control of an essential commodity or service (as, for example, air transport) is in effect one of the most far-reaching powers which can be conferred on any authority. And as there is scarcely anything which could not be justified by "technical necessities" which no outsider could effectively question—or even by humanitarian and possibly entirely sincere arguments about the needs of some specially ill-favored group which could not be helped in any other way—there is little possibility of controlling that power. The kind of organization of the resources of the world under more or less autonomous bodies, which now so often finds favor in the most surprising quarters, a system of comprehensive monopolies recognized by all the national governments, but subject to none, would inevitably become the worst of all conceivable rackets—even if those intrusted with their administration should prove the most faithful guardians of the particular interests placed in their care.

One need only seriously consider the full implications of such apparently innocuous proposals, widely regarded as the essential basis of the future economic order, such as the conscious control and distribution of the supply of essential raw materials, in order to see what appalling political difficulties and moral dangers they create. The controller of the supply of any such raw material as gasoline or timber, rubber or tin, would be the master of the fate of whole industries and countries. In deciding whether to allow the supply to increase and the price or the income of the producers to fall, he would decide whether some country is to be allowed to start some new industry or whether it is to be precluded from doing so. While he "protects" the standards of life of those he regards as specially intrusted to his care, he will deprive many who are in a much worse position of their best and perhaps only chance to improve it. If all essential raw materials were thus controlled, there would indeed be no new industry, no new venture on which the people of a country could embark without the permission of the controllers, no plan for development or improvement which could not be frustrated by their veto. The same is true of international arrangement for "sharing" of markets and even more so of the control of investment and the development of natural resources.

It is curious to observe how those who pose as the most hard-boiled realists, and who lose no opportunity of casting ridicule on the "utopianism" of those who believe in the possibility of an international political order, yet regard as more

practicable the much more intimate and irresponsible interference with the lives of the different peoples which economic planning involves; and believe that, once hitherto
undreamed-of power is given to an international government, which has just been represented as not even capable
of enforcing a simple Rule of Law, this greater power will be
used in so unselfish and so obviously just a manner as to
command general consent. If anything is evident, it should
be that, while nations might abide by formal rules on which
they have agreed, they will never submit to the direction
which international economic planning involves—that while
they may agree on the rules of the game, they will never
agree on the order of preference in which the rank of their
own needs and the rate at which they are allowed to advance
is fixed by majority vote. Even if, at first, the peoples should,
under some illusion about the meaning of such proposals,
agree to transfer such powers to an international authority,
they would soon find out that what they have delegated is
not merely a technical task but the most comprehensive
power over their very lives.

What is evidently at the back of the minds of the not altogether unpracticable "realists" who advocate these schemes
is that, while the great powers will be unwilling to submit to
any superior authority, they will be able to use those "international" authorities to impose their will on the smaller
nations within the area in which they exercise hegemony.
There is so much "realism" in this that by thus camouflaging
the planning authorities as "international" it might be easier
to achieve the condition under which international planning
is alone practicable, namely, that it is in effect done by one
single predominant power. This disguise would, however,
not alter the fact that for all the smaller states it would mean
a much more complete subjection to an external power, to

which no real resistance would any longer be possible, than would be involved in the renunciation of a clearly defined part of political sovereignty.

It is significant that the most passionate advocates of a centrally directed economic New Order for Europe should display, like their Fabian and German prototypes, the most complete disregard of the individuality and of the rights of small nations. The views of Professor Carr, who in this sphere even more than in that of internal policy is representative of the trend toward totalitarianism in England, have already made one of his professional colleagues ask the very pertinent question: "If the Nazi way with small sovereign states is indeed to become the common form, what is the war about?"[5] Those who have observed how much disquiet and alarm some recent utterances on these questions in papers as different as the London *Times* and the *New Statesman*[6] have caused among our smaller Allies will have little doubt how much this attitude is even now resented among our closest friends, and how easy it will be to dissipate the stock of good will which has been laid up during the war if these advisers are followed.

Those who are so ready to ride roughshod over the rights of small states are, of course, right in one thing: we cannot hope for order or lasting peace after this war if states, large or small, regain unfettered sovereignty in the economic sphere. But this does not mean that a new superstate must be given powers which we have not learned to use intelli-

5. Professor C. A. W. Manning, in a review of Professor Carr's *Conditions of Peace* in the *International Affairs Review Supplement*, June, 1942.

6. It is significant in more than one respect that, as was once observed in one of the weekly journals, "one had already begun to expect a touch of the Carr flavour in the *New Statesman* pages as well as in those of *The Times*" ("Four Winds" in *Time and Tide*, February 20, 1943).

gently even on a national scale, that an international authority ought to be given power to direct individual nations how
to use their resources. It means merely that there must be a
power which can restrain the different nations from action
harmful to their neighbors, a set of rules which defines what
a state may do, and an authority capable of enforcing these
rules. The powers which such an authority would need are
mainly of a negative kind; it must, above all, be able to say
"No" to all sorts of restrictive measures.

Far from its being true that, as is now widely believed, we
need an international economic authority while the states
can at the same time retain their unrestricted political sovereignty, almost exactly the opposite is true. What we need
and can hope to achieve is not more power in the hands of
irresponsible international economic authorities but, on the
contrary, a superior political power which can hold the economic interests in check, and in the conflict between them
can truly hold the scales, because it is itself not mixed up in
the economic game. The need is for an international political authority which, without power to direct the different
people what they must do, must be able to restrain them
from action which will damage others.

The powers which must devolve on an international authority are not the new powers assumed by the states in recent times but that minimum of powers without which it is
impossible to preserve peaceful relationships, i.e., essentially
the powers of the ultra-liberal "laissez faire" state. And, even
more than in the national sphere, it is essential that these
powers of the international authority should be strictly circumscribed by the Rule of Law. The need for such a supernational authority becomes indeed greater as the individual
states more and more become units of economic administration, the actors rather than merely the supervisors of the

economic scene, and as therefore any friction is likely to arise not between individuals but between states as such.

The form of international government under which certain strictly defined powers are transferred to an international authority, while in all other respects the individual countries remain responsible for their internal affairs, is, of course, that of federation. We must not allow the numerous ill-considered and often extremely silly claims made on behalf of a federal organization of the whole world during the height of the propaganda for "Federal Union" to obscure the fact that the principle of federation is the only form of association of different peoples which will create an international order without putting an undue strain on their legitimate desire for independence.[7] Federalism is, of course, nothing but the application to international affairs of democracy, the only method of peaceful change man has yet invented. But it is a democracy with definitely limited powers. Apart from the more impracticable ideal of fusing different countries into a single centralized state (the desirability of which is far from obvious), it is the only way in which the ideal of international law can be made a reality. We must not deceive ourselves that, in the past, in calling the rules of international behavior international law, we were doing more than expressing a pious wish. When we want to prevent people from killing each other, we are not content to issue a declaration that killing is undesirable, but we give an authority power to prevent it. In the same way there can be no international law without a power to enforce it. The

7. It is a great pity that the flood of federalist publications which in recent years had descended upon us has deprived the few important and thoughtful works among them of the attention they deserved. One which in particular ought to be carefully consulted when the time comes for the framing of a new political structure of Europe is Dr. W. Ivor Jennings' small book on *A Federation for Western Europe* (1940).

obstacle to the creation of such an international power was
very largely the idea that it need command all the practically
unlimited powers which the modern state possesses. But
with the division of power under the federal system this is
by no means necessary.

This division of power would inevitably act at the same
time also as a limitation of the power of the whole as well as
of the individual state. Indeed, many of the kinds of planning which are now fashionable would probably become altogether impossible.[8] But it would by no means constitute an
obstacle to all planning. It is, in fact, one of the main advantages of federation that it can be so devised as to make most
of the harmful planning difficult while leaving the way free
for all desirable planning. It prevents, or can be made to
prevent, most forms of restrictionism. And it confines international planning to the fields where true agreement can be
reached—not only between the "interests" immediately concerned but among all those affected. The desirable forms of
planning which can be effected locally and without the need
of restrictive measures are left free and in the hands of those
best qualified to undertake it. It is even to be hoped that
within a federation, where there will no longer exist the
same reasons for making the individual states as strong as
possible, the process of centralization of the past may in
some measure be reversed and some devolution of powers
from the state to the local authorities become possible.

It is worth recalling that the idea of the world at last find-
ing peace through the absorption of the separate states in
large federated groups and ultimately perhaps in one single
federation, far from being new, was indeed the ideal of al-

8. See on this the author's article on "Economic Conditions of Inter-
state Federation," *New Commonwealth Quarterly*, Vol. V (September, 1939).

most all the liberal thinkers of the nineteenth century. From Tennyson, whose much-quoted vision of the "battle of the air" is followed by a vision of the federation of the people which will follow their last great fight, right down to the end of the century the final achievement of a federal organization remained the ever recurring hope of a next great step in the advance of civilization. Nineteenth-century liberals may not have been fully aware *how* essential a complement of their principles a federal organization of the different states formed;[9] but there were few among them who did not express their belief in it as an ultimate goal.[10] It was only with the approach of our twentieth century that before the triumphant rise of *Realpolitik* these hopes came to be regarded as unpracticable and utopian.

We shall not rebuild civilization on the large scale. It is no accident that on the whole there was more beauty and decency to be found in the life of the small peoples, and that among the large ones there was more happiness and content in proportion as they had avoided the deadly blight of centralization. Least of all shall we preserve democracy or foster its growth if all the power and most of the important decisions rest with an organization far too big for the common man to survey or comprehend. Nowhere has democracy

9. See on this Professor Robbins' already quoted book, *op cit.*, pp. 240–57.

10. As late as the closing years of the nineteenth century Henry Sidgwick thought it "not beyond the limits of a sober forecast to conjecture that some future integration may take place in the West European states: and if it should take place, it seems probable that the example of America will be followed, and that the new political aggregate will be formed on the basis of a federal polity" (*The Development of European Polity* [published posthumously in 1903], p. 439).

ever worked well without a great measure of local self-government, providing a school of political training for the people at large as much as for their future leaders. It is only where responsibility can be learned and practiced in affairs with which most people are familiar, where it is the awareness of one's neighbor rather than some theoretical knowledge of the needs of other people which guides action, that the ordinary man can take a real part in public affairs because they concern the world he knows. Where the scope of the political measures becomes so large that the necessary knowledge is almost exclusively possessed by the bureaucracy, the creative impulses of the private person must flag. I believe that here the experience of the small countries like Holland and Switzerland contains much from which even the most fortunate larger countries like Great Britain can learn. We shall all be the gainers if we can create a world fit for small states to live in.

But the small can preserve their independence in the international as in the national sphere only within a true system of law which guarantees both that certain rules are invariably enforced and that the authority which has the power to enforce these cannot use it for any other purpose. While for its task of enforcing the common law the supernational authority must be very powerful, its constitution must at the same time be so designed that it prevents the international as well as the national authorities from becoming tyrannical. We shall never prevent the abuse of power if we are not prepared to limit power in a way which occasionally may also prevent its use for desirable purposes. The great opportunity we shall have at the end of this war is that the great victorious powers, by themselves first submitting to a system of rules which they have the power to enforce, may at the same time acquire the moral right to impose the same rules upon others.

An international authority which effectively limits the powers of the state over the individual will be one of the best safeguards of peace. The international Rule of Law must become a safeguard as much against the tyranny of the state over the individual as against the tyranny of the new super-state over the national communities. Neither an omnipotent superstate nor a loose association of "free nations" but a community of nations of free men must be our goal. We have long pleaded that it had become impossible to behave in international affairs as we thought it desirable because others would not play the game. The coming settlement will be the opportunity to show that we have been sincere and that we are prepared to accept the same restrictions on our freedom of action which in the common interest we think it necessary to impose upon others.

Wisely used, the federal principle of organization may indeed prove the best solution of some of the world's most difficult problems. But its application is a task of extreme difficulty, and we are not likely to succeed if in an overambitious attempt we strain it beyond its capacity. There will probably exist a strong tendency to make any new international organization all-comprehensive and world-wide; and there will, of course, be an imperative need for some such comprehensive organization, some new League of Nations. The great danger is that, if in the attempt to rely exclusively on this world organization it is charged with all the tasks which it seems desirable to place in the hands of an international organization, they will not in fact be adequately performed. It has always been my conviction that such ambitions were at the root of the weakness of the League of

Nations: that in the (unsuccessful) attempt to make it world-wide it had to be made weak and that a smaller and at the same time more powerful League might have been a better instrument to preserve peace. I believe that these considerations still hold and that a degree of co-operation could be achieved between, say, the British Empire and the nations of western Europe and probably the United States which would not be possible on a world scale. The comparatively close association which a federal union represents will not at first be practicable beyond perhaps even as narrow a region as part of western Europe, though it may be possible gradually to extend it.

It is true that with the formation of such regional federations the possibility of war between the different blocs still remains and that, to reduce this risk as much as possible, we must rely on a larger and looser association. My point is that the need for some such other organization should not form an obstacle to a closer association of those countries which are more similar in their civilization, outlook, and standards. While we must aim at preventing future wars as much as possible, we must not believe that we can at one stroke create a permanent organization which will make all war in any part of the world entirely impossible. Not only would we be unsuccessful in such an attempt but we would thereby probably spoil our chances of achieving success in a more limited sphere. As is true with respect to other great evils, the measures by which war might be made altogether impossible for the future may well be worse than even war itself. If we can reduce the risk of friction likely to lead to war, this is probably all we can reasonably hope to achieve.

16
Conclusion

THE purpose of this book has not been to sketch a detailed program of a desirable future order of society. If with regard to international affairs we have gone a little beyond its essentially critical task, it was because in this field we may soon be called upon to create a framework within which future growth may have to proceed for a long time to come. A great deal will depend on how we use the opportunity we shall then have. But, whatever we do, it can only be the beginning of a new, long, and arduous process in which we all hope we shall gradually create a world very different from that which we knew during the last quarter of a century.

It is at least doubtful whether at this stage a detailed blueprint of a desirable internal order of society would be of much use—or whether anyone is competent to furnish it. The important thing now is that we shall come to agree on certain principles and free ourselves from some of the errors which have governed us in the recent past. However distasteful such an admission may be, we must recognize that we had before this war once again reached a stage where it is more important to clear away the obstacles with which human folly has encumbered our path and to release the creative energy of individuals than to devise further machinery for "guiding" and "directing" them—to create conditions favorable to progress rather than to "plan progress." The first need is to free ourselves of that worst form of contemporary obscurantism which tries to persuade us that what we have done in the recent past was all either wise or inevitable. We shall not grow wiser before we learn that much that we have done was very foolish.

If we are to build a better world, we must have the courage to make a new start—even if that means some *reculer pour mieux sauter.* It is not those who believe in inevitable tendencies who show this courage, not those who preach a "New Order" which is no more than a projection of the tendencies of the last forty years, and who can think of nothing better than to imitate Hitler. It is, indeed, those who cry loudest for the New Order who are most completely under the sway of the ideas which have created this war and most of the evils from which we suffer. The young are right if they have little confidence in the ideas which rule most of their elders. But they are mistaken or misled when they believe that these are still the liberal ideas of the nineteenth century, which, in fact, the younger generation hardly knows. Though we neither can wish nor possess the power to go back to the reality of the nineteenth century, we have the opportunity to realize its ideals—and they were not mean. We have little right to feel in this respect superior to our grandfathers; and we should never forget that it is we, the twentieth century, and not they, who have made a mess of things. If they had not yet fully learned what was necessary to create the world they wanted, the experience we have since gained ought to have equipped us better for the task. If in the first attempt to create a world of free men we have failed, we must try again. The guiding principle that a policy of freedom for the individual is the only truly progressive policy remains as true today as it was in the nineteenth century.

BIBLIOGRAPHICAL NOTE

The exposition of a point of view which for many years has been decidedly out of favor suffers from the difficulty that, within the compass of a few chapters, it is not possible to discuss more than some aspects of it. For the reader whose outlook has been formed entirely by the views that have been dominant during the last twenty years this will scarcely be sufficient to provide the common ground required for profitable discussion. But although unfashionable, the views of the author of the present book are not so singular as they may appear to some readers. His basic outlook is the same as that of a steadily growing number of writers in many countries whose studies have led them independently to similar conclusions. The reader who would like to acquaint himself further with what he may have found an unfamiliar but not uncongenial climate of opinion may find useful the following list of some of the more important works of this kind, including several in which the essentially critical character of the present essay is supplemented by a fuller discussion of the structure of a desirable future society. The earliest and still the most important of these works is that by von Mises, originally published in 1922.

CASSEL, G. *From Protectionism through Planned Economy.* Cobden Memorial Lecture, London, 1934.

CHAMBERLAIN, W. H. *A False Utopia: Collectivism in Theory and Practice.* London: Duckworth, 1937.

GRAHAM, F. D. *Social Goals and Economic Institutions.* Princeton: Princeton University Press, 1942.

GREGORY, T. E. *Gold, Unemployment, and Capitalism.* London: King, 1933.

BIBLIOGRAPHICAL NOTE

HALÉVY, ÉLIE. *L'Ere des tyrannies*. Paris: Gallimard, 1938. (English versions of two of the most important essays in this volume will be found in *Economica*, February, 1941, and in *International Affairs*, 1934.)

HALM, G.; MISES, L. VON; *et al. Collectivist Economic Planning*, ed. F. A. HAYEK. London: Routledge, 1937.

HUTT, W. H. *Economists and the Public*. Cape, 1935.

LIPPMANN, WALTER. *An Inquiry into the Principles of the Good Society*. London: Allen & Unwin, 1937.

MISES, L. VON. *Socialism*, trans. J. KAHANE. London: Cape, 1936.

———. *Omnipotent Government*. New Haven: Yale University Press, 1944.

MUIR, RAMSAY. *Library and Civilization*. London: Cape, 1940.

POLANYI, M. *The Contempt of Freedom*. London: Watts, 1940.

QUEENY, EDGAR M. *The Spirit of Enterprise*. New York: Scribners, 1943.

RAPPARD, WILLIAM. *The Crisis of Democracy*. Chicago: University of Chicago Press, 1938.

ROBBINS, L. C. *Economic Planning and International Order*. London: Macmillan & Co., 1937.

———. *The Economic Basis of Class Conflict and Other Essays in Political Economy*. London: Macmillan & Co., 1939.

———. *The Economic Causes of War*. London: Cape, 1939.

ROEPKE, W. *Die Gesellschaftskrisis der Gegenwart*. Zürich: Eugen Rentsch, 1942.

———. *Civitas Humans*. Zürich: Eugen Rentsch, 1944.

ROUGIER, L. *Les Mystiques économiques*. Paris: Librairie Medicis, 1938.

VOIGT, F. A. *Unto Caesar*. London: Constable, 1938.

The following "Public Policy Pamphlets" were published by the University of Chicago Press:

SIMONS, HENRY. *A Positive Program for Laissez Faire: Some Proposals for a Liberal Economic Policy.* 1934.

GIDEONSE, H. D. *Organized Scarcity and Public Policy.* 1939.

HERMENS, F. A. *Democracy and Proportional Representation.* 1940.

SULZBACH, WALTER. *"Capitalist Warmongers": A Modern Superstition.* 1942.

HEILPERIN, M. A. *Economic Policy and Democracy.* 1943.

There are also important German and Italian works of a similar character which, in consideration for their authors, it would be unwise at present to mention by name.

To this list I add the titles of three books which more than any others known to me help one to understand the system of ideas ruling our enemies and the differences which separate their minds from ours:

ASHTON, E. B. *The Fascist: His State and Mind.* London: Putnam, 1937.

FOERSTER, F. W. *Europe and the German Question.* London: Sheed, 1940.

KANTOROWICZ, H. *The Spirit of English Policy and the Myth of the Encirclement of Germany.* London: Allen & Unwin, 1931.

and that of a remarkable recent work on the modern history of Germany which is not so well known abroad as it deserves:

SCHNABEL, F. *Deutsche Geschichte im 19. Jahrhundert.* 4 vols. Freiburg i.B., 1929–37.

Perhaps the best guides through some of our contemporary problems will still be found in the works of some of the great political philosophers of the liberal age, De Tocqueville or Lord Acton, and, to go even further back, Benjamin Constant, Edmund Burke, and *The Federalist* papers of Madison, Hamilton, and Jay—generations to whom liberty was still a problem and a value to be defended, where ours at the same time takes it for granted and neither realizes whence the danger threatens nor has the courage to emancipate itself from the doctrines which endanger it.

INDEX

Lensch, Paul, 195; *Three Years of World Revolution,* 191–94
Leviathan, 209n
Lewis, W. Arthur, 215n
Ley, Robert, 148
liberalism, 13, 15–18, 21–23, 28, 95, 193, 196–97; change of meaning of term, xxxv; long-run character of, 89–90
liberals, 200
liberty, 17; "collective," 173. *See also* freedom
Lippincott, B. E., 160n
Lippmann, Walter, 32
List, Friedrich, 25, 207
Locke, John, 17, 91n

Macaulay, Thomas Babington, 236
Mackenzie, Findlay, 157n
Macmillan Report, 15n
Maine, Sir Henry, 87
Man, Hendrick de, 129n
Mannheim, Karl, 25, 76, 173
Manning, C. A. W., 253n
Marx, Karl, 25, 116, 158, 159n, 185, 187–88, 204, 206
Marxism, 32, 33, 49–50, 127, 177, 184–85, 187–88, 210, 212
means and ends, 37–39, 64–67, 101, 103. *See also* ends
Medicare and Medicaid, xvi
Michels, Robert, 33n
middle class, dispossession of, 127–28

middle-class socialism, 128, 213
Middle East, xiv
middle way, 47–48
military organizations of Central Europe, 151
military type of society, 140–41; in Germany, 145
Mill, John Stuart, 9, 124, 236
Milton, John, 17, 231, 237
minorities, 77, 95–96
Modern Law Review, 215n
Moeller van den Bruck, Arthur, 194, 196
money, 98–100
monopoly, 46–47, 49–52, 56–58, 102, 213–18, 220
Montaigne, Michel Eyquem de, 17
moral basis and effects of collectivism, 149–67
moral code, 64–68, 170–71, 175
moral standards, 230–37
Morley, Lord, 9n, 201, 236
Mosley, Sir Oswald, 75
motives, economic or pecuniary, 98–100
motor roads of Germany, 60–61
Muggeridge, M., 119n
Mussolini, Benito, 33, 53, 172
myths of totalitarian leaders, 171–72

Napoleon, 194
National Planning Board, xxxii